of

First English-language edition

Library of Congress Cataloging in Publication Data

Piccinardi, Antonio.
The gourmet's tour of Italy.

"A New York Graphic Society book".
Includes index.
1. Restaurants, lunch rooms, etc. – Italy –
Directories. 2. Cookery, Italian. I. Johnson,
James M., 1936 - II. Tittle.
TX910.18P53 1986   647'.945'025   86-15263
ISBN 0-8212-1628-7

New York Graphic Society books are published by
Little, Brown and Company (Inc.).

Published simultaneously in Canada by
Little, Brown & Company (Canada) Limited.

Printed in Japan

The Gourmet's Tour of ITALY

30 GREAT ITALIAN RESTAURANTS AND THEIR FAVORITE RECIPES

Text by:	*Antonio Piccinardi*
	James M. Johnson
Photographs by:	*Ian Berry*
	Patrick Zachmann
Introduction by:	*Count Giovanni Nuvoletti Perdomini*

A New York Graphic Society Book / Little, Brown and Company•Boston

30
Gourmand
Localities

Contents

People these days are increasingly discussing cuisine and writing about it, yet they are eating less or, what is worse, badly. And that is to put it mildly. That assessment applies in general to just about every place in the world, including Italy, of course. However, we can perhaps still find in Italy a secure anchorage or something of a life preserver in the attributes of simplicity and naturalness, which have been for centuries the touchstones of our customs and, therefore, of our cuisine. Curiously, both features of Italian life and diet are now in vogue, whether in Italy or elsewhere.

But we know all too well that fashion is no real guarantee of quality. And there are many signs that the defense of our cuisine and the values of the long, refined, and civilized tradition that underlies it is only a rearguard action. In the near future, we can expect that culinary tradition to be humiliated further by the fast pace of modern life, to be sterilized by a rationality that is more or less scientific, and to be parched by dieting and fasting. Simultaneously, we are witnessing an extraordinary boom in sales of slick, lavishly illustrated and printed – and therefore, expensive – books on cuisine, while serious talks and idle chat on the subject are dominated by the squalor of fat and lean. The true triumphs of modern cuisine appear to be subjected to the tyranny of the scales, which assign the victor's crown to dried-out, skeletal ascetics. Have we, therefore, any reason for confidence in contemplating the future of our beloved cuisine?

Many centuries ago, a saint, the great Thomas Aquinas, observed that "this art of nourishing mortals holds the first rank." Despite the sad signs of the times, we remain firmly within the traditional culinary faith and, with the master, we continue to believe that God, in setting man upon the earth, inflicted hunger and famine upon him, perhaps as a punishment, but He also blessed man with an appetite.

That belief places us firmly on the side of Descartes. When the arrogant Duc de Duras criticized an intellectual's interest in gastronomy, the philosopher angrily replied: "Do you perhaps think that the Lord made good things only for imbeciles?"

Even in this jumbled world of fast food and amid the chaos of prefabricated pizzas, premasticated hamburgers, and explosive Coca-Cola, we stubbornly hold to the view that the considered choice of a menu, bolstered by the selection of a fine bottle of wine, is a fitting homage to a civilization that has been enhanced by those glorious arts that serve to enrich life. In this respect, Madame de Sévigné wrote to her daughter, "Yes, it is true that we as well, like beasts, eat and make love, but, in any event, a bit better."

In contemplating his cuisine, the Italian is not fettered by a provincial chauvinism but readily admires and respects the achievements and the discoveries of others. Secure in his own, ancient tradition, he can appreciate without any trace of an inferiority complex or exaggerated sense of reverence the contributions of other cuisines, especially that of the French, who have made of the table a monument to art.

Twenty centuries or so ago, the Roman legionnaires in Gaul reproved their general, saying, "Caesar, you told us that we had come to fight against barbarians, but we eat soup and they eat roasted meats." Despite their complaints, the soldiers clung to their soups, but a compliment to the cuisine of another people was implicit in their grumbling.

In presenting this aristocratic selection of the finest Italian restaurants, I believe that I must first say that I do so without presumption and with an easy conscience, because I know that I am only doing honor to a highly refined cuisine, one that is the heir to many golden centuries. Obviously, because of my regard for the selectors and because of the impartiality I am obliged to observe as president of the Italian Academy of Cuisine, I have not wanted to intervene in any way in the choosing of the restaurants. However, I believe that on the whole I can endorse the selection. This occasion provides me an opportunity to express my satisfaction over the development of Italian cuisine, which, after having descended to a low level, has in recent years been giving many brilliant indications of renewal. This revival has been due especially to the reestablishment among the young cooks of that professional enthusiasm and spirit of sacrifice that seemed at one point to have been lost forever. In performing a sort of apprenticeship, many of our young cooks, who have studied their art and are often the descendants of cooks, go on pilgrimage to the most select Italian and French culinary sanctuaries. The result has been a revival of the Italian table, with a cuisine that is young and energetic, one that is open to all that is new yet faithful to our great past.

In Italy as in France, it is still and too often possible to come across some encumbering residues of the past that should be cleared up if not eliminated entirely. They bear the names, now empty rhetoric, of grande cuisine or bourgeois cuisine, gourmand and minceur, classic or nouvelle.

I still have faith that the young, especially, will know how to create in the near future a cuisine that is adapted to the times, that changes to meet new requirements and to explore the possibilities of further development as they evolve. In short, I believe they will be able to create a "good" cuisine. Now, we, the ancient pupils and friends of Maurice Sailland and the unforgettable Curnonsky, must resign ourselves to the fate of the aged and to nostalgia for a time that will never return.

We are the survivors of the wreck of the Medusa, the final witnesses of a world in which the lights have gone out for the last time in the last sublime restaurants in which the Baudelairean rhymes of the "Invitation au voyage" could still resound: "There, all is order and beauty, calm, luxury and voluptuousness." And, "there, colors and sounds correspond." Yes, the snows of yesteryear are gone and no one dares evoke the pearls of Amphitryon in speaking of caviar or the slaves of Neptune in citing oysters.

Drawing comfort in the last years of a long, epicurean, and well-nourished life, we regard ourselves as fortunate that there should be a group of emulators of Carême and Escoffier in this new, resurgent Italy, cooks who are prepared to welcome their guests honorably with ancient courtesy and modern understanding. That ensures the continuation of an ancient tradition of which the history of my country provides numerous examples. I would like to cite two, involving the ancient city of Mantua and the experiences of Henri III and Napoleon.

Abandoning Poland to rush to Paris to take possession of a much more glorious crown, Henri slackened his pace in passing through Italy.

After leaving Venice with a charming dancer, the gift of the Doge, he stopped off at Mantua for a sumptuous banquet given by the Duke. The dinner culminated in the serving of the famous pavone (or peacock) dei Gonzaga as the pièce de résistance. The dish involved fifty-five lapwings, a European plover, whose delicately savory meat was accompanied by a secret. Below the multicolored mantle of the proud bird's plumage was concealed the much more flavorful meat of guinea fowl.

The same sapid surprise can still be obtained, upon request, by modern visitors to the beautiful city in the north of Italy, along with another treat that won the favor of Napoleon. During the siege of Mantua, the conquering general fell into a foul temper, because the fortress seemed to be impregnable. To put him in a better mood, an attractive peasant girl offered to prepare for him a Mantuan speciality, the famous risotto alla pilota. The risotto consists of rice mixed with salamelle mantovane, a typical sausage of the Mantua area, which has been broken up and stewed in butter, and Parmesan cheese. The preparation's name is derived from piloti, the name given the workers who carried out the husking or pilatura of rice grains. Although he was no gourmand and even less of a gourmet, Napoleon was so taken by the preparation that it seems that he wanted to try another dish, the cook. While the latter cannot be guaranteed, the visitor will still find the first, the risotto, which is an authentic gastronomic triumph. And it can be savored along with the works of Mantegna, Raphael, and Giulio Romano that adorn the historic city.

This combination of Italian and French tastes that underlies the two accounts from the history books can be appreciated as well in a recipe, one of my favorites, that I would like to propose for the connoisseur's palate.

Granseola alla Nuvoletti (Crab Nuvoletti). Cook the crabs in a fish court bouillon for 15 to 20 minutes, according to their size. Cut them in half, extract the meat, and cut it into small pieces. Lightly sauté in butter the pieces of meat along with some finely chopped shallots for about 5 minutes. Add a large cup of cream and a good splash of fine Cognac. Blend, then add dry white wine and finely chopped tarragon. Meanwhile, prepare a bechamel with some fish broth. Add to it, in addition to the usual ingredients, two egg yolks, some grated Parmesan cheese, and a tablespoon of mustard. Pass this sauce through a sieve. Fill the empty shells with the meat blended with the sauce. Gratiné in the oven.

Buon appetito!

Giovanni Nuvoletti Perdomini,
President of the Italian Academy of Cuisine

CAVALLO BIANCO

Color is an essential element of the cuisine of the Cavallo Bianco as interpreted by Franco and Paolo Vai, the owners. Paolo, the chef, has based his culinary chromatic variations on the inspirations of such artists as Henri Matisse so that food becomes a treat for eye and palate.

Paolo Vai, chef and owner of the Cavallo Bianco, is without doubt the most attentive interpreter of "visual cuisine" in Italy. This results from his special sensibility that links him to the wider world of art. His most recent decorations for the dishes issuing from his kitchen, carefully executed for the benefit of each guest, were inspired by Henri Matisse. He says that he thirsts for colors, so that he first procures the products and the ornamental elements, inspired by the colors desired, and afterward he composes the preparation within the opalescent form of the plate. In that way, he succeeds in providing original decorations for each dish, which, although they are carefully thought out, seem totally fresh and spontaneous.

Tucked away in the shadows of the tallest mountains in Italy, the Aosta Valley is a tiny region but one that is incredibly beautiful. It has soaring peaks of spectacular appeal, such as Mount Blanc, Monte Rosa, Cervino, Gran Paradiso, and Grand Combin. There is, too, the National Park of the Gran Paradiso, and there are green valleys, vast forests, and innumerable icy streams and waterfalls. The traces of the past are just as abundant. Over the course of many millennia, man has left numerous relics. The valley was settled in Neolithic times. Aosta, or Augusta Praetoria, was founded in 25 B.C., during the Roman period. Later, at the end of the year 1000, the valley was of great importance because it was part of the principal chain of communications between southern and northern Europe and because of the strategic role it played in the numerous wars of the epoch. Even later, up until the eighteenth century, the valley was a duchy of considerable significance. The long struggle to preserve Aostan cultural and linguistic independence was rewarded, after 1945, with the creation of a special autonomous administration. This local government assures continuing bilingualism (French and Italian) and economic development.

Aosta possesses fine Roman ruins. The center of the city is enclosed by the ancient walls, which are almost completely intact. There are, as well, the forum, the amphitheater, and the Arch of Augustus. The valley itself is dotted with well-preserved medieval castles, many of which have an extraordinarily photogenic quality.

In the heart of the Aosta Valley, at Aosta, is the Cavallo Bianco. It was already established as a restaurant in the first half of the nineteenth century, taking its present name around 1865. After 1945, it was owned by the Sarteur family, the latest descendant of which is Paolo Vai, the chef as well as the current owner, along with Franco Vai. Up until 1980, the Cavallo Bianco offered the traditional cuisine of the Aosta Valley.

Afterward, there were modifications that produced a cuisine that was ever more personal but still closely linked to the tradition. Even more recently, the establishment, which displays old pewter and wood carvings in an atmosphere of great refinement, has been reconstructed, along with the four levels of the cellar, where the great crus of the Aosta Valley as well as the finest wines of the rest of Italy and other countries are carefully stored under stone vaults and on pavements of the Roman era. At that time, five suites and seven rooms in perfect Aostan style were installed.

The biographies of the preceding owners abound in references to great apprenticeships and periods of work in London, Liège, the great hotels, the House of Escoffier, and France. Vai, however, is a dedicated but self-taught man. Not everyone can reach the level he has attained, especially if they have done everything

The Cavallo Bianco is located in the heart of Aosta, the capital of the valley of the same name that is a border region between French and Italian cultures. The local dialect is, as well, a unique blend of the two languages. The restaurant's cuisine, therefore, draws strength from two venerable traditions, although Paolo Vai has added a new and personal dimension in his treatment of foods and their preparation and presentation. The Aosta Valley is a popular resort in the winter, when skiers flock to the snow-covered mountain slopes that surround it, and in the summer as well when many tourists halt there for a night or several days on their way to the sun and sandy beaches to the south. For the Mount Blanc Tunnel has made the valley a main artery of communications between Northern Europe and the Mediterranean.

Via E. Aubert 15 - 11100 Aosta. The restaurant is closed Sunday evenings, Mondays and from June 20 to July 10.
The restaurant, two stars in the **Guide Michelin,** is located in the center of the city between the Piazza della Repubblica and the Hôtel de Ville (Municipio or City Hall) in the Piazza Chanoux. Aosta is 113 kilometers (70 miles) northwest of Turin on Autostrada (Superhighway) A-5. AE, Diners, Visa cards accepted.
Tel. (0165) 362214

on their own and without the "right" schooling. Fortunately, the family tree has borne its fruit, endowing Vai with a character that strongly predisposed to haute cuisine. In this valley, however, great heights are natural, and those who are accustomed to the altitude will not be afflicted by vertigo.

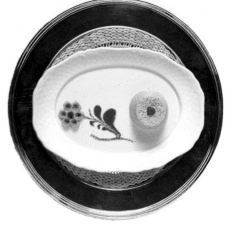

Duck Salad

Insalata d'anatra

Serves 4
1 breast of duck
1 head of lettuce
2 small heads of red chicory or ¹/₂ head
   of red cabbage
Several drops balsamic vinegar (or another aromatic vinegar)
Several drops raspberry vinegar
4 tablespoons (60 g) *extra-vergine* olive
   oil
Salt and pepper
1 orange

Sauté the breast of duck in its own fat, cooking it only until the meat is rare. Allow the
breast to cool and then cut it into thin slices.
Wash the lettuce and red chicory or cabbage,
drain, and cut in julienne slices.
Place the greens in a bowl. Prepare a vinaigrette with the balsamic vinegar (or aromatic
vinegar), raspberry vinegar, oil, salt and
pepper. Pour the vinaigrette over the salad.
Peel the orange and separate it into sections.
Arrange the lettuce and red chicory or cabbage on the dishes and place the slices of
duck atop the salad. Put the orange sections
at the base of the duck and decorate with
myrtle-berries.

Wine: Enfer d'Arvier (Aosta Valley), 5-6
years

Cabbage Mold

Sformato di cavolo

Serves 4
¹/₂ head of cabbage
1 onion
2 tablespoons (30 g) butter
2 bay leaves
4 eggs
³/₄ cup (200 g) cream
Several basil leaves
Salt and pepper

Chop the cabbage and onion into extremely
fine pieces and stew them in the butter along
with the bay leaves. Salt and pepper to taste.
When the cabbage is tender, put it and the
onion along with the basil leaves into a blender
and puree. Pass the puree through a sieve.
Add the eggs and cream to the puree and
beat well with a whisk.
Butter 4 small molds and pour in the mixture. Place the molds in a large pan partly
filled with water and bake in a 350 °F (180 °C)
oven until the mixture becomes firm.
Pour some fonduta sauce (see next recipe) in
each plate and place a cabbage mold on the
sauce. Decorate by making a flower pattern
with pieces of raw carrot partly hollowed out
and finely chopped parsley.

Wine: Vin des Chanoines (Aosta Valley), 3-5
years

Fonduta*

10 ¹/₂ ounces (300 g) fontina cheese
   from the Aosta Valley
³/₄ cups (1 ¹/₂ dl) milk
4 teaspoons (20 g) butter
3 egg yolks

Cut the cheese into small cubes and soak
them in the milk for at least 2 hours.
Melt the butter in a pan, add the cheese (and
any unabsorbed milk), and stir constantly
over low heat until the cheese has melted
and blended with the butter. The cheese
should form a thread when the spoon is

dipped in it. Raise the heat and continue to stir rapidly as, one by one, the egg yolks are mixed in. Blend well. The cheese mixture should be creamy and rather thick.
* The same sauce is used in a recipe appearing on page 16.

Fillet a la Carbonade

Filetto a la carbonade

Serves 4
1 carrot, chopped
1 onion, chopped
1 celery stalk, chopped
1 cup red wine (approximate)
4 slices of fillet of beef
1 garlic clove
Rosemary
Salt and pepper
1 teaspoon (15 g) butter

Put the chopped vegetables in the wine and simmer, reducing the liquid until it becomes thick and transparent.
In a separate pan, sauté the pieces of fillet in a bit of oil, cooking them for 2 minutes on each side, along with the garlic, rosemary, salt and pepper. Add the wine sauce. Cook the meat in the sauce for a few minutes. Remove the meat from the pan and stir ¹/₂ tablespoon of butter into the sauce. Serve the pieces of fillet with the sauce poured over, and a sliver of butter on top. Garnish with small slices of polenta (cornmeal mush), browned in a little butter.

Wine: Donnaz (Aosta Valley), 5-6 years

Frogs' Legs in Broth with Parsley

Cosce di rane al brodetto di prezzemolo

Serves 4
48 frogs' legs
2 tablespoons olive oil
1 tablespoon butter
1 garlic clove
Salt and pepper
1 tablespoon chopped parsley
<u>Basil sauce:</u>
The leaves of 2 basil stalks
1 garlic clove
1 tablespoon white flour
2 tablespoons butter
¹/₂ cup meat broth

Stew the frogs' legs for 10 minutes in the oil and butter along with the garlic. Salt and pepper. Then bone the legs and keep the meat warm.
Put all the ingredients of the basil sauce into a blender and reduce to a smooth liquid. Pass the liquid through a fine sieve. Heat the sauce and pour it over the meat of the frogs' legs placed in the center of each plate. Sprinkle with chopped parsley and serve.

Wine: Blanc de Morgex (Aosta Valley), 1-2 years

Lemon Bavarian Cream

Bavarese al limone

Serves 4
1 ¹/₂ teaspoons (1 ¹/₂ sheets) powdered gelatin
4 ¹/₃ cups (10 dl) milk
Peel of 1 lemon
1 egg yolk
8 teaspoons (40 g) sugar
2 egg whites
<u>Pineapple sauce</u>
1 fresh pineapple weighing 1 pound (500 g)
1 cup (200 g) sugar
1 cup carbonated mineral water
Juice of ¹/₂ lemon

Dissolve the gelatin in a small amount of cold water. Bring the milk, with the peel of the lemon added, to a boil. Remove from the heat and discard the peel.
Beat the egg yolk with 4 teaspoons (20 g) of sugar and put in another saucepan. Add the milk to the beaten egg yolk and sugar, over low heat, and stir steadily until a rather consistent cream is obtained. Remove the pan from the heat and add the dissolved gelatin. Blend in well and allow the mixture to cool. Beat the egg whites until they are firm then blend in the remaining sugar. When the cream is cool, delicately fold in the beaten egg whites. Pour the cream into 4 small molds, previously chilled in the refrigerator. Put the molds in the refrigerator and leave for 4-5 hours.
Make the pineapple sauce by dipping the whole fresh pineapple in boiling water for a couple of minutes. Remove the pineapple from the water, peel it, cut it into pieces, put them in the blender and reduce to a puree. Blend in the sugar, mineral water and lemon juice. Pass the puree through a fine sieve and pour some of the sauce into each of 4 dishes. Remove the Bavarians from the molds and place atop the sauce. Decorate with slices of fresh fruits.

Wine: Passito di Chambave (Aosta Valley), or Malvoisie de Nus (Aosta Valley)

LA CONTEA

Tonino Verro is an avid collector of old recipes of the Piedmontese cuisine and he has rescued many unique preparations from oblivion, re-presenting them in the antique and comfortable inn, La Contea, which he and his wife, Claudia, operate in the center of the hilltop village of Neive.

Piazza Cocito 8 - 12057 Neive (Cuneo). The restaurant is closed Sunday evenings and all day Monday. In truffle season, October and November, the restaurant is also open Sunday night. Neive is about 70 kilometers (44 miles) southeast of Turin. There is a turnoff to Neive on the Alba-Asti highway.
AE and Visa cards accepted.
Tel. (0173) 67126, 67367

Claudia and Tonino Verro are among the few restaurateurs who have succeeded in capitalizing on the severe cuisine of Piedmont or, more precisely, that of the Langhe. Their restaurant is something of a gastronomic island, with specialties that are linked not only to history, habit, and the influence of ancient invaders but also to the products of a land that is rich and generous.

The Langhe is a hilly area of southern Piedmont with the city of Alba as its "capital." The towns and villages in the Langhe are all perched on hills, a necessary precaution in the days of repeated invasions and raids. The Piedmontese are hard, strong people with little imagination, who are more inclined to the traditional than to the poetic, practical yet aristocratic in their habits. In the markets of Piedmont, too, the people and their gestures are rigorous, as are the foods themselves, which are of great intensity, such as the truffles, the *tome* (fermented cheeses), and the *sanato Piedmontese* (veal). And the preparations are as imposing as the foods, such as the beef braised in Barolo *(brasato)*, which is austere, intense, and concentrated, or the *fonduta*, consisting of Fontina cheese, egg yolks, cream, and truffles, which is richly full-bodied and persistent in aroma and flavor. The *bagna caôlda*, hot oil flavored with anchovies and garlic in which raw vegetables are dipped, is another Piedmontese dish that is stern and uncompromising, and as such matches the landscape. The richness of the cuisine does not arise solely from the truffle, the white variety, it must be understood, which is overpoweringly aromatic, unique, and irreplaceable and which lends greatness to a host of dishes such as *risotti* (rice preparations), *tagliolini* (fine noodles), meats, eggs, and game. The richness is found as well in the meats, cheeses, and especially in the vegetables, which thrive in this area. This is all true as well of Barolo, Barbaresco, and Nebbiolo, penetrating wines that are austere and full-bodied, dry but substantial and noble.

The Langhe offers a soft landscape of gentle and productive hills that are protected from climatic extremes by the chain of the Alps that partly encircles them. The small town of Neive is an example of the Langhe's subtle fascination, which does not shout for attention but utters its appeal in a whisper. It is entirely circular and from above resembles a *panettoncino*, a round and compact cake.

La Contea is ensconced in the center of that *panettoncino* in an ancient building that was once inhabited by the counts of Neive. It is now one of the most outstanding restaurants in the country. Operated with great ability by the Verros, La Contea serves as a confirmation that the best Italian restaurants are to be found in the countryside, and in the least populous areas – in hamlets or small towns that are seldom if ever mentioned in the columns of the daily newspapers. The stubbornness and constancy of persons like the Verros is to be found in such places. They have put those traits to good use in exploring the gastronomic traditions of Piedmont and discovering local dishes of another time and of another culture. Some of those preparations had, to all appearances, vanished, but they were still there, an integral part of the daily life of the people. The Verros crisscrossed the countryside of the Langhe and persuaded the people to describe what was once done in the district and to recall the feasts of another day and what foods were consumed on such occasions. In so doing, the Verros have succeeded in "unearthing" a hidden and abundant treasure.

The restaurant La Contea is situated in the heart of the Barolo and Barbaresco wine production area. The austere Barolo and the warmer and more spontaneous Barbaresco have been highly regarded for more than two centuries and both are used in numerous dishes served at the restaurant. Naturally, there is a good selection of both wines, as well as other products of the region and country, in La Contea's cellar. The restaurant is in every way a country inn, relaxed and unassuming, with emphasis upon good food, tranquility and comfort. The pace is unhurried and there is none of the hustle and bustle, the clatter and constant chatter of an establishment in the city. Instead, guests are encouraged to take their time, savor the dishes prepared by Claudia Verro and her staff, and drink in the good wines of Piedmont and the atmosphere of another, easier day. La Contea is a beautifully preserved inn with painted ceilings, wallpaper of elaborate design, and cream-painted paneling. And the village in which it is located, Neive, is something of a preserve of "old Piedmont" with large buildings with severe but self-assured facades lining nar-

row streets and small squares. The most elaborate structure in the community is the church with its dome and pinnacled belltower. All the towns and villages of this part of Piedmont, the Langhe, are perched on the tops of steep hills, for when they were founded, a millennium and a half ago, the area was subjected to repeated raids by freebooters landing on the coast of Liguria beyond the mountains. Immediately below the settlements on the tops of the hills are the vineyards, with rows of vines planted so close together that it is often impossible to work the soil with standard tractors.

Truffle Pastry

Pasticcini di tartufo

Serves 4
For the pastry:
1 cup (100 g) white flour
1 egg yolk
2 ¹/₂ tablespoons (35 g) butter, softened
1 tablespoon milk
Salt
For the filling:
¹/₄ cup (60 g) black truffle
1 tablespoon (15 g) butter
1 tablespoon (15 g) olive oil
1 garlic clove
¹/₂ tablespoon chopped parsley
1 tablespoon (5 g) grated Parmesan
Juice of 1 lemon

Pour the flour onto a doughboard and add the egg yolk, the butter, the milk, and a pinch of salt. Combine the ingredients and work until a smooth dough is obtained. Let the dough rest in a cool place for at least an hour.
Preheat the oven to 425 °F (220 °C).
Cut the truffle into paper-thin strips. Heat the butter and oil in a pan, if possible over wood coals, and lightly brown the clove of garlic. Remove the garlic and discard it. Cook the truffle slices briefly in the butter and oil. Add the chopped parsley, grated Parmesan, and the lemon juice. Cook for 10 minutes, then allow the truffles to cool. Butter 4 small pastry pans. Roll out dough and divide into eight pieces. Place a layer of pastry dough in each pan and pour in the truffle filling. Cover each pan with a disk of pastry. Bake in the oven for 20 minutes. The pastries should then be covered with some Piedmontese *fonduta* (the recipe appears on page 12), and lightly gratinéd under the grill. Serve hot with some fine slivers of white truffle, if available, sprinkled over the *fonduta*.

Wine : Arneis dei Roeri (Piedmont), 1-2 years or Gavi dei Gavi (Piedmont), 2-4 years

Onion Custard

Tartra o tartrà

Serves 4
2 herb bouquets (1 bay leaf, 3 sage leaves, several sprigs of parsley, 1 sprig rosemary)
1 ³/₄ cups (4 dl) cream
¹/₂ cup (1 dl) milk
3 eggs, separated
¹/₂ onion, sliced
4 teaspoons (20 g) butter
1 tablespoon grated aged Robiola (or another soft cow's milk cheese)
Nutmeg
Salt and pepper

Put one of the herb bouquets in the cream and milk, mixed together, and allow to infuse for an hour.
Preheat the oven to 425 °F (220 °C).
Coarsely chop the second bouquet and stew in the butter with the sliced onion. Pass the butter through a sieve.
Beat the egg yolks until they have thickened slightly. Beat the egg whites until they are stiff. Remove the bouquet from the cream and milk and add the butter, the grated Robiola or other cheese, the egg yolks, a pinch each of salt and pepper, and a small pinch of nutmeg. Blend well and fold in the egg whites.
Pour the mixture into a deep, buttered baking dish. Put the baking dish in a larger pan partly filled with hot water and bake for 30 minutes.

Wine : Dolcetto d'Alba (Piedmont), 1-3 years

Fine Noodles with Veal and Tomato

Tagliolini con vitello e pomodore

Serves 4
For the pasta:
2 cups (200 g) white flour
6 egg yolks
Salt
For the sauce:
1 garlic clove
2 tablespoons (30 g) olive oil
2 ripe tomatoes
1 medium-size onion, chopped
1 celery stalk, chopped
1 carrot, chopped
8 basil leaves
1 tablespoon chopped parsley
1 bay leaf
1/4 pound (100 g) ground veal
Salt

Pour the flour onto a doughboard, add the egg yolks and a pinch of salt, and work into a dough, kneading for 10 minutes. Let the dough rest for 30 minutes. With a rolling pin, roll the dough into a thin sheet. Let the pasta dry for several minutes. Then roll it into a tube and, using a sharp knife, slice finely across the tube. Uncurl the slices and scatter the noodles about on the board so that they do not stick together.
Lightly brown the clove of garlic in the oil. Peel, seed and chop the tomatoes, and add them to the pan. Then add the chopped onion, celery and carrot, the basil leaves, parsley, and bay leaf. Salt lightly. Simmer gently for 10 minutes, then add the ground veal and cook for a further 15 minutes.
Cook the noodles in boiling salted water for 5 minutes. Drain and dress the noodles with the sauce.

Wine: Barbera d'Asti (Piedmont), 2-5 years

Duck alla Favorita

*Anatra alla Favorita**

Serves 4
1 duck, about 2 1/2 -3 pounds (1.2 K)
5 garlic cloves
2 bay leaves
10 pitted black olives
2 tablespoons of rosemary, chopped
2 tablespoons (30 g) *extra-vergine* olive oil
2 cups (1/2 L) white wine
Salt

Cut the duck into pieces and remove as much of the fat as possible. Finely chop together the garlic, bay leaf, olives, and rosemary and brown in the oil. Add the pieces of duck to the pan and fry on both sides for several minutes. Salt the meat and douse it with some of the white wine. Cover the pan with a lid and cook over low heat. As the wine evaporates, add more until the duck is cooked.

Wine: Barbaresco (Piedmont), 4-8 years

* Favorita refers to the mistress of the king Vittorio Emanuele II, probably the Bella Rosina.

"Bonnet" Chocolate Cake

Bonet al cioccolato

Serves 4
3 eggs, separated
3 tablespoons (45 g) butter
1 cup (1/4 L) milk
1/4 cup (1/2 dl) cream
1/2 cup (50 g) amaretti (almond cookies), crumbled
5 tablespoons (50 g) bitter cocoa
6 tablespoons (90 g) sugar

Preheat oven to 425 °F (220 °C).
Beat the egg yolks with 3 tablespoons of butter. Add the milk, the cream, the crumbled *amaretti*, the cocoa, and the egg whites beaten until they are stiff. Blend, working carefully so that the egg whites remain fluffy.
Pour into a mold coated with caramel.* Place the mold in a larger pan partly filled with hot water and bake for 40 minutes.
Let the cake cool, remove it from the mold, and serve it cut in slices, decorating the plate with crumbled torrone and cornmeal or almond cookies.

* To make caramel coating for dessert molds, heat 1 cup sugar in a very heavy nonferrous pan over low heat. Stir constantly with a wooden spoon for 8-10 minutes. Remove from heat. Add 1/4 cup very hot water slowly. Return to heat and stir for another 8-10 minutes.

Wine: Malvasia delle Lipari (Sicily), or Erbaluce di Caluso (Piedmont)

CÀ PEO

Melly and Franco Solari have made the Cà Peo into a stronghold of Ligurian traditional cuisine, although they have updated and refined this ancient combination of fresh products from the sea and wild herbs and garden vegetables of the mountains that rise steeply from its shores.

Strada Panoramica 77 - 16040 Leivi (Genoa). The restaurant is closed all day Monday, at lunch Tuesday, and throughout November. It is easily reached from the Genoa-La Spezia superhighway (A-12). From the Chiavari exit, it is five kilometers (about three miles) to the top of the hill where the Michelin one-star restaurant is situated with a fine view of the sea. Several small, rustic apartments are available. Visa card honored.
Tel. (0185) 319090.

The cuisine of Liguria is one of the country's most fascinating, for it has two aspects, one linked to the sea and the other derived from the countryside. A few professional and many domestic cooks of Liguria have from earliest times drawn upon every resource of nature, using vegetables and seasonings with great fantasy, to create dishes of notable harmony.

The Cà Peo restaurant is, in a sense, the heir of that impressive tradition. Peo, or Pietro, was the grandfather of Franco Solari. His home, an old farmhouse, was transformed into a restaurant by Solari and his wife, Melly, after they had had many years of experience in hotels along the Ligurian coast and in other parts of the world.

The restaurant is a few miles from Chiavari, an historic place where great archaeological finds have been made. The restaurant offers a sweeping view of the marvelous Gulf of Tigullio, a large inlet of the sea that extends from Chiavari to Portofino and on the shores of which are situated Zoagli, Rapallo, Santa Margherita, and Paraggi. It is without doubt the most appealing area in Liguria. The three hills that give Portofino its unique profile were created by ancient volcanic eruptions. The prehistoric crater can still be seen amid the maritime pines that now cover the entire territory so lushly that it has been declared a national park. The volcanic formation is evident in the composition of the rocks and the shape of the coastline.

Until the tenth century, all the hills around Leivi, a small village close to the Ligurian Apennines, were still covered by the *macchia* (brush) characteristic of the Mediterranean. Then a community of monks was established and the brothers planted olives and chestnuts. The monks are perhaps responsible in part for the oil made today by Solari, the purest fruit of the press, as pure as the panorama of lush olive orchards that can be viewed through the restaurant's large windows.

Understated luxury pervades the establishment, which is spacious although arranged to accommodate only a relatively few guests. It is the refuge of a cuisine that is known superficially by many but prepared and endowed with greater competence by extremely few. The dishes offered on the Cà Peo menu each day represent country specialities in updated fashion. The *trenette al pesto* (a traditional pasta flavored with a basil sauce) and *pansotti* (large ravioli in walnut sauce), both well-known Ligurian dishes, need only be mentioned. But another preparation of rustic origin deserves attention and appreciation. It is a dish of potatoes, fava beans and tuna in broth, although in its new form it is a mold.

The taste for tradition updated and modernized has also determined Solari's choice of wines. In addition to the most prestigious products of other regions, such as the Sassicaia of the Marchesi Incisa della Rocchetta and the Lungarotti Rubesco, the Cà Peo offers an extraordinarily large selection of Ligurian wines. Solari loves the wines of his own area and assiduously seeks them out. The more limited the production of a certain wine, the more determined he is to acquire some of it for his clientele. The result is that the Cà Peo has all the best wines of Liguria, a collection that includes gems of great rarity. It was precisely this steadfast dedication that led Solari to create a prize to encourage the rediscovery and promotion of the wines of Liguria, the Ronseggin d'Ou (the device, in gold, that is used for pruning the vine). It is awarded each year to the vintner whose wine a jury of experts considers the best.

Cà Peo, an old farmhouse that once belonged to the grandfather of Franco Solari, perches on the slopes of the mountains that rim the Gulf of Tigullio, a deep blue inlet of the Mediterranean that is protected from storms by the promontory on which the well-known resort of Portofino is situated.

The village of Leivi seems to have derived its name from that of the ancient Ligurian tribe of the Laevi. The remains of a megalithic wall are still visible on the hill, on which a castle, constructed a couple of thousand years later, stands. There are

numerous other relics of the pre-Roman, Roman, and Renaissance periods scattered about the heavily forested area, which has been declared a national park. Franco Solari is a dedicated collector and promoter of the wines of Liguria, which are not well known to the general public, whether in Italy or abroad. The entire region is mountainous so that properties are generally small and difficult to work. As a result, production is highly fragmented and wines, often of excellent quality, must be deliberately sought out. Solari has been a highly successful wine hunter and he has accumulated an immense trove in the cellar of the Cà Peo, a treasure that he has not hoarded but made available to his guests with great discernment and enthusiasm. The restaurant, with huge windows overlooking the sea far below, is light and airy. The Cà Peo also provides a few rooms for those who want to pass the night or a day or two in one of Italy's most attractive regions.

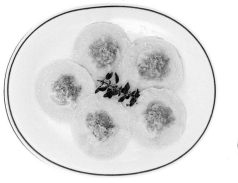

Cappellacci with Marjoram

Cappellacci al profumo di maggiorana

Serves 4
For the pasta:
3-3 ½ cups (300 g) flour
3 eggs
Salt
For the filling:
2 bunches of mixed wild herbs, such as
  wild thyme and borrage
¾ cup (180 g) ricotta cheese
⅔ cup (80 g) grated Parmesan
2 eggs
Salt and pepper
For the sauce:
4 tablespoons (60 g) butter
1 sprig of fresh marjoram
⅓ cup (40 g) grated Parmesan

Pour out the flour on a doughboard, make a well, and put in the eggs and a pinch of salt. Blend with a fork, then knead the dough for 10 minutes or until it is well blended and soft.
Wash the herbs, simmer them in salted water for a few minutes, then drain and squeeze them dry. Chop the herbs. Add to the herbs the ricotta cheese, ⅔ cup Parmesan, 2 eggs, a pinch of salt and pepper. Blend well.
Roll out a sheet of pasta and cut out disks about 2 ½ inches (6 cm) in diameter. Place dollops of filling on the centers of half of the disks. Cover with the remaining disks, pressing down the edges to seal. Cook the *cappellacci* in abundant boiling salted water.
Meanwhile, melt the butter and flavor it with the sprig of marjoram. Drain the *cappellacci*, sprinkle them with Parmesan, pour over the flavored butter, and serve.

Wine : Pigato, Riviera di Ponente (Liguria), 1-2 years.

Capuchin Pie

Torta cappuccina

Serves 4
For the pasta:
7 cups (1 K) flour, ½ cup (1 dl) olive oil
Water, salt and pepper
For the filling:
4 ½ pounds (9 cups) beet greens
½ onion, chopped
2 tablespoons (30 g) butter
3 ¼ cups (800 g) ricotta cheese
5-6 sprigs fresh marjoram
3 eggs
1 ⅔ cups (200 g) grated Parmesan
Salt and pepper

Make a dough with the flour, oil, a little water, a pinch of salt and pepper. Knead well so that a soft dough is obtained. Divide the dough into 5 pieces. Cover them with a damp cloth and then with a dry cloth. Allow the dough to rest. Preheat the oven to 350 °F (180 °C). Remove the stalks from the beet leaves. Wash the leaves and cook them until they are tender in a little salted water. Squeeze them dry and sauté them with the chopped onion in the butter. Remove the pan from the heat and allow to cool. Add the ricotta cheese, marjoram, eggs, salt and pepper.
Grease a baking sheet with a bit of oil and sprinkle it with flour. Take one of the pieces of dough and roll it out into a thin sheet. Put it on the baking sheet, brush the surface with oil, spread a quarter of the filling on the dough, and sprinkle grated Parmesan over the filling. Roll out the second piece of dough, slightly smaller than the first. Put it atop the filling, brush with oil, spread over another quarter of the filling and sprinkle with Parmesan. Continue in that way until all layers of pasta dough and the filling have been used. The top layer should be the same size as the first. Put it atop the pie. Press the overlapping edges of the first and fifth layers together, and fold to make a rim. Brush the top of the fifth disk with oil and bake for about an hour.

Wine : Cinqueterre (Liguria), 1-2 years, or Gavi dei Gavi (Piedmont), 2-4 years

Stuffed Lettuce in Broth

Lattughe ripiene in brodo

Serves 4
8 ounces (200 g) lean veal
1 tablespoon (15 g) butter
2 bay leaves
4 ounces (100 g) sweetbreads
¾ cup (100 g) grated Parmesan
4 ounces (100 g) brains
1 bunch parsley
1 garlic clove
1 sprig of fresh marjoram
½ ounce (15 g) dried mushrooms
1 egg plus 1 egg yolk
Dash of nutmeg
Salt and pepper
3 heads of lettuce
2 quarts (2 L) meat broth
2 tablespoons Genoese-style meat sauce
  (see following recipe)

Cut the veal into small pieces and brown in the butter along with the bay leaves. Parboil the brains and sweetbreads in boiling water. Drain, remove the membranes and add them to the veal. Brown for a further couple of minutes. Chop the meat and put it in a terrine. Finely chop the parsley, garlic, and marjoram together. Cut the mushrooms, softened in water and squeezed dry, into fine pieces. Add the chopped herbs and mushrooms to the meat, along with the eggs, and egg yolk, Parmesan, and a pinch of grated nutmeg, salt and pepper, then blend well.
Discard the outer leaves of the heads of lettuce. Carefully separate all the others. Wash them well, then scald them in boiling water for 2 minutes. Drain the leaves and spread them out on a towel. Put a little filling on each leaf and roll it up in a cylinder. Tie with kitchen string and cook in the broth. Remove the strings just before serving the lettuce rolls.
Serve in the broth with the meat sauce added.

Wine : Ormeasco, rosé, Riviera di Ponente (Liguria), 1-2 years, or Lagrein Rosato or Lagrein Kretzer (Trentino-Alto Adige), 1-2 years

For the Genoese Meat Sauce (Sugo di carne alla Genovese)
Yields about 1 cup
$^1/_2$ pound (200 g) beef, chopped
1 carrot, coarsely chopped
$^1/_2$ onion, coarsely chopped
2 $^1/_2$ teaspoons (15 g) olive oil
1 $^1/_2$ teaspoons (7 $^1/_2$ g) butter
$^1/_2$ cup ($^1/_8$ L) red wine
1 tomato
$^1/_3$ ounce (10 g) dried boletus mushrooms, softened
1 teaspoon (2 $^1/_2$ g) flour
Meat broth, as required

In a dutch oven brown the meat, along with the onion and carrot, in oil and butter. When the meat has browned nicely, add the red wine, the tomato, peeled, seeded, and chopped, the softened boletus mushrooms and the flour. Cook for 15 minutes.
Add sufficient broth to cover the meat. Cover the pot and cook for 2 $^1/_2$ hours over low heat. Pass the sauce through a food mill and use it with the stuffed lettuce in broth.

Blancmange in Caramel Sauce

Biancomangiare in salsa al caramello

Serves 4
8 tablespoons (80 g) cornstarch
$^1/_2$ cup (150 g) sugar
1 $^1/_3$ cups (3 dl) hot milk
$^1/_4$ cup ($^1/_2$ dl) kirsch
$^3/_4$ cup (2 dl) cream
$^1/_2$ cup (1 dl) almond milk*
For the caramel:
1 cup (300 g) sugar
1 teaspoon (3 g) cornstarch
$^1/_2$ cup (1 dl) water
For the crema inglese:
$^3/_4$ cup (2 dl) milk
$^1/_2$ teaspoon (2 g) vanilla extract
2 egg yolks
2 tablespoons (20 g) sugar
1 teaspoon (3 g) cornstarch

* Pound 4 ounces (100 g) of almonds in a mortar, gradually adding 2 tablespoons ($^1/_4$ dl) of water and $^1/_4$ cup ($^1/_2$ dl) of milk. Strain the liquid through a cloth.

Sift the 8 tablespoons of cornstarch and $^1/_2$ cup of sugar into a pan and add the hot milk, a little at a time, stirring constantly so that the cornstarch and sugar dissolve. Cook over low heat until the mixture thickens. Blend in the kirsch and cream, then the almond milk. Remove from the heat and allow to cool. Pour the mixture into 4 small molds. Put the molds in the refrigerator for several hours.
To prepare the caramel, put the sugar, cornstarch, and water in a pan and cook until the sugar has colored, but not too darkly. The flavor should be slightly bitter.
To make the *crema inglese*, boil the milk and add the vanilla. In a deep double boiler beat the egg yolks with 2 tablespoons of sugar and 1 teaspoon of cornstarch. Stirring constantly, add the milk little by little. Do not allow the mixture to boil. When the liquid coats the spoon, remove the pot from the heat. Cool the cream by putting the pot in a basin containing ice and water.
Pour some caramel in each dish. Remove the blancmange from the molds and place atop the caramel. Pour the *crema inglese* over the blancmange and decorate with bits of chocolate and fresh fruit.

Wine: Cinque Terre Sciacchetrà (Liguria), 5-10 years, or Malvasia delle Lipari Passito (Sicily)

Fricassee of Lamb with Artichokes

Fricassea di agnelletto con carciofi

Serves 4
2 pounds (900 g) lamb
2 garlic cloves
3 tablespoons (50 g) olive oil
Small bunch of parsley, chopped
1 cup white wine
Salt
7 artichokes
$^1/_2$ cup (1 dl) meat broth
1 egg yolk and 1 lemon

Wash and dry the lamb, and cut into pieces. In a pan, sauté the garlic in the oil. When the garlic has turned brown, remove and discard it. Add the chopped parsley, then immediately add the lamb pieces and brown over high heat. Reduce heat, pour the wine over, salt the lamb and cook for about 10 minutes. Remove the meat from the pan and keep it warm.
Meanwhile, prepare the artichokes. Remove the tough outer leaves, cut off the spiky tips, and then cut the artichokes into quarters. Remove the chokes and put the artichoke quarters in water acidulated with lemon juice so that they will not discolor.
Put the artichokes in the pan in which the lamb was browned, add the broth and salt, and simmer for 10 minutes. Add the pieces of lamb and continue cooking for an additional 20 minutes. When the meat is done, add the egg yolk blended with the juice of one lemon. Stir energetically with a wooden spoon and serve.

Wine: Dolceacqua (Liguria), 2-5 years, or Nebbiolo d'Alba (Piedmont), 3-6 years

PARACUCCHI – LOCANDA DELL'ANGELO

*Angelo Paracucchi knew exactly the sort of restaurant
he wanted when he created his Locanda dell'Angelo
near the Ligurian-Tuscan border, for he had had
many years' experience in Italy and other countries
directing hotels or teaching others that art.*

Viale 25 Aprile 60 – 19031 Ameglia (La
Spezia). The restaurant, which has one
star in the Guide Michelin, is open every
day throughout the year, as is the
attached hotel with 37 rooms. The
Locanda is 3 kilometers (2 miles) southeast of Ameglia on the Sarzana-Marinella
road. Ameglia is 16 kilometers (10 miles)
east of La Spezia from which it can be
reached by SS (Highway) 437.
AE, Visa, Eurocard, Comites cards honored.
Tel. (0187) 64391, 64392, 64393

Angelo Paracucchi's Locanda dell'Angelo is the temple of a key personality in
the Italian culture of gastronomy. He has
provoked debate and dissent but, for that
reason, too, he has been a central figure
in the renewal of the country's cuisine.
He is a generous, extroverted man, who is
impetuous yet mild, fiery yet sensitive,
and who possesses an active imagination
and an indomitable will. As a cook, he is
dedicated to discovering and creating,
no matter what difficulties or opposition
he may encounter along the way. First in
the town of Sarzana and now in Ameglia,
Paracucchi has established a citadel of
Italian cuisine that is also a shrine at
which the rites of food as feast are cele-
brated. The dishes Paracucchi offers at
his restaurant grow out of his impetuous
creativity, which, however, is accompanied by a refined intuition and a critical
spirit that ensures that the foods will be
new and immediate whether in substance or in presentation.

Fish plays a leading role in the cuisine of
the Locanda dell'Angelo and is prepared
partly according to regional tradition
and partly by the new approach that
Paracucchi has introduced into this
beautiful area – between the point where
the Magra River empties into the Tyr-
rhenian Sea and the beginning of the
Versilia. The dishes initiating a meal
have the impact of main courses, with
pasta and rice sensitively combined with
seafood, fish, and shellfish or just as
appealingly matched with vegetables.
Meats, game, and poultry are offered
with equally well-calibrated flair, in
which fantasy is linked with tradition.
Paracucchi chose the site of his restaurant after careful deliberation. It is an area
of borders, no longer Liguria but still not
quite Tuscany, a frontier hemmed in by
the Apuanan Alps, as the Apennines are
known in the district. Yet the land still
has the appearance of Liguria, a strip of

land between sea and mountain peaks, between the azure luminescence of the water and the stark white of the Apuana Alps' marble pinnacles and cliffs.

Designed by architect Vico Magistretti, the Locanda dell'Angelo represents the realization of Paracucchi's dream. The building, completed in 1975, manages to combine rustic characteristics and great refinement. Soberly elegant, in various shadings of white and laid out on horizontal lines, the building with its vast windows does not enclose its occupants but offers them a contact that is virtually physical with the surrounding greenery. Here, light has full liberty, flooding every room and corridor. All is bright, inside and out, in the open countryside and fields amid which the inn is situated. The brilliance illuminates each corner of the dining room, each table, and each vase of flowers. This same sensitivity is apparent as well in the annexed hotel.

Paracucchi, an Umbrian by birth, having been born at Cannara in the province of Perugia, inaugurated the Locanda in the mid-1970s after many years of experience in Italy and abroad as a teacher in hotel schools and as a hotel manager. In setting up his own restaurant, he adopted a philosophy of gastronomy in which it is recognized that, in presenting foods, as in selecting wines, it is essential to provide the guest the possibility of living within a particular style, of making choices, and of being offered alternatives so that among them the best composition can be achieved. After his considerable experience in Italy, Paracucchi decided to carry his message of gastronomic generosity and intuition to another bastion of cuisine, Paris, where he has opened the Carpaccio restaurant.

The Locanda dell'Angelo is situated in a land of borders – between regions and between the Apennines and the sea. The gentle hills around the restaurant are pressed between craggy summits and marine expanses and they shelter villages and towns that are rich in history. The leading community of the area is La Spezia, of medieval origin, which was dominated by the noble Fieschi family in the thirteenth century and became a Genoese possession in 1274. Other places, such as Ortonovo, Castelnuovo Magra, Nicola, and Fosdinovo abound in treasures of art, ancient castles, and fragments of a history that is often unknown to all outsiders, including inhabitants of other districts of Liguria and Tuscany.

The hotel-restaurant is located in a green declivity and can easily be recognized at a distance because of its sloping roof, clean lines, and large windows. The atmosphere and the style with which the visitor is welcomed are refined and properly discreet. Angelo Paracucchi created his restaurant literally from nothing, for before he set the builders to work the site was a vacant field. He is still building, adding to the restaurant and hotel structures other satellite buildings that will, apparently, be used for a variety of purposes. Assisting Paracucchi in realizing his designs are Giuseppe Nappini, the chef, and Ivano Brusciantella, a professional sommelier, who is in charge of the cellar.

Pasta Ribbons with Jumbo Shrimp and Asparagus

Stracci agli scampi e asparagi

Serves 4
For the pasta:
1 ¹/₂ cups (200 g) white flour
2 eggs – 1 egg yolk – salt
For the dish:
20 asparagus stalks
2 tablespoons (30 g) *extra-vergine* olive oil
2 tablespoons (30 g) butter
1 teaspoon chopped onion
20 fresh shelled jumbo shrimp
Salt and pepper
4 tablespoons (¹/₂ dl) dry Sherry
1 cup fish or vegetable broth
1 garlic clove

Pour the flour on the doughboard, make a well, and place in it the eggs and the egg yolk. Add a pinch of salt. Blend the flour and eggs, working the dough energetically for about 10 minutes until it becomes smooth and soft. Roll out the dough into a thin leaf and cut with an irregularly ridged roller so that small ribbons or shreds of pasta are obtained.
Boil or steam the asparagus, then remove the tough ends. Remove and set aside 12 tips. Cut the rest of the asparagus into small pieces. Put a tablespoon of oil and a tablespoon of butter in a pan and brown the chopped onion. Add the shrimp and the chopped asparagus, salt and pepper. Baste with the Sherry and cook until it evaporates. Cook the pasta in abundant salted water until it is done but still has a bite *(al dente)*. As the pasta is boiling, put a peeled garlic clove in 1 tablespoon olive oil.
Drain the pasta and put it in the pan with the shrimp. Stir rapidly and cook over high heat to evaporate any remaining juices. Remove the garlic from the oil and add the oil to the pan, with some tablespoons of broth and the remaining butter cut into small pieces. Remove from the heat, stir rapidly, and serve, garnishing each dish with the asparagus tips.

Wine: Riesling Renano del Collio (Friuli-Venezia Giulia), 1-2 years

Capri Salad

Caprese

Serves 4
For the tomato sauce:
¹/₂ pound (250 g) ripe tomatoes
¹/₃ pound (150 g) unripe bitter tomatoes
2 teaspoons (10 g) vinegar
1 teaspoon (5 g) fresh chives
¹/₂ celery heart
³/₄ cup (200 g) *extra-vergine* olive oil
Salt and pepper
10 ¹/₂ ounces (300 g) mozzarella cheese
   (if possible, made from buffalo milk)
20 basil leaves, both large and small

Prepare the sauce by blending together all the ingredients except the cheese and basil along with 2 tablespoons of oil. When everything is well blended, add salt and pepper and then, using the blender, add all the remaining oil a little at a time. Blend until the sauce is quite smooth.
Chop the largest basil leaves finely. Cut the mozzarella into slices about ¹/₄ inch (¹/₂ cm) thick. Using a small cutter, cut little holes in the slices. Put 2 ¹/₂ tablespoons of sauce on each dish. On the sauce, place 3 mozzarella slices, side by side. Sprinkle with the chopped basil and garnish the dish by placing a few small basil leaves between the slices of cheese.

Wine: Müller Thurgau (Trentino-Alto Adige), 1-3 years

Bream Fillets, Date-Shells, and Spinach with Balsamic Vinegar

Filetti di dentice, datteri e spinaci all'aceto balsamico

Serves 4
4 ounces (100 g) date-shells (or 6 ounces mussels)
2 garlic cloves
4 bream (or porgy) fillets, each weighing about 6 ounces (150 g)
Salt and pepper
4 tablespoons balsamic (or aromatic) vinegar
3 tablespoons (50 g) butter
8 ounces (200 g) cleaned raw spinach

Put the date-shells or mussels and 1 garlic clove in a deep pot. Cover the pot with a lid and put it over high heat, shaking the pot regularly. When the shells have opened, remove the pot from the heat and the meat from the shells. Pour the liquid remaining in the pot through a fine cloth and set it aside. Keep the shellfish warm. Butter an oven-proof glass dish. Arrange the bream fillets in the dish and add a garlic clove cut in quarters. Pour over the date-shell liquid. Salt and pepper. Cover the dish with a lid and put it in an oven heated to 400°F (200°C). Cook for about 8 minutes.
Remove the fillets from the oven, pour the cooking liquid into a pan, and keep the fish warm.
Add the balsamic vinegar to the cooking juices and reduce quickly. Blend in half the butter. Put the remaining butter and the cleaned raw spinach in a deep pot and cook over high heat, stirring repeatedly, for 8 minutes. Salt and pepper to taste.
Divide the spinach into 4 portions. Put each in a plate.
Place the date shells and bream fillets atop the spinach. Pour over the sauce, which should be quite hot, and serve.

Wine: Montecarlo Bianco (Tuscany), 1-2 years

Breast of Quail with Salsify

Petto di coturnice con scorzonera

Serves 4
4 quail
$^1/_2$ onion, chopped
$^1/_2$ leek, chopped
1 celery stalk, chopped
1 tomato, chopped
1 bay leaf
2 cups (1/4) water
2 $^1/_4$ pounds (1 K) black salsify (*scorzonera*; parsnips may be substituted)
3 tablespoons (50 g) butter
1 tablespoon balsamic vinegar (or a highly aromatic vinegar)
1 $^1/_2$ tablespoons (25 g) *extra-vergine olive* oil
Salt and pepper
$^1/_2$ cup Armagnac

Preheat the oven to 425°F (220°C).
Pluck and singe the birds, remove the intestines and wash them. Remove the breasts and set them aside. Brown the carcasses including the legs in a pot along with the onion, leek, celery, tomato and bay leaf. Then put the pot in the oven for 10 minutes. When the carcasses have browned, remove from the oven, add a pint of water and cook over a moderate flame until the liquid has been considerably reduced. Pass the sauce through a fine sieve. Turn oven down to 375°F (190°C).
Heat the oil in a pan, add the quail breasts and salt and pepper them. Brown on both sides and then put the pan in the oven for 15 minutes. Remove the quail from the oven, baste with the Armagnac and cook until the liquor has evaporated. Remove the quail from the pan and keep them warm.
Clean the salsify and cut it into $^1/_2$-inch (1-cm) cubes. Boil the salsify in salted water for 3 minutes, then drain.
Put a little butter in a pan, add the salsify, brown briefly and then put the pan in the oven. When the butter has been absorbed, add the vinegar and 2 tablespoons of cooking liquid from the quail. When the liquid has evaporated, remove the pan from the oven and keep warm.
Put the previously prepared sauce in the pan in which the quail were cooked and thicken with the remaining butter. Pour some sauce on each plate. Remove the breastbone from each quail breast and cut the meat into scallops. Arrange the scallops on the sauce and garnish with the salsify cubes.

Wine: Villa Trefiano (Bonacossi, Tuscany), 4-6 years, or Carmignano (Tuscany), 4-6 years

Sea-bass Slices with Artichokes

Trance di branzino con carciofi

Serves 4
6 small Jerusalem artichokes
1 tablespoon lemon juice
1 sprig of marjoram
7 tablespoons (80 g) *extra-vergine* olive oil
1 unpeeled garlic clove
Salt and pepper
8 slices of sea-bass, each weighing about $^1/_3$ pound (100 g)

Clean the artichokes and cut 4 of them into slices, which should be soaked in water acidulated with lemon juice. Put the 2 remaining whole artichokes in boiling salted water and cook for 5 minutes. Drain them and chop them finely along with the marjoram. Brown the chopped artichokes for several minutes in 3 tablespoons (50 g) of oil along with the garlic clove. Add salt and pepper.
Put 4 tablespoons of oil in another pan and heat the oil until it is quite hot. Cook the slices of sea-bass over high heat, 2 to 3 minutes per side. Salt and pepper the fish. Remove the pan from the heat, keeping it warm.
With the remaining oil, brown the artichoke slices for one minute, turning them for an additional minute. Pour some chopped artichoke sauce in each plate. Put the sea-bass slices in the center of the dish and arrange slices of raw artichoke around the fish. Pour over a little sauce and serve.

Wine: Torre di Giani Vigna al Pino Riserva (Umbria), 3-4 years

Raspberry Puffs with Zabaione

Sfogliata di lamponi e zabaione

Serves 4
9 ounces (250 g) puff pastry dough
1 beaten egg
9 ounces (250 g) raspberries
For the zabaione:
4 egg yolks
4 tablespoons (80 g) sugar
4 tablespoons ($^1/_2$ dl) Muscat wine

Preheat the oven to (350°F; 180°C).
Roll out the puff pastry dough into a sheet about $^1/_4$ inch ($^1/_3$ cm) thick. Cut four disks of about 4 inches (10 cm) in diameter. Cut a hole in the center of each disk so that 4 rings of pastry are obtained. Roll dough out again, to a sheet $^1/_4$ inch ($^1/_3$ cm) thick. Cut four more disks the same diameter as the rings. Put the whole disks on a cookie sheet. Place the rings atop the whole disks and brush them on top with beaten egg. Bake for about 10 minutes.
Prepare the *zabaione* by putting the egg yolks in the deep pot of a double boiler, off the stove. Add sugar and mix well, then add the Muscat wine and place the top of the double boiler over the boiling water, whisking constantly until the *zabaione* has thickened and puffed up. Remove from the heat.
Put the puffs on dishes. Put a layer of raspberries in the center of each disk and top with the hot *zabaione*.

Wine: Moscato d'Asti (Piedmont), 1 year

GUALTIERO MARCHESI

In establishing his restaurant at Milan, which was recently awarded its third Michelin star, the first Italian restaurant to have achieved that distinction, Gualtiero Marchesi decided to take an elegantly modern line in design and decor. And he has consistently followed the same policy in preparing and presenting a cuisine that is innovative and provocative.

Via Bonvesin de la Riva 9 - 20127 Milan. The restaurant is closed Sundays and for lunch Mondays, as well as throughout August and at all holidays. The restaurant is located just outside the nineteenth-century boulevard that encircles the city. In the vicinity is the Rotonda della Besana, an old hospital that now houses an important collection of modern art.
AE cards accepted.
Tel. (02) 7386677

Gualtiero Marchesi is, without any doubt, the chef who has shaped the Italian restaurant of the eighties. After considerable experience in Italy and in France, he opened his restaurant in 1977 with the intention of revising the way in which cuisine was conceived and presented. And he has shown himself to be a restless researcher rather than an unbridled creator in the way in which he shapes and offers his preparations. In appearance and in architecture his dishes are envisaged and constructed as visual works of art.

Marchesi respects the primary characteristics of each food, eschewing needless elaboration and refusing to compromise the aromas and flavors of a meat or a fish with contradictory ingredients, seasonings, or sauces. That stance is based on the understanding that tastes are not static but rather in continuous evolution, as in the worlds of art, fashion and customs. Marchesi has taken that dynamism into account in developing his recipes. He has been most innovative in the aesthetic presentation of his creations: there is a sculptural quality to the dishes, in which meats, fish, and vegetables in small but carefully modulated portions are clearly distinguished from their accompanying sauces.

Marchesi and his restaurant share many characteristics with Milan. It is a city that astounds and dazzles without descending to the vulgar, a metropolis that knows how to be preeminent without being ostentatious. Milan boasts one of the most appealing picture galleries in the world, the Brera, the world's best-known fresco, *The Last Supper* by Leonardo da Vinci, the most discussed piece of sculpture, the Rondanini Pietà by Michelangelo, the most famous of theaters, La Scala, the most spiritual and imposing cathedral, and the largest shopping gallery, which is dedicated to Victor Emma-

nuel II. Milan has been the birthplace of Italy's most important and lively cultural movements, such as Futurism, and two of its restaurants made history, first Savini and then Giannino.

In this city of ancient primacy, Gualtiero Marchesi gleams with the light of its "three stars," the first and only Italian restaurant to have received such recognition in the *Guide Michelin*. In this Milan, Marchesi, who is Milanese by birth, is truly at home. There he has created his model of cuisine and there he has been discussed and understood.

Although trained in Switzerland, Marchesi as a youth acquired his first practical experience in Milan at the Mercato, his family's restaurant. Therefore, his inventiveness has always been solidly linked to professional competence and to a mastery acquired in the city itself and in travels throughout the world.

In appearance, Marchesi's restaurant is simple, perhaps a bit cold, but quite refined. The arc lamps by Castiglioni combined with numerous green plants form, in the center of the two rooms, small, luminous forests in opposition to the linear character of the rooms. On the tables, in place of the customary bouquets, there are objects created by such artists as Arnaldo Pomodoro, Man Ray, Duchamp, and Pardi, which serve as a tangible affirmation of the cultural engagement of the restaurant.

There is a fine wine list, the fruit of a careful selection carried out by Marchesi himself. Among the impressive choices are the Torcolato and Cabernet of the Veneto produced by Maculan and the appealing Champagne-method sparkling wine of the Cà del Bosco of Franciacorta to the northeast of Milan.

Gualtiero Marchesi has suppressed the traditional bouquets as centerpieces for his tables. Instead, he sets out objects created by such artists as Arnaldo Pomodoro and Man Ray, for the restaurateur is a man of eclectic taste and considerable culture. In preparing his dishes, Marchesi displays the same flair and feeling for color and proportion. Quite recently, he drew up the recipes and oversaw the production of some tasty and attractive dishes for a leading Italian frozen-food company. That initiative was another indication of Marchesi's modern attitude. For he never hesitates to break with ancient traditions and patterns of thought, although, because of his long experience both in Italy and abroad, he has mastered all the fundamentals of his art and craft and his forays into the new and untried nearly always succeed.

The filigree has been banished and the essential emphasized at Marchesi's restaurant. He does not believe in a cuisine of pretense nor in one that is repetitious and uninspired. If he makes a dish, it becomes his dish. Its preparation is not determined by a recipe but his intuition.

For Marchesi has no respect for the past but only for his own creativity. He is loved and detested, hymned and derided, because he represents in the small cosmos of contemporary Italian cuisine the principle of novelty. He is the bearer of a revolutionary message that the tradition-haunted world of Italian cuisine finds disturbing. As cuisine, Marchesi's work is a plunge into creativity, one that is at times disturbing but always impressive. It is an approach that has attracted a wide following, especially at Milan, which responds to innovation.

Single Fish Dish

Piatto unico di pesce

Serves 4
For the Seabass Tartar (Tartare di branzino)
6 ounces (160 g) fillet of seabass
Salt and pepper
Juice of $^1/_2$ lemon
2 tablespoons olive oil
$^1/_2$ tablespoon tarragon, chopped
4 lettuce leaves

Finely chop the seabass fillet with a knife. Just before serving, dress the chopped fish with salt, pepper, the lemon juice, and olive oil. Form the chopped seabass into small ovals, place them on lettuce leaves, and sprinkle with chopped tarragon.

For the Marinated salmon (Salmone marinato)
6 ounces (160 g) salmon, thinly sliced
2 tablespoons olive oil
Juice of $^1/_2$ lemon
Salt and pepper

Marinate the slices of salmon in the oil, lemon juice, salt, and pepper for 15 minutes, in the refrigerator. Drain the fish slices and serve.

For the Fine Spaghettini and Caviar Salad (Insalata di spaghettini al caviale)
2 $^1/_2$ ounces (60 g) spaghettini
4 tablespoons *extra-vergine* olive oil
2 $^2/_3$ tablespoons (40 g) caviar
$^1/_2$ scallion, chopped
Some chervil leaves

Cook the spaghettini in boiling salted water. Drain the pasta and cool it under running water. Drain, dress with the oil, and serve out on dishes. Put a dollop of caviar in the middle of each portion of spaghettini, sprinkle with the chopped scallion, and decorate with some chervil leaves.

For the Shrimp Tails in Sweet Red-Pepper Sauce (Code di gamberi in salsa di peperoni rossi)
3 $^1/_3$ tablespoons (4 cl) olive oil
$^1/_2$ garlic clove
$^1/_2$ cup (120 g) onion, chopped
1 pound (400 g) sweet red peppers, cubed
$^1/_2$ cup (140 g) fresh tomato pulp
Salt and pepper
1 $^1/_4$ cups (24 cl) water
10 tablespoons (12 cl) cream
8 large shrimp or *mazzancolle tails*
Some basil leaves

Heat the olive oil in a pan and add the garlic, finely chopped, and onion. Cook over a low flame, stirring constantly, for 2 minutes. Do not let the onion brown. Add the cubed peppers and the tomato pulp. Salt and pepper. Baste with the water, cover the pan, and cook over moderate heat for about 30 minutes. Allow the mixture to cool, put it in a blender, and blend thoroughly. Pass the puree through a fine sieve. Put the puree in a bowl and incorporate the cream. Mix well.
Shell, salt, pepper, and steam the shrimp tails. Let them cool.
Put a tablespoon of the pepper puree on a plate. Put 2 shrimp tails atop the puree in each plate. Garnish with basil leaves.

For the Sole Mousse with Chives (Mousse di sogliola all'erba cipollina)
$^1/_2$ pound (250 g) fillet of sole
1 egg
Salt and pepper
1 cup (250 g) cream
1 tablespoon chives, finely chopped
1 tablespoon butter

Cut the fillet of sole into fine cubes. Put the fish in the blender, blend, and pass through a sieve. Incorporate the egg in the puree. Salt and pepper. Put the puree in the refrigerator for about 2 hours.
Delicately blend in the cream and mix in the chopped chives.
Salt and pepper, if needed.
Butter a small terrine. Pour in the mousse and put the terrine in a pan partly filled with hot water. Bake in a 350 °F (180 °C) oven for 25-30 minutes.

Allow the mousse to cool completely. Place 2 slices of mousse on each plate.

Wine : Riesling Renano del Collio (Friuli-Venezia Giulia), 1-2 years

Chicken-Liver, Truffle, and Lettuce Salad

Insalata di fegati di pollo, tartufi e lattuga

Serves 4
$^1/_4$ pound (120 g) butter
$^1/_2$ pound (240 g) chicken livers
Salt and white pepper
A small head of lettuce
3 tablespoon (4 cl) *extra-vergine* olive oil
2 teaspoons (1 cl) lemon juice
6 tablespoons (80 g) black truffle, thinly sliced

Clarify the butter in a pan over moderate heat. Skim off the foam and carefully pour off the melted butter, leaving the residue at the bottom of the pan. Put the butter in the refrigerator, pending use.
Carefully clean the livers and salt and pepper them. Melt the clarified butter in a pan, add the chicken livers, and cook them over moderate heat for about 20 minutes. Stir them delicately and make sure that, during the cooking, they are always covered by the butter.
Using a slotted spoon, remove the livers from the pan and put them in a bowl, terrine, or mold. The livers should almost entirely fill the bowl. Using a strainer, pour the butter over the livers in the bowl. The butter should cover the livers. Place the bowl in the refrigerator. When the butter is cold and firm, remove the bowl from the refrigerator. Separate the butter from the livers. Thinly slice the livers. Dress the lettuce with salt, pepper, olive oil, and lemon juice. Place the salad on plates and arrange atop it alternating slices of liver and of black truffle.

Wine : Grignolino d'Asti (Piedmont), 2-3 years

Veal and Ham Slices

Piccata di vitello a prosciutto

Serves 4
7 ounces (200 g) veal fillet
Generous 2 ounces (60 g) raw ham
  sliced paper-thin
Salt
A small head of young lettuce
3 tablespoons (4 cl) *extra-vergine* olive
  oil
2 tablespoons lemon juice
2 tablespoons (25 g) butter
1 tablespoon dense meat broth

Cut the veal fillet into thin slices. Pound the slices with a meat hammer. Place a slice of raw ham of the same size atop each of the veal slices. Salt the veal on the other side. Dress the lettuce with salt, olive oil, and lemon juice and arrange it on the dishes. Melt the butter in a pan. Place the veal pieces in the pan with the side covered by the ham down. Sauté over moderate heat for a few minutes. Turn the pieces and cook for a few minutes more.
Remove the veal-ham pieces from the pan and place them on the dishes with the salad. Pour off the butter and deglaze the pan with about 3 tablespoons of water. Scrape the bottom of the pan with a wooden spatula to release the cooking juices solidified by the heat and blend them with the water. Reduce the liquid, add the dense meat broth, reduce slightly, and pour over the veal slices. Serve immediately.

Wine: Chianti Rufina (Tuscany), 2-3 years

Gratinéed Freshwater Crayfish, Sweet Peppers and Zucchini

Gratin di gamberi d'acqua dolce, pepperoni e zucchine

Serves 4
60 freshwater crayfish
¹/₄ cup (¹/₂ dl) reduced crayfish broth
  (coulis)
2 tablespoons (30 g) cream
<u>For the garnish:</u>
2 tablespoons (50 g) olive oil
16 small cubes sweet red pepper
16 small cubes zucchini
Salt and pepper
<u>For the zabaione:</u>
1 egg yolk
6 tablespoons (3 cl) of water

Cook the crayfish in lightly salted boiling water for 3 minutes. Remove them from the pot, reserving the liquid. Remove the tails and shell them. Prepare a concentrated broth (coulis) by simmering the heads of the crayfish in the liquid left from their cooking. Reduce until there is about ¹/₄ cup (¹/₂ dl) of broth left. Then add the cream and allow to thicken over low heat.
Meanwhile, heat the oil and cook the small cubes of sweet pepper and zucchini, adding salt and pepper, over a moderate flame until the pieces are cooked *al dente* (retaining a bite).
Make a *zabaione* by blending the egg yolk and the water. Add it to the *coulis* and blend well. Pour in equal portions into 4 heated dishes. Arrange the crayfish atop the sauce and top them with the cubes of peppers and zucchini. Put the dishes in the oven for a few minutes to gratinée.

Wine: Riesling Renano del Collio (Friuli-Venezia Giulia), 1-2 years

Sea Crayfish with Herbed Rice

Riso alle erbe e aragosta

Serves 4
2 live sea crayfish or rock lobster, about
  1 pound (500 g) each (American lobster
  can be substituted)
4 tablespoons (60 g) butter
2 teaspoons (10 g) finely chopped onion
²/₃ cup (160 g) rice
4 tablespoons (¹/₂ dl) fish essence
  (fumetto)
4 teaspoons (20 g) fresh fine herbs
  (parsley, chervil, tarragon, and young
  green onions or chives)
Salt and pepper

Remove the tails from the crayfish and cook the heads in boiling salted water to produce about 2 cups of broth.
Melt 4 teaspoons (20 g) of butter in a pan and stew the onion, finely chopped, until golden. Add the rice. Cook one minute, then finish cooking the rice, adding boiling fish essence from time to time, and, when it is used up, boiling water. Make sure that the rice is quite soft (about 20-30 minutes) and, at the end, whisk into it the herbs, which have been finely chopped, and 4 teaspoons (20 g) of butter.
Cut the tails in half, making 4 steaks. Salt and pepper them lightly and brown them on both sides in 4 teaspoons butter. Then extract the meat from the crayfish or lobster legs. Pour the rice into dishes, as if it were a sauce. Arrange atop it the crayfish "steaks" and the meat from the legs.

Wine: Chardonnay di Miralduolo (Umbria), 3-5 years

SCALETTA

*In creating Milan's most elite and intimate restaurant,
Giuseppina Cantori Bellini and her close associate,
Ernesto Maestri, have effectively blended tradition and
imagination, a combination that has made the
restaurant a culinary shrine.*

Piazza Stazione Genova 3 - 20144 Milan.
The restaurant, which has two stars in the
Guide Michelin, is closed on Sundays
and Mondays, the entire month of
August, 15 days at Christmas, and 15 days
at Easter. La Scaletta is near the Porta
Genova and faces the Porta Genova Rail-
road Station.
The establishment does not accept any
cards.
Tel. (02) 8350290

For the gourmets of Milan, Pina Bellini is
something of an institution. For they
remember her as the unsurpassable
cook of many night spots, refined restaurants, and an "oasis" in the Brianza district just outside Milan. In cooking, Pina
Bellini succeeds not only in renewing an
ancient tradition, in which she has had
great experience, but also in applying to
the preparation of foods the sensitivity,
communicativeness and fresh and
immediate fantasy that are typical of a
woman who is both reflective and highly
imaginative. Her compositions are new
and original in part but they are still
linked in every way to the flavor of the
food. And it is obvious that she never seeks
to astound her guests or puzzle them with
abstractions. Everything at the Scaletta –
furnishings, paintings, sculpture, and
rare books, along with the cordial and
friendly but professional style of service
– clearly indicates that the restaurant
and all who work there have deep roots in
the culinary profession.

Giuseppina Cantori Bellini is one of the
few women in the "Who's Who" of cuisine, Italian and otherwise. She has had
great experience in other restaurants,
large and small. Unquestionably Emilian in origin, she has progressed from
"roller-out" of pasta years ago to the
deserved fame of Scaletta, where diners
must reserve a table considerably in
advance. Pina Bellini's story is that of a
courageous and knowledgeable woman,
who is full of initiative. Perhaps a certain
amount of courage was required to open
a restaurant on the foggy periphery of
the city amid the clanging of trolleys and
the whistles of the trains in the nearby
station, between Porta Genova and the
old network of canals. Perhaps in selecting this location she was seeking a contrast, the creation of a mirage or refuge
for the weary traveler from the rumble
and fumes of trucks, cars and trains. And

she has succeeded, for the candles on the
tables, the flowers, and the enticing
scents make her guests forget the deafen-
ing world of the city's outskirts, and this
juxtaposition of calm and chaos is typi-
cally Milanese. Milan loves contrast,
photographs in black and white, and dis-
sonance, and it loves Pina Bellini. A sen-
timent that is reciprocated, it must be
understood.

The cuisine of Pina Bellini and her close
associate, Ernesto Maestri, is founded on
a philosophy that is quite precise and
concise : "to love cuisine and guests and
to earn respect in return." Therefore,
there is no single style that must be followed at any cost but the wisdom of seeking the good in every shading, in every dif-
ference, and in every variation. Fantasy
and imagination complete the transfor-
mation. In one case, she begins with an
idea based on the practice of Calabrian
fishermen, marinated raw cod. After
modifications, variations, and additions,
the result is a salad of cod marinated in
oil, lemon juice, and chives. Tripe, a dish
of the poor, is similarly converted into a
terrine.

Pina's son, Aldo, is the sommelier as well
as the attentive director of the dining
room. In addition to the wines, he takes
great pride in his list of grappas (a
liqueur distilled from grape pressings).
There are more than one hundred types
based on the variety of the grapes used.
Among the wines, there are the crus of
Borgo Conventi, Mastroberardino, and
Lungarotti. It is rare to find a restaurant
such as this in which every detail of the
surroundings has been so carefully
selected. The atmosphere itself, which is
warmly intimate and extremely refined,
bears the creative stamp of Gianfranco
Frattini, who has given the contemporary structure a personal touch and
impact.

La Scaletta's smart decor and chic color scheme are in considerable contrast with the neighborhood in which it is situated. It is the Milan of studios and artists but also the Milan of craftsmen and workshops, of poor and popular traditions. It is an interesting area to stroll, for in the streets and along the canals it is possible to savor an atmosphere that is almost nineteenth century in character. There is the Naviglio as well, an ancient link between the city and the countryside, a canal that served as a major communications route for many centuries. Milan, however, thrives on contrasts and the Milanese have found the combination of "old" neighborhood and "new" restaurant stimulating, so much so that a table in the relatively small establishment must be reserved a considerable time in advance.

Salad of Salt Cod Marinated in Oil and Lemon with Chives

Insalata di baccalà in olio, limone e erba cipollina

Serves 4
10 ¹/₂ ounces (300 g) of fillets of salt cod
1 cup (¹/₄ L) *extra-vergine* olive oil
Juice of 2 lemons
Freshly ground pepper
10 chive shoots
Handful of dried brown beans, boiled
Bunch of rucola (mustard greens may
  be substituted)

Remove the salt from the cod by soaking it in running water for 48 hours. After having drained and dried it well, cut it into thin slices. Place the slices in a glass baking dish and cover them with a sauce made with the oil, lemon juice, freshly ground pepper, and half of the chive shoots, finely chopped. Allow to marinate for 24 hours.
Serve on individual dishes garnished with the beans, a salad made with the rucola (or greens), and chives, chopped extremely fine.

Wine: Bianco di Pitigliano (Tuscany), 1-2 years

Terrine of Tripe in Gelatin

Terrina di trippa in gelatina

Serves 4
2 tablespoons (50 g) olive oil
2 tablespoons (50 g) butter
1 carrot, chopped
1 celery stalk, chopped
1 garlic clove
1 onion, chopped
³/₄ pound (800 g) mixed tripe
Salt and pepper
1 cup (¹/₄ L) white wine
4 cups (1 liter) meat broth
¹/₂ envelope powdered gelatin (2 sheets
  softened fish glue)
¹/₄ cup (50 g) fresh, cooked peas
1 ripe tomato, peeled, seeded, and
  cubed
1 tablespoon parsley

Heat the oil and butter in a pot. Add the carrot, celery, and garlic. After 10 minutes, add the onion and cook until the ingredients have softened. Cut the tripe into extremely thin strips. Put the strips in the pot and allow the tripe to absorb the flavors of the seasonings. Add salt and pepper. Then pour in the wine and cook for 3 hours. Baste the tripe from time to time with 2 cups (¹/₂ L) of broth so that it does not dry out. Allow to cool.
Combine 2 cups (¹/₂ L) of broth and the gelatin. Place a layer of tripe in a rectangular mold. Add some peas, some cubes of ripe, raw tomatoes, and a little parsley. Pour over some liquid gelatin. Continue layering until the mold is full.
Put the mold in the refrigerator and leave until the gelatin has set. To serve, cut the terrine in slices. Place the slices on individual plates and garnish with fresh vegetables seasoned with oil and lemon.

Wine: Sauvignon del Collio (Friuli-Venezia Giulia), 1-2 years

Tortellini with Asparagus Stuffing and Sauce

Tortellini con ripieno e ragù di asparagi

Serves 4
For the pasta:
2 cups (300 g) white flour
2 eggs
White wine, as needed
For the filling:
$^{1}/_{2}$ pound (1 cup) (200 g) asparagus tips
$^{1}/_{3}$ cup (100 g) ricotta cheese
$^{1}/_{3}$ cup (40 g) grated Parmesan
3 tablespoons (45 g) cream
Salt and pepper
For the sauce:
$^{3}/_{4}$ pound (350 g) asparagus
2 tablespoons (50 g) butter
$^{1}/_{3}$ cup (40 g) grated Parmesan
Salt

Using the flour, eggs, and as much white wine as is necessary, make a pasta dough and roll it out quite thin. Cut into squares of 1 $^{1}/_{4}$ inches (3 cm) a side.
To make the filling, boil $^{1}/_{2}$ pound (200 g) of asparagus tips until they are thoroughly cooked. Drain them. Pass them through a sieve and blend them with the ricotta cheese, Parmesan, cream, salt and pepper.
Put a little filling in the center of each square. Fold the dough over and press down around the edges to seal the "envelopes."
Scald $^{3}/_{4}$ pound (350 g) of asparagus in boiling salted water. Remove the tips, setting aside 12 to decorate the dishes. Slice the remaining asparagus in small rounds and stew briefly in 2 tablespoons (50 g) of butter. Cook the tortellini in abundant salted water. Drain them and arrange them on individual dishes. Sprinkle with grated Parmesan. Pour the asparagus sauce over and garnish with the extra tips.

Wine: Chardonnay (Trentino-Alto Adige) 1-2 years

Veal Kidneys with Boletus Mushrooms and Watercress

Rognone di vitello con funghi porcini e crescione

Serves 4
1 pound (400 g) veal kidneys
$^{1}/_{2}$ cup (1 dl) olive oil
1 garlic clove
1 pound (400 g) fresh boletus mushrooms
2 tablespoons (50 g) butter
Salt and pepper
1 tablespoon chopped parsley
$^{1}/_{2}$ cup (1 dl) fruity white wine
$^{1}/_{2}$ pound (200 g) watercress

Cut the kidneys in slices and put them in a pan with the garlic clove and the oil. Cook them over high heat for 3 to 4 minutes, then put them in a sieve, after discarding the garlic, and allow to drain for about 10 minutes. Clean and slice the mushrooms. Cook them for 5 minutes in a drop of oil and butter. Salt and pepper. When the kidneys have drained well, put them again in a pan over high heat for 3 to 4 minutes, adding the previously cooked mushrooms along with the chopped parsley, white wine, and a pinch of salt and pepper, and stir frequently.
Pick over and wash the watercress, then dry it in a towel. Arrange the cress in circles on hot plates. Put the kidneys and mushrooms in the center, as soon as they have cooked, and serve.

Wine: Tignanello (Tuscany) 7-10 years

Cantaloupe Mousse with Kiwi, Strawberry and Pineapple Sauce

Mousse di melone con salsa di kiwi, fragole e ananas

Serve 4
1 cantaloupe, about 1 pound (500 g)
1 cup (130 g) powdered sugar
$^{1}/_{4}$ envelope powdered gelatin (1 scheet fish glue)
3 kiwis
15 strawberries
$^{1}/_{2}$ small pineapple
Juice of 1 lemon

Skin and seed the cantaloupe, and cut into rough small pieces. Blend in a blender along with the sugar. In a bowl placed on a bed of crushed ice, combine the blended cantaloupe with the gelatin dissolved in a little warm water. Carefully blend the ingredients, stirring until the mixture develops considerable consistency. Pour into 4 small molds and chill in the refrigerator for several hours. Separately, blend the kiwis with a bit of the remaining sugar and several drops of lemon juice in the blender. Do the same for the strawberries, then for the pineapple. Turn out each mousse onto a small dish and serve with each of the three sauces.

Wine: Malvasia delle Lipari (Sicily)

ANTICA OSTERIA DEL PONTE

*Renata and Ezio Santin have made an old inn along
the ancient course of the Naviglio Canal into an oasis
of innovative cuisine that is attracting an ever-growing
number of food fanciers to a quiet, little-known corner
of Lombardy.*

Piazza G. Negri 9 - 20081 Cassinetta di
Lugagnano (near Milan). The restaurant,
which has two stars in the *Guide Michelin*, is closed Sundays and Mondays,
throughout August, and for the first 15
days of January. Cassinetta is three kilometers (two miles) north of Abbiate-
grasso, which is 24 kilometers (15 miles)
southwest of Milan. The highway begins
at Milan's Piazza 24 Maggio, near the
Genova railroad station, and passes along
the Naviglio Canal.
AE card accepted.
Tel. (02) 9420034

It is a brief but fascinating journey along
the banks of the Naviglio Grande from
Milan to Cassinetta di Lugagnano, which
was a favorite summer resort of Milanese
nobles in the eighteenth century. Passing along the former tow path bordering
the Naviglio Grande, the motorist soon
enters a dreamy landscape. A lot of water
has flowed rapidly and murmuringly
along the canal since it was excavated in
1177, so long ago that it now appears a
part of nature, an original feature of the
environment of the great plain of Lombardy. The water is still clean, and it is
drawn from the Ticino, which is often
described as the most beautiful river in
Italy. The route is lined by delightful villas constructed in the seventeenth and
eighteenth centuries by Milanese nobles
as cool retreats during the hot summer
months. Among the most impressive
mansions are the Villa Visconti, now the
Villa Castiglione, the Villa Pallavicini di
Persia, the Villa Rovasenda di Bel-
gioioso, and the Villa Calderari.

Along the road flanking the Naviglio,
there are numerous pleasant villages
with inviting inns that were once popular
stops for boatmen and passengers of the
famous "Boffalora packet," a sort of fer-
ryboat that linked the western extremity
of Lombardy with Milan. In its descent of
the canal, carried along by the current,
the boat loaded with passengers and
merchandise required eight hours to
reach its destination, including stops
along the way. The ascent took more
time, twelve hours altogether when the
craft was drawn by horse teams moving
along the towpath.

The Antica Osteria del Ponte has now
become a popular "port of call," one of
the most fascinating, along this ancient
stretch of waterway. It was in 1976 that
Ezio Santin discovered the graceful
house in which the Antica Osteria is now
installed on the banks of the Naviglio,

Lombardy west and south of Milan is generally flat and monotonous, although appealing in its own way, especially in spring and autumn when fogs blanket the fields, creating a mood of mystery and remoteness. On such days and evenings, the fireplace in the Antica Osteria's principal dining room provides not only warmth but also a sensation of coziness that endows the word hospitality with fresh meaning. The inn is set among a cluster of appealing eighteenth-century villas, among the parks with hedges pruned low and planted in labyrinths. The canal in front of the inn, once a busy avenue of commerce, is now a limpid mirror that reflects the building's serene and uncluttered facade.

Renata Santin, who oversees service in the dining room, was responsible for the decoration and furnishing of the Antica Osteria. Antique furniture is effectively set off by contemporary drawings and paintings on the wall and their juxtaposition is a clear sign that this is an establishment that knows how to select the best from each place and time and to meld them in lively and stimulating fashion. The cuisine is as

beside one of the twenty-seven attractive bridges that span the canal. Ezio Santin is a cook by avocation, who decided, midway through his life and after a varied business career, to dedicate himself to cuisine, not just for the benefit of himself and his friends but for a wider public. He sought an appropriate site for his new profession and found it along the Naviglio in the fine house in a pure Lombardy style with attractive roof tiles and chimney pots and small windows.

At first, he experimented with some dishes of the traditional regional cuisine of Italy, but he soon came to apply his own creativity, intuitively working out a personal cuisine that was due to his own sensibilities rather than to the standards, which were at that time rather confused, of Italian restaurants in general. Ezio Santin plunged into the world of cuisine in company with his wife, Renata, whose artistic sensibilities found expression in the furnishing and then the direction of the dining room. The kitchen, however, is a male preserve, where Ezio Santin, now seconded by his son Maurizio, interprets and creates, exercising his vocation while expressing his sensitivity. Although he has forged ahead in creative terms, Ezio Santin has never forgotten his earlier dishes, which are a highly personal expression of Italian cuisine. The Antica Osteria del Ponte always features *risotti* (rice dishes) that are imaginative and tasty and ravioli that are traditional in form but innovative in composition. Santin also offers a considerable range of fish and shellfish dishes, which are always prepared with interpretive and creative flair. This particular area of cuisine is clearly one that stimulates Santin's imagination to the fullest.

elegant, for Ezio Santin's preparations acquire a personal character, taking on a personality of their own without any culinary affectation. It is obvious that he loves beauty, art, and festivity. There is a tactile quality to his preparations, where appearance is equaled in force and effect by flavors and aromas. The cuisine has a magnetism and vital force that are balanced by a delicacy and grace that are immediately apparent to all those who take a place at his table.

Sea Crawfish (or Lobster) Ravioli
Ravioli di aragosta

Serves 4
For the pasta:
1 ³/₄ cups (250 g) flour
2 eggs
Pinch salt
For the filling:
1 crawfish (or lobster), approximately
    1 pound (500 g)
4 ounces (100 g) zucchini, cut into small
    pieces
4 ounces (100 g) raw salmon
1 egg
1 egg yolk
2 fresh tomatoes, seeded and chopped

Pour the flour onto a doughboard, make a well, and break the eggs into it. Add a pinch of salt, blend with a fork, and then knead energetically by hand for about 10 minutes so that a soft, smooth dough is obtained. Roll out the dough into a thin leaf.
For the filling: drop the crawfish (or lobster) into boiling water and cook for 5 minutes. Set aside to cool, then remove the meat from the shell. Cut the meat into pieces and add the pulp from the claws and feet. Reserve the body with the tomalley. Boil the small pieces of zucchini for 2 minutes in salted water. Put the salmon, egg, egg yolk, zucchini, and crawfish (or lobster) meat in the blender. Blend until all the ingredients are well amalgamated.
Cut the sheet of dough in half and place small lumps of filling in rows on the dough. Each should be separated from the other by a distance of slightly more than an inch (3 cm). Place the second sheet of dough over the first and the filling. Using the fingers, press down the dough between the lumps of filling to seal the ravioli. Cut into squares with an indented pastry cutter. Cook in abundant boiling, salted water 4-5 minutes, or until they rise to the top.

With a small spoon, remove the tomalley (the greenish or sometimes almost blackish soft matter in the chest cavity or "head" of the lobster). Add it to the chopped tomatoes and cook for 3 minutes. Use the resulting sauce to flavor the ravioli.

Wine: Riesling Renano di Capriva (Friuli-Venezia Giulia), 1-2 years.

Jumbo Shrimp and Zucchini Squash Salad
Insalata di scampi e zucchine

Serves 4
12 jumbo shrimp
¹/₄ cup (100 g) *extra-vergine* olive oil
1 teaspoon (5 g) soy sauce
2 medium-size zucchini
4 tablespoons (10 g) breadcrumbs
Salt and pepper
1 tomato
Vinaigrette made with *extra-vergine*
    olive oil

Shell the shrimp and marinate the tails for 15 minutes in the olive oil and the soy sauce blended together. Cut the zucchini in thin slices lengthwise and poach in salted water for 2 minutes. Drain and allow the slices to cool.
Remove the shrimps one by one from the marinade and dredge them in the breadcrumbs. Salt and pepper the shrimp and put them under a broiler or on a hot grill for 2 minutes.
Arrange the zucchini slices in the form of a star on each plate. Peel, seed, and chop the tomato and place in the center of each plate. Arrange the shrimp in the spaces between the zucchini slices. Baste with the *vinaigrette*, made with three parts *extra-vergine* olive oil, and one part vinegar with a pinch of salt and pepper, and serve.

Wine: Spumante Classico Crémant (Cà del Bosco, Lombardy)

Red Mullet with Herbs

Triglie alle erbe aromatiche

Serves 4
12 filleted mullet (sea bass, perch, rock-
   fish, or snapper may be substituted)
1/4 cup (100 g) *extra-vergine* olive oil
2 tablespoons (40 g) dry white wine
3 basil leaves, torn into small pieces
1 tablespoon chopped parsley
2 sprigs chives cut into fine pieces
8 grains of coriander
16 green peppercorns
4 tablespoons ripe tomato, cut into
   small pieces

Preheat the oven to 425 °F (220 °C).
Place the fillets of mullet or other fish in aluminium foil or tinfoil. Sprinkle the various
ingredients over the fish, seal the foil, and
place the envelope in the oven. Cook for
about 5 minutes.

Wine: Soave Classico (the Veneto), 1-2 years.

Saddle (or Loin) of Rabbit with Basil and Olives

Sella di coniglio al basilico e olive

Serves 4
2 saddles of rabbit, approximately
   2 pounds (800 g) total weight
2 tablespoons (50 g) *extra-vergine* olive
   oil
1 garlic clove
5 tablespoons (100 g) of butter
1/2 cup (1 dl) dry white wine
1/4 cup (50 g) black olives
2 ripe tomatoes, skinned, seeded, and
   cut into slices
1 tablespoon chopped fresh basil
Salt and pepper

Preheat oven to 425 °F.
Put the saddles of rabbit in a pan with the oil,
garlic, and 2 tablespoons (30 g) of butter.
Roast for about 20 minutes, basting the meat
repeatedly with the cooking juices. Salt the
meat. When the rabbit is cooked, remove it
from the pan. Remove and discard the garlic.
Discard the cooking fat, pour the white wine
in the pan, and boil it down, scraping the
juices that have coagulated on the bottom of
the pan. Add the black olives and the tomato
cut into slices and cook until the wine has
completely evaporated. Add about 1/2 cup of
water and reduce by half. Add the basil, salt
and pepper to taste and then bind the sauce
with the remaining butter.
Remove the fillets from the saddles and cut
them lengthwise into thin slices. Arrange
the slices on hot plates and baste with the
black olives and tomato sauce.

Wine: Tignanello (Tuscany), 7-10 years

Pears with Chocolate Sauce

Pera con salsa di cioccolato

Serves 4
2 1/2 cups (500 g) sugar
1 quart (1 L) water
Juice of 2 lemons
Pinch cinnamon
2 large Williams pears
5 tablespoons cream
1/2 cup dense *espresso*-type coffee
3 1/2 ounces (100 g) bitter chocolate
   (coarsely chopped)
1 tablespoon butter
4-6 hazelnut pralines (or almond
   cookies), coarsely chopped

Dissolve the sugar in a quart of water. Bring
the sugar solution to a boil and add the juice
of 2 lemons and a pinch of cinnamon. Boil
for 5 minutes.
Peel the pears but leave them whole. Carefully lower them into the sugar syrup and
cook over moderate heat for 10 minutes.
Remove the pears from the syrup and let
them cool.
Combine the cream and the coffee in a small
pan. Cook over moderate heat for 4 minutes
or until the mixture thickens. Add the coarsely chopped chocolate. Stir until the chocolate melts and blends with the cream and
coffee. Stir in the butter.
Pour out some of the sauce, which should be
hot, on each dish. Cut the pears in half and
place a half on the chocolate sauce in each
plate. Sprinkle over some hazelnut pralines
or almond cookies that have been coarsely
chopped. The pears can be served with pis-
tacchio ice cream.

Wine: Malvasi delle Lipari Passito (Sicily)

DEL SOLE

*In the stifling heat of the summer months, the shade of
the thickets around the restaurant Del Sole, on the banks
of Lago Maggiore, is extremely inviting to travelers.
And the welcome that awaits them inside from the
owners, Carlo and Itala Brovelli, only completes the
nexus of enchantment.*

Piazza Venezia 5 - 21020 Ranco (Varese).
The restaurant is closed Monday evenings and Tuesdays, as well as throughout January. Ranco is 67 kilometers
(42 miles) northwest of Milan, from
which it can be reached by taking Autostrada (Superhighway) A-8. The superhighway divides, one branch going to
Varese, the other to Sesto Calende. From
Sesto Calende, Ranco is 12 kilometers
(7 1/2 miles) to the north.
Diners, AE, Visa, Eurocard cards accepted.
Tel. (0331) 969507

*Ranco, the village in which the restaurant
is situated, is near Angera, which possesses
a fortress founded by the Torriani family.
It passd in 1314 to the Visconti of Milan
but was acquired in the 15th century by
the Borromeo family, which still owns it.
The fortress consists of a thirteenth-cen-
tury keep and a palace that was steadily
enlarged for centuries. The building's judg-
ment hall is embellished with fourteenth-
century frescoes. The Del Sole is not as old*

The trip to Ranco, a small village
perched virtually on the edge of Lake
Maggiore in northern Italy, has something of a dreamlike quality. After reach-
ing Angera with its small basin full of
boats, the traveler takes the road along
the shore overlooking the lake. The road
twists and turns, and on one side there
are lush gardens and villas half-hidden
by shrubbery, while on the other is the
green shoreline, edged with gravel, and
beyond it the limpid waters of the lake.
In June, the air is heavy with the intense,
penetrating, and honey-sweet scent of
the blossoms of the lime trees that line
the route. It is an odor that is captivating
yet melancholy, as is the lake itself,
which, even if it is bright and sunny, has
dark, intimate, and saddening places. It
is without doubt one of the most appealing roads in Lombardy.

After the brief run along the lake, the traveler reaches "port" in a spacious courtyard. From the clump of trees in which
the parking lot is situated, it is a short distance, down a steep flight of steps and
along a path through a labyrinth of
hedges, to the restaurant's large terrace.
From it, most of the lake can be seen. The
greeting that awaits the diner after his
journey is as pleasant and relaxing as the
trip itself. It is extended by Itala Brovelli,
who, along with her husband, Carlo, is
the owner. She is also the master sommelier and the sensitive and attentive director of the restaurant. It is rare to find so
much care, pride, intimacy, and discipline combined in such a proper balance, one that achieves a surprising, even
unforgettable impact.

The establishment was opened in 1872
as an inn complete with stables and wineshop. Since then, it has been uninterruptedly owned by the Brovelli family. Carlo
Brovelli, in the kitchen, interprets the
recipes of a renewed cuisine, which,
however, does not reject the influence of

but it has a long tradition as an inn, having been founded in 1872. And it has been uninterruptedly owned by the Brovelli family since its inception. In addition to the restaurant and a small hotel with eight attractive apartments, the complex operated by the Brovellis includes an interesting wineshop where the finest oenological products of the whole of Italy can be found.

the ancient regional tradition. The methods that he has applied for years now in his cooking, which are quite revolutionary in comparison with the preexisting family tradition, are the result of a new type of interpretation of foods and of a methodical process of research conducted in Europe as well as in America. The pure and immediate character of his culinary creativity, even if some of its aspects have distant origins, does not conflict with the formulas of Lombardy's regional cuisine. But he is too dedicated to cuisine to rest content with formula and he continues to select and deepen the unique and particular character of the foods he serves.

Ranco is located at the beginning of the long road that, paralleling the coast of Lake Maggiore, extends as far as the Swiss border. The lake ends where it meets the Ticino, known as the "azure river" because of the limpidness of its waters and the reflection of the sky on its glassy surface. Along the lake, the vegetation is lush and varied, with woods and flowery meadows in which herons, egrets, and pheasants roam freely. Both river and lake with their abundant fish, such as trout, salmon trout, pike, lavarello, and perch, provide the basis of numerous preparations. Del Sole di Ranco offers this freshwater bounty in dishes derived, although transformed, from the traditional cuisine.

The foods served follow in a natural way the alteration of the seasons, and this steady progression seems more apparent on the menu here than in other districts. Whether in summer or in winter, the restaurant serves as an anchorage for extended voyages of discovery, for it has an annexed hotel with eight comfortable apartments that are spacious and appealing. Del Sole is also furnished with a dock on the lake, a private beach, and even a landing pad for helicopters. Yet all those modern features are linked, if only in contrast, with a respect for the traditional that is so pronounced that the establishment even prepares and bakes its own breads. The wines offered by Del Sole are of considerable interest, since they represent not only the finest wineries but also the best crus of Italy. The list is of such breadth that Itala is able to propose with the various dishes a wide range of wines, including the superb whites of the Collio of Mario Schiopetto, the Rosa del Golfo, a rosé from the extreme south of Italy, and even the elegant and austere Barolo di Bricco Rocche.

IL GRISO

Il Griso was planned and founded by Bruno Gobbi, who thereby launched a new dynasty in the professions of cuisine and hospitality. His son Roberto tends to the cellar and greets guests in the dining room, while chef Claudio Prandelli oversees preparation of a light and appealing cuisine.

Via Provinciale 51 - 22040 Malgrate (Como). The restaurant never closes. The hotel, with 30 rooms, is attached to the restaurant, which has one star in the *Guide Michelin*. Malgrate is 3 kilometers (1 1/2 miles) northwest of the town of Lecco, which is 56 kilometers (35 miles) northeast of Milan, from which it can be reached by SS (Highway) 342.
AE, Visa, Eurocard, Diners cards accepted.
Tel. (0341) 375235

Il Griso is situated in one of the most appealing parts of Italy, on the edge of Lake Lecco, overlooking Lecco itself and a large stretch of water, a ribbon of brilliant light among the dark green mountains that form an enclosing and protective barrier.

Lake Lecco is a major tourist attraction of inspiring beauty. The panorama during the long periods of serene weather when the air is brightly limpid is incomparable. In the winter, meals are served on Il Griso's flowery, glass-enclosed veranda overlooking the water, while in the summer guests are served in a lush and lovely garden.

The name of the restaurant is derived from a character in Alessandro Manzoni's novel *I Promessi Sposi*. Il Griso is a "bravo," who comes to a brutal end. Yet he is one of the figures in *I Promessi Sposi* who remains most indelibly fixed in the memory. "Two men stood, facing each other, at the confluence, it might be said, of two narrow lanes. One of them partly straddled a low wall, with his arms folded across his chest.... Both of them had green hairnets around their heads that fell to their left shoulders and ended in big tassles. Bushy forelocks emerged from the nets and dipped down over their foreheads. Long mustaches twisted to points. A gleaming leather belt to which were attached two pistols. A small horn full of gunpowder hung across the chest like a necklace. The handle of a large knife extending from a small pocket in the large and billowy trousers. A sword, with a perforated guard of copper strips contrived in some coded design, polished and bright. They advertised themselves, to be recognized at first sight, as members of the species known as bravos" (Alessandro Manzoni, *I Promessi Sposi*, Chapter 1). It is an impression that endures, as is true of the impact made by the restaurant that bears the same name.

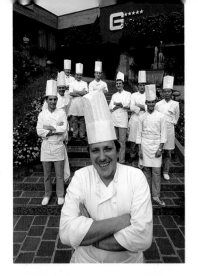

Il Griso itself is the result of a great effort, now nearly twenty years past, undertaken by a devotee of cuisine, Bruno Gobbi. After previous, highly successful experiences, Gobbi decided to settle down in the Lake Lecco area, and in 1967 he created the hotel-restaurant Il Griso. Gobbi belongs as well to that squad of perfectionists who are the pride of Italian gastronomy. In fact, not content with his knowledge of his own country's culinary achievement, he went to France to expand his understanding. It was a tour of exceptional interest. It is unnecessary, perhaps, to observe that that experience made a considerable contribution to Gobbi's cultural background. Gobbi's son Roberto takes care of the wine cellar and also greets the guests. Claudio Prandili is the chef. With the help of these competent collaborators, and in only a few years, Gobbi has succeeded in bringing Il Griso to a top level among Italian restaurants and in maintaining the highest standards.

At the moment a cook selects a vegetable or other food, it belongs no longer to nature but to the fantasy of the chef himself. Cuisine is thus understood as a projection, for the recipe has become a motive and an occasion for interpretation and creation in which the practitioner externalizes his own sensibility and gives it an image. All that presupposes special attitudes and sensibilities in respect to food or something of a fundamental faith in cuisine such as Bruno Gobbi has demonstrated for many years now in tirelessly and insatiably seeking a new culinary language, one that is rich in possibilities.

The restaurant can accomodate 100 guests. In the winter, they are served on a glass-enclosed and flowery veranda overlooking Lake Lecco with a range of mountains beyond. In the summer, guests are served in a lush and tranquil garden. Owner Bruno Gobbi decided in the Sixties to open a restaurant and embarked upon a program of preparation such as few of his contemporaries in Italian cuisine have pursued. Not content with his knowledge of Italian culinary achievement, he made a journey to France to expand his understanding of culinary approaches that were both traditional and contemporary. Only a few years after opening Il Griso, Gobbi had attained the highest levels of Italian gastronomy and his restaurant is still today a magnet in the "lake country" for food lovers from the south and vacationers from northern Europe. The Lake Lecco area is a major area for tourism in northern Lombardy, for it offers water sports of every sort in the summer and in the winter the ski slopes are near at hand. However, the climate is extremely mild, pleasantly cool and fresh in summer and far from frigid in winter. The numerous large lakes at the foot of the Italian Alps serve as a moderating factor. Il Griso, with its terrace and garden far above the lake, enjoys superb views of the water below and the mountains above. In atmosphere, the restaurant is placid and serene, comfortable and unassuming, although the cuisine is as delicate and refined as the most demanding critic could wish and the service warm and efficient at the same time. The Gobbis have struck exactly the right balance between total professionalism and easygoing Italian charm, which is entirely appropriate in an area of vacations and relaxing weekends.

Ravioli Stuffed with Cheese and Spinach with Basil

Ravioli di magro al basilico

Serves 4
1 ¹/₂-2 cups (200 g) white flour
1 egg
Salt
1 scallion (or shallot)
5 tablespoons (70 g) butter
2 tablespoons (30 g) cooked pureed spinach
3 ounces (80 g) farmer's cheese
¹/₄ cup (30 g) grated Parmesan
Nutmeg
Salt and pepper
1 tablespoon (15 g) fresh basil

Pour the flour onto a board, make a well, and break the egg into it. Add a pinch of salt, blend with a fork, then knead the dough by hand until it is soft and smooth. Make the pasta into a ball and wrap it in a sheet of waxed paper. Put in the refrigerator for 30 minutes.
Chop the scallion (or shallot) and sauté it in 1 tablespoon (10 g) of butter. Add the spinach and stew for 2 minutes. Remove the pan from the heat, add the fresh cheese, two-thirds of the Parmesan and a pinch of nutmeg. Blend well and add salt and pepper.
Divide the pasta into 2 parts and roll each into a thin sheet. Put dollops of filling on one sheet of pasta. Using a brush dipped in water, moisten the pasta around the lumps of filling. Lay the second sheet of pasta atop the first. Press down with the fingers around the lumps so that the ravioli are completely sealed. Cut out with a toothed roller. Cook the ravioli in boiling salted water for 4-5 minutes.
Drain the ravioli and put them in 4 pasta dishes. Melt the remaining butter, adding the basil leaves. Pour the butter over the ravioli and sprinkle with the remaining Parmesan.

Wine : Clastidium (Ballabio, Lombardy), 4-8 years

Rabbit Salad with Truffle Vinaigrette

Insalata di coniglio con vinaigrette al tartufo

Serves 4
1 ¹/₄ pounds (600 g) saddle of rabbit
8 tablespoons (100 g) butter
³/₄ cup (150 g) fine green beans
¹/₄ pound (100 g) cultivated mushrooms
2 tablespoons olive oil
2 tablespoons vinegar
Salt and pepper
1 ripe tomato
Chives
Watercress
Lettuce
2 teaspoons (10 g) truffle
¹/₄ cup (2 dl) cream

Bone the saddle of rabbit and cut into pieces. Lightly brown the pieces in 4 teaspoons (20 g) of butter. Allow the pieces to cool and then cut them into thin slices.
Boil the green beans and cut the mushrooms into thin slices. Put the beans and mushrooms in a bowl and marinate with the olive oil, 1 tablespoon vinegar, salt and pepper. Sauté the slices of rabbit in the remaining butter. Add salt and pepper and sprinkle over a bit of vinegar. Add the tomato, which has been peeled, seeded, and cut into small cubes, the chives, chopped, and the watercress. Cook for 4-5 minutes.
Put some lettuce on each plate. Place the slices of rabbit atop the greens and pour over the tomato, chives, and cress. Make a vinaigrette with the truffle, cut into tiny pieces, fresh cream, 1 tablespoon of vinegar, and salt to taste. Pour over the rabbit. Accompany the rabbit salad with the green beans and mushrooms.

Wine : Riviera del Garda Bresciano, Chiaretto or rosé (Lombardy), 1-2 years

Lavarello in White Wine

Lavarello al vino bianco

Serves 4
2 $^1/_2$-3 pounds (1.2 K) lavarelli (a firm-
 fleshed freshwater fish of mild flavor
 may be substituted)
2 chopped scallions (or shallots)
2 carrots
2 leeks
1 celery heart
2 cups ($^1/_2$ L) white wine
1 cup ($^1/_4$ L) fish broth
Salt
For the sauce:
4 teaspoons (20 g) butter
$^1/_2$ teaspoon white flour
1 cup ($^1/_4$ L) fish broth
4 teaspoons (20 g) cream
1 egg yolk
Salt and pepper

Fillet the fish. Butter a large saucepan,
arrange the fillets in it, and add the scallions
(or shallots), carrots, leeks, and celery cut
into julienne slices, the white wine, and
1 cup of fish broth. Add salt, if desired. Cover
the pan, bring the liquid to a boil, and stew
gently for at least 5 minutes.
Prepare the sauce by melting the butter, stirring in the flour and, after it has cooked a few
moments but before it colors, adding the cup
of fish broth. Blend well, then, stirring constantly, cook for 10 minutes. Add the cream
and continue to stir until a well-blended
sauce is obtained.
Remove the sauce from the heat, stir in the
egg yolk, and add salt and pepper to taste.
Drain the fish fillets. Arrange them on a
heated serving dish, garnish with the vegetables with which they were cooked, pour
over the sauce, and serve.

Wine: Lugana (Lombardy), 1-2 years

Veal Fillets Mignons
with Mushrooms

Filetti mignon con funghi

Serves 4
1 $^1/_4$ pounds (600 g) thick fillet of veal
Salt
Flour
8 mushroom caps
2 tablespoons olive oil
$^1/_2$ cup (2 dl) white wine
Juice of $^1/_2$ lemon
1 bay leaf
4 teaspoons (20 g) butter
Cognac
2 sweet peppers, roasted and peeled
For the sauce:
2 scallions (or shallots), finely chopped
4 teaspoons (20 g) butter
$^1/_2$ cup (2 dl) red wine
2 crushed peppercorns
1 teaspoon (5 g) chopped thyme
1 cup ($^1/_4$ L) strong meat broth
3 ounces (80 g) beef-bone marrow cut
 into small cubes
Salt

Cut the fillet into 8 pieces, each about 1 $^1/_4$
inches (3 cm) thick. Salt them and dredge
them lightly in flour.
To prepare the sauce, stew the finely
chopped scallions (or shallots) in the butter,
baste with the red wine, add the crushed
peppercorns and thyme. Reduce by a third.
Add the meat broth and cook slowly for
15 minutes. Add the beef bone marrow and
cook for 10 minutes more. Skim off the
grease, remove from the heat and pass
through a fine sieve. Press the lumps of
marrow with a spoon so that they dissolve
completely.
Brown the mushroom caps in the olive oil.
Baste with the white wine and lemon juice.
Add the bay leaf and salt to taste. Cook for
5 minutes.
Melt 4 teaspoons (20 g) of butter in a frying
pan and cook the veal fillets for 5 minutes on
each side over a slow fire. Remove the grease.
Baste with a few drops of Cognac, add the

sauce, already prepared, and cook for
1 minute. Remove the fillets from the pan
and keep them warm. Quickly reduce the
sauce and pass it through a sieve. Put the fillets in the center of a serving dish. Put 2
mushroom caps on each fillet. Pour over the
sauce. Garnish with the sweet peppers cut
into thin strips and serve quite hot.

Wine: Sassella (Lombardy), 6-8 years

Gratinéed Fruit Cup

Coppa gratinata

Serves 4
Generous $^1/_3$ cup (100 g) sugar
5 teaspoons (25 g) water
$^1/_2$ teaspoon vanilla extract
 (or $^1/_2$ vanilla bean)
$^1/_4$ lemon
$^1/_4$ orange
3 egg yolks
7 tablespoons (100 g) cream, whipped
4 scoops vanilla ice cream
8 tablespoons (100 g) fresh fruit, cut
 into small cubes
4 *amaretti* (almond cookies)

Bring the water to a boil, add the sugar,
vanilla, the peels and the juice of $^1/_4$ lemon
and $^1/_4$ orange. Boil for 5 minutes.
Remove the pan from the heat and allow the
liquid to cool. Pass through a sieve and put
the sugar solution in the upper half of a
double boiler. Add the egg yolks and cook in
the double boiler, whipping with a whisk
until the mixture becomes thick and
creamy. Remove from the heat but continue
to whip the mixture until it cools. Carefully
fold in the whipped cream. Put the mixture
in the refrigerator.
Take 4 ovenproof dessert cups, put a scoop
of ice cream in each along with an almond
cookie and the fruit cut into small cubes.
Cover with the sauce and gratiné under the
grill for several minutes. Serve immediately.

Wine: Malvasia delle Lipari (Sicily)

IL SOLE

At Maleo, about an hour's drive southeast of Milan, Franco and Silvana Colombani, now aided by their son Mario, create dishes derived from recipes of Italian culinary masterpieces of earlier ages and from the local tradition, which is an extraordinarily rich and stimulating one.

A restaurant for the thinking gourmand, yet one that has something of the fabulous about it, Il Sole was cut to the measure of those who want to forget the workaday world and savor a cuisine that is personal and stimulating. To experience fully all that the food and the ambience of Il Sole have to offer, it is absolutely necessary to consider in some depth both the structure of the establishment, which to all appearances is simple but in reality is quite refined, and the dynamics of the dishes that emerge from its kitchen.

Franco and Silvana Colombani have succeeded in reinterpreting recipes that range in time from the sixteenth century to the twentieth and in origin from the rich Po Valley, where their restaurant is located, to Russia, giving these ancient preparations new life and immediacy. They do not take refuge in a fixed formula but constantly renew their repertoire, drawing upon the past but creating in the present. The foods they offer their guests have a certain completeness and breadth that generate strong sensations of physical and aesthetic satisfaction, the effects of an artistic combination of thought and spontaneous inspiration.

Franco Colombani was one of the leaders of the movement to renew Italian cuisine that began in the early seventies. And his approach was a characteristic combination of research into the history of cuisine and a dedication to the modern virtues of freshness and originality. His contribution was fundamental in the renovation of Italian culinary philosophy. Silvana, Franco's wife, who is now the heart and soul of the kitchen, is a sensible and sensitive cook who knows how to remain faithful to tradition but at the same time how to re-create, how to go to the heart of a recipe and how to select and present it in modern fashion.

Maleo is deep in the heart of the Po Valley, sixty kilometers (thirty-seven miles) south-east of Milan, and it offers two distinct faces to the world, one wintry, the other summery. During the cold months, the countryside is often blanketed by thick fog. In the spring, the atmosphere changes completely. In the fine weather, it is eminently satisfying to lunch outside under the restaurant's fifteenth-century portico of exposed brick mellowed by the centuries, at the edge of the magnificent, sunny, internal courtyard that is enclosed by the wings in which wood is stored and *aceto balsamico* (balsamic vinegar) is made. This is a special, premium vinegar, produced most extensively in the region of Emilia-Romagna to the south and especially around Modena. The vinegar is aged in a variety of barrels to give it a complexity of flavors and often made in the Sherry fashion, one "vintage" being blended with another in an unending process.

Il Sole is installed in two buildings joined together. It was a functioning inn as long ago as 1464. It has gone through many remodelings, the last in 1985, but the structure has not been radically modified. The exterior suggests a coziness that is only confirmed inside. Beyond the spacious entry room is the corner where guests wait to be seated. It leads into the dining room with a fireplace, which is furnished with appealing and costly antique objects, including an incredibly long table made from one massive piece of wood. In the corner to the right is a secondary kitchen that supports the house's principal facility and in it the dishes are given their finishing touches, as they were a century ago. The fire blazing in the dining room's fireplace, with its fine frame and mantel and its ancient but still functioning device for roasting meats on the spit, creates a stimulating ambience. The eye is immediately drawn to the fine collection of old copper pots and utensils, which are still used in the cooking.

Maleo is a small town in the great plain of Lombardy that largely depends upon agriculture for its livelihood. The setting, therefore, accounts for the many rustic touches in the appearance of Il Sole, which was functioning as an inn as long ago as 1464. Yet it is also a highly sophisticated restaurant that offers a fascinating cuisine that blends an ancient tradition and modern culinary sensitivity. Much of the preliminary preparation of foods occurs in the complex of buildings surrounding its arcaded courtyard. Il Sole, for example, makes its own balsamic vine-

Via Trabattoni, 22 – 20076 Maleo (Milan). The restaurant is closed Sunday evenings, all day Mondays and during the months of January and August. Maleo can be reached from the Milan-Rome Autostrada del Sole by leaving it at the Casalpusterlengo exit and proceeding in the direction of Cremona. The Adda is crossed just outside Maleo, and it is necessary to pass through Pizzighettone enroute.
AE cards honored
Tel. (0377) 58142

gar, which is then used to flavor many dishes. Wood for the fireplace, where meats are spit-roasted, is stored in another wing, and yet another section contains a large stock of wines that includes some of the finest crus and vintages of Italy and other countries.

Il Sole can accommodate fifty guests and the easygoing atmosphere of the establishment encourages exchanges of views and opinions among the diners, who quickly cease to be strangers and become friends, or at least warm acquaintances. This is especially true of the ambience of the res-

taurant's first room, where Silvana Colombani and her husband, Franco, do much of the cooking in view of their guests. The second dining room is more formal, since, rather than a single, large table, there are many arranged in the customary style, separated one from another. But most guests seem to prefer the relaxed, informal atmosphere of the first room, where, seated all together at the big table before the fireplace, they enjoy conversing while eating and drinking well.

Pike in Sauce

Luccio in salsa

Serves 4
1 pike, about 2 ¼ pounds (1 K) (freshwater bass can be substituted)

For the marinade:
1 onion, thinly sliced
1 carrot
½ celery stalk
½ lemon
2 cloves
Pinch of cinnamon
6 black peppercorns
8 cups (2 L) water
2 cups (½ L) white vinegar
Salt

For the sauce:
6 tablespoons (10 cl) *extra-vergine* olive
   oil
2 anchovies with the salt removed
3 garlic cloves
1 tablespoon capers
1 tablespoon finely chopped onion
1 strip red sweet pepper, pickled in
   vinegar
1 tablespoon chopped parsley
Salt and pepper

Clean the pike, remove the intestines, and
wash. Poach it in the marinade, then allow to
cool. Remove the bones and put the fish in a
soup tureen.
To prepare the sauce, melt the anchovies in
the olive oil in a pan placed over moderate
heat. Add the garlic cloves, leave them for a
few minutes, and then remove them. Add
the chopped capers, onion, sweet red pepper, and parsley as well as a pinch of salt.
Simmer for 15 minutes, then pour the sauce
over the fish and sprinkle with a bit of pepper. Allow to cool. The dish is better if it is
made a day before it is served. The pike in
sauce can be accompanied with slices of
toasted *polenta* (cornmeal mush).

Wine: Spumante (Champagne Method) Brut
(Franciacorta in Lombardy or Trentino-Alto
Adige).

Capon Salad

Insalata di cappone

Serves 4
1 tablespoon (10 g) sultana raisins
2 tablespoons (20 g) candied citron
1 ⅓ cups (300 g) boiled capon or hen
Salt and pepper
4 tablespoons (7 cl) *extra-vergine* olive
   oil
3 drops balsamic vinegar (if available)
½ tablespoon of vinegar
½ head of lettuce

Soak the sultana raisins in water for 3 hours.
Cut the candied citron into thin slices. Bone
the meat and cut into fine strips that are
about ½ inch (1 cm) thick. Put the meat in a
soup tureen and add the raisins, chopped,
and the citron slices. Salt and pepper to taste.
Pour over the olive oil, balsamic vinegar, and
vinegar. Mix carefully. Serve out onto individual plates on a bed of lettuce.

Wine: Soave Classico (Veneto), 1-2 years

Mushroom Soup

Zuppa di funghi

Serves 4
14 ounces (400 g) porcini (boletus)
   mushrooms
4 tablespoons (7 cl) *extra-vergine* olive
   oil
1 tablespoon (15 g) of butter
½ onion, chopped
2 garlic cloves
2 tomatoes, cut up into small pieces
4 cups (1 L) meat broth
Salt
1 egg
4 tablespoons grated Parmesan
1 tablespoon chopped parsley
4 slices of bread
Pepper

Clean and wash the mushrooms, then chop
them into large pieces. Put the mushroom
pieces in a dutch oven along with the oil, butter, chopped onion, and crushed garlic. Simmer for several minutes. Add the tomatoes
cut into small pieces and the broth. Add salt
and cook over moderate heat for 15 minutes.
Meanwhile, beat an egg and mix in the Parmesan and parsley. Pour the mixture into
the broth, after taking the pot from the heat.
Smear the slices of bread with a bit of olive
oil and put the slices in an oven, leaving
them until they become crisp. Then rub the
slices with garlic and put one each in a soup
dish. Pour the mushroom soup over the
slices of toasted bread, sprinkle with pepper,
and serve.

Wine: Chianti Classico (Tuscany), 2-3 years

Noodles with Eggs and Truffles

Tagliatelle con uova e tartufo

Serve 4
For the noodles:
2 cups (300 g) white flour
3 eggs
Salt
For the sauce:
5 tablespoons (80 g) butter
4 eggs
Pinch of salt
⅓ cup (40 g) grated Parmesan
2 ounces (60 g) white truffles

Pour out the flour onto a doughboard, make a well in the center, and drop in the eggs along with a pinch of salt. Blend the flour and eggs with a fork and then knead by hand until the dough is smooth and all the ingredients perfectly amalgamated. Using a rolling pin, roll out the dough, makinbg a leaf that is not too thin. Roll up the leaf of dough and, using a sharp knife, cut it into strips that are about a ¼ inch (½ cm) wide. Unroll the strips and spread them out on a doughboard, taking care that they do not stick together; allow them to dry for at least 6 hours. Boil the noodles in salted water until they are *al dente* (done but still with a bite).
Melt the butter in a pan and cook the eggs, keeping them separated from each other. Salt them and make sure that they romain soft. Remove the cooked white from around the yolk. Put the noodles in individual dishes, sprinkle with some grated Parmesan, and atop the pasta, using a spatula, place one egg yolk per serving. Pour over the melted butter and then sprinkle each dish with finely shaved white truffles.

Wine: Pinot Grigio del Collio (Friuli-Venezia Giulia), 1-2 years

Mantis Shrimp and Beans

Sparnocchi e fagioli

Serve 4
7 ounces *cannellini* (200 g) (dried white beans)
1 ¼ pounds (600 g) prawns *(mazzan-colle)* or shrimp
2 tomatoes, skinned, seeded, and chopped into small pieces
6 basil leaves, roughly chopped
¼ cup (½ dl) *extra-vergine* olive oil
Salt and pepper

Cook the beans, drain them and place them in a salad bowl. Plunge the prawns or shrimp in boiling salted water. Boil them for 5 minutes, then remove their shells while they are still warm.
Add the shrimp tails to the beans along with the tomatoes and basil. Dress with olive oil and salt and pepper to taste. Mix carefully and serve warm.

Wine: Vernaccia di San Gimignano (Tuscany), 1-2 years

Quails in Sweet Peppers

Quaglie nel peperone

Serve 4
1 strip (about ¼ ounce; 20 g) *pancetta* (or bacon)
4 tablespoons *extra-vergine* olive oil
8 small quails
Salt and pepper
4 large sweet peppers
4 grape leaves

Finely chop the bacon and put the pieces in a sauteing pan along with the oil. Add the quails and brown them for several minutes, turning them frequently. Salt and pepper the birds.
Slice the peppers crosswise at about three-quarters of their height, making small vessels of them. Clean out the seeds and filaments and arrange the peppers in a pan. Put two quails in each pepper and pour into each some of the juices from the pan in which the birds were browned. Place a grape leaf atop the birds in each of the peppers. Use the quarters removed from the peppers as lids. Add a bit of water to the pan containing the peppers and cover loosely with a sheet of aluminium foil. Roast in a moderate oven (350°F; 180°C) for 20 minutes.

Wine: Valpolicella Superiore (Veneto), 3-5 years

AL BERSAGLIERE

*Roberto, maître d' and sommelier, and Massimo, chef,
are cousins, the latest generation of the Ferrari family
to be involved in the operation of Al Bersagliere at Goito,
which is owned by Gino Ferrari. The family founded
the restaurant in the vicinity of Mantua in the early
nineteenth century.*

Via SS Goitese 258 - 46044 Goito (Mantua). The restaurant, which has been accorded one star by the *Guide Michelin*, is closed Mondays, for 15 days in August and 10 in January. Goito is 16 kilometers (10 miles) northwest of Mantua on SS (Highway) 236.
AE, Diners, Visa cards accepted
Tel. (0376) 60007

The atmosphere of the restaurant, some of the foods offered, and the nearness of Mantua (the seat of a splendid duchy in the sixteenth century) establish a link with Bartolemeo Scappi, who was one of the greatest cooks and authors of books on cuisine in Italian literature.

The treatise Scappi has left to us is titled *Opera* and concerns the art of cooking. The first edition is dated 1570 and was printed in Venice. "It is the synthesis of a doctrine proved in everyday practice by a professional and an educational function translated in terms of example," as Emilio Faccioli has written in the second volume of *Arte della cucina* (The Art of Cooking). Al Bersagliere's link with the *Opera*, the most complete and exhaustive Italian gastronomic treatise of the Renaissance, grows out of the fact that the Ferrari family, the owners, are identified with a modern cuisine that draws upon centuries-old experience, for they interpret ancient recipes in a modern key, rendering them more current by filtering them through a contemporary sensibility.

Some entries on the menu are directly derived from ancient tradition, such as the frogs' legs with rice *(risotto con le rane)*, sturgeon *(storione)*, eels *(anguilla)*, the typical Emilian *culatello* sausage and *tortelli di zucca* (large ravioli stuffed with pumpkin). Others are the result of a modern intuition, such as the scallops with orange juice and the puff pastry with seafood.

"Goito or death!" seems to have been the battle cry of La Marmora to his troops, the Bersaglieri, in 1848. For the town of Goito witnessed all three Italian wars of independence. At the time of Austrian domination, Goito was an Italian outpost and it was inevitable that it would be the site of many battles. It is a small village, a bit anonymous yet with a great deal of history behind it. Its name, it seems, is

The restaurant is appealing and intimate, warmed by the light reflected from the Mincio, which flows just outside the veranda. The establishment offers a cuisine that is inspired by regional traditions, which in this region are deep-rooted and substantial, since nearby Mantua was the seat of the powerful Gonzaga family, all of whose members knew how to live – and dine – well. Chef Massimo Ferrari, reappraising the ancient culinary approach, combines an interpretive intuition with a sensitivity that permits him to prepare dishes of particular appeal. The restaurant also provides a panoramic view of the traditional foods of Mantua, envisaged and executed in coherence with a modern conception. The cellar stocks fine wines, including hard-to-find vintages.

For many decades, Al Bersagliere was a virtual border post, for the river Mincio was the boundary between Italian and Austrian territory. Passage of the river involved tolls and customs duties and later, when Italy surged toward national unification, it was an area of skirmishes and battles. Son has succeeded father in the direction of the restaurant for many gener-

derived from the word *barbara* or "barbarian," a reference to the Goths, who constructed an imposing castle on the banks of the Mincio. Quite probably, the Etruscans and Romans were already acquainted with the place, but the Goths installed themselves on the site and grafted a new community onto the preexisting settlement.

The Po Valley, a land of verdant fields and water, would not be the same without its rivers. A large part of the fascination of Goito, as is true of many other small centers, is due to its position on the blue, placid ribbon of the Mincio. It is one of Italy's most attractive rivers. It issues from Lake Garda and, flanking the Colli Morenici, descends into the sunny plain to join the Po. The river flows at the side of the building in which the restaurant is installed.

Since the beginning of the nineteenth century, the Ferrari have operated a public establishment at Goito next to the bridge over the Mincio. It was once called the Trattoria al Ponte. After April 8, 1848, and the historic battle in which La Marmora, the Bersaglieri, Goito, and the Austrians were the principal actors, the Ferraris changed the name. It became the Al Bersagliero restaurant. As patriotic people, the Ferraris regarded the alteration as a virtual obligation. Here, the family has pursued its profession generation after generation. The current owner is Gino Ferrari, although his son Massimo has assumed a directing role, while his nephew Roberto is in charge of the kitchen.

ations with a rhythm imposed by time and
with a fluidity that is virtually fluvial, a
tempo that suggests security, a sense of
trust, and an understanding that everything is a part of history, even small matters.
A visit to the Padania, a region watered
by the Po, takes the traveler back to an
ancient tradition that is still alive at Goito.
It can be found in the Cuisine, in the welcome, which is correct yet also intimate
and cordial, and in the atmosphere, with
the dining rooms overlooking the Mincio
and the terrain that was once stoutly occupied and defended by the Austrians.

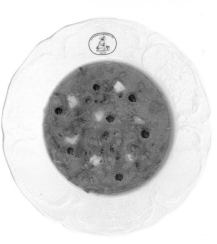

Loin of Hare in Salad

Insalata di lombo di lepre

Serves 4
1 pound (500 g) saddle of hare
  (or rabbit)
2 tablespoons (30 g) butter
1 cup (1/4 L) Dolcetto d'Alba wine
$^1/_3$ cup (50 g) sultana raisins
2 tablespoons (30 g) capers preserved in
  vinegar
2 $^1/_2$ tablespoons (30 g) toasted pinenuts
3 tablespoons (30 g) candied orange
  peel
1 celery heart
$^1/_2$ ounce (20 g) black truffle, cut into
  slivers
$^1/_2$ ounce (20 g) pomegranate seeds or
  gooseberries
4 tablespoons (60 g) olive oil
1 teaspoon balsamic vinegar (or aromatic
  vinegar)
Salt and pepper
Cinnamon, nutmeg, coriander

Brown the saddle of hare in butter, salt, pepper, and spices, basting it with the wine, in a 400 °F (200 °C) oven for 5 minutes. Reserve the meat juices. Cool and bone the hare.
Soak the raisins in water for 30 minutes, then squeeze them lightly to expel excess moisture. Wash the capers in water.
Slice the rabbit and put it in a salad bowl along with the pinenuts, the candied orange peel, the raisins, capers, celery cut into small cubes, the black truffles, and the pomegranate seeds (or gooseberries).
Meanwhile, prepare a sauce with the oil, balsamic vinegar, 2 tablespoons of the cooking juices of the meat, salt and pepper. Pour the sauce over the salad, mix well, and serve.

Wine: Soave Classico (Veneto), 1-2 years

Artichoke Soup

Minestra di fondi di carciofo

Serves 4
1 garlic clove
4 tablespoons (60 g) olive oil
1 onion, chopped
1 leek
2 ounces (50 g) cocks' combs (optional)
8 artichokes
Salt and pepper
2 quarts (2 L) chicken broth
2 ounces (50 g) beef-bone marrow
$^1/_3$ cup (50 g) chopped pistachios
$^1/_3$ cup (50 g) red currants
1 egg yolk
1 tablespoon cream

Brown the garlic in the olive oil, then remove it. Add the chopped onion, the leek cut into small pieces, and the cocks' combs. Stew gently.
Clean the artichokes, retaining only the hearts. Cut the artichoke hearts into slivers and add them to the pan. Salt and pepper. Add the chicken broth and simmer for 30 minutes.
Meanwhile, steam the beef marrow or poach it in stock for several minutes and cut it into small cubes. Place some marrow, chopped pistachios, and the currants in each soup dish. Bind the soup with the egg yolk blended with the cream. Pour the soup into the dishes and serve.

Wine:
Terre Alta (Livio Felluga, Friuli-Venezia Giulia), 2-3 years or Sauvignon del Collio (Friuli-Venezia Giulia), 1-2 years

Sturgeon in Anchovy Sauce

Storione con salsa di acciughe

Serves 4
For the broth:
3 cups (³/₄ L) white wine
4 tablespoons (80 g) butter
1 bay leaf
Peppercorns
Salt
4 slices of sturgeon, ¹/₃ pound (150 g)
   each
8 anchovy fillets
5 tablespoons (80 g) olive oil
2 tablespoons white wine
1 teaspoon of balsamic vinegar
   (or aromatic vinegar)
2/3 cup (100 g) pinenuts
4 teaspoons (20 g) sugar
Pinch of cinnamon
2 cloves
6 tablespoons (100 g) capers preserved
   in vinegar
14 ounces (400 g) Belgian endive
2 tablespoons (30 g) butter
Salt and pepper

Combine 3 cups white wine, 4 tablespoons butter, bay leaf, peppercorns, and salt and simmer for 5 minutes. Add the sturgeon slices and poach for 10-15 minutes.
Chop the well-washed anchovy fillets and cook them slowly in the olive oil until they have dissolved. Baste with the white wine and balsamic vinegar (or aromatic vinegar). Cook for 1 minute and pass through a sieve. Blend the pinenuts with the sugar and add them to the sauce. Add the cinnamon and cloves and reduce the sauce without boiling. Add the capers and remove from the heat. Cut the endive in strips and braise them in the butter with a bit of broth. Add salt and pepper. When the endive is cooked and dried, arrange it on the dishes. Place the sturgeon slices atop it. Warm the sauce and put a tablespoon of it on each portion.

Wine: Vintage Tunina (Jermann, Friuli-Venezia Giulia), 3-5 years

Turkey Stuffed with Chestnuts

Tacchinella ripiena alle castagne

Serves 4
1 turkey breast, about 2 pounds (1 K)
Salt and pepper
¹/₄ cup (170 g) butter
4 sage leaves
1 sprig of rosemary, 1 carrot
1 celery stalk, 1 onion, finely chopped
¹/₂ cup (1 dl) white wine
For the stuffing:
¹/₄ pound (100 g) turkey meat
¹/₄ pound (100 g) pork
¹/₄ cup (50 g) cream
4 teaspoons (20 g) egg white
Salt and pepper
2 ounces (50 g) fatty bacon
¹/₃ cup (50 g) walnut meats
2 tablespoons (20 g) softened sultana
   raisins
2 teaspoons (10 g) black truffle
2 ounces (50 g) glazed chestnuts

Prepare the stuffing by mincing the turkey meat and pork. Then put the meat in a blender, add the cream, the egg white, salt and pepper and blend thoroughly. Put the mixture in a bowl and blend in the fatty bacon cut into tiny cubes, the walnuts, raisins, truffle (cut into small cubes), and the glazed chestnuts. Allow the stuffing to rest. Spread out the turkey breast, taking care not to remove the skin. Put the skin side down, and salt and pepper the meat. Spread the stuffing on the breast, roll it up and tie it. Put the meat in a roasting pan along with 6 tablespoons (100 g) of butter, sage, and rosemary. Brown the stuffed breast, then add the carrot, celery, chopped onion, and the white wine. Roast the turkey breast in a 350 °F (170 °C) oven for about 50 minutes, adding water to the pan if necessary. When the meat is done, set aside but keep it warm.
Pass the cooking juices through a strainer and bind with the remaining butter. Cut the breast in slices and put two slices on each

dish. Pour over the sauce and garnish with glazed onions, glazed chestnuts, and, if available, mostarda di Cremona (fruits pickled in mustard).

Wine: Barbaresco (Piedmont), 4-8 years

Blancmange with Caramel Cream

Bianco mangiare con crema al caramello

Serves 4
For the blancmange:
¹/₂ cup (150 g) milk
2 tablespoons blanched almonds
1 teaspoon (8 g) cleaned bitter almonds
1 teaspoon (8 g) gelatin
³/₄ cup (100 g) powdered sugar
3 tablespoons (40 g) cherry brandy
1 ¹/₄ cup (280 g) cream, whipped
For the caramel cream:
¹/₂ cup (150 g) sugar
2 teaspoons (10 g) cornstarch
¹/₃ cup (100 g) sugar
2 cups (¹/₂ L) milk
5 egg yolks. Vanilla (to taste)

To make the blancmange, chop the white and bitter almonds and blend with the milk. Pass the purée through a cheesecloth folded over. Meanwhile, soak the gelatin in a little cold water. Add the powdered sugar, the cherry brandy, the dissolved gelatin and the whipped cream. Pour the mixture into 4 small molds and place it in the refrigerator for 4 hours.
For the caramel cream, caramelize ¹/₂ cup (150 g) of sugar in a little water. Separately, combine the egg yolks with ¹/₃ cup (100 g) of sugar, the cornstarch, and the vanilla. Bring the milk just to a boil, and add to the vanilla mixture. Add to the caramel when it is ready and allow to cool.
Pour some cold sauce into each plate. Unmold the blancmange and place on the cream. Garnish with toasted almonds.

Wine: Moscato d'Asti (Piedmont), 1 year

IL CIGNO

Gaetano Martini, the owner of Il Cigno, serves as the establishment's maître d' and sommelier, while his wife, Alessandra, supervises the kitchen. The restaurant is installed in an old palace in the ancient heart of Mantua in rooms long occupied by an inn.

Mantua is situated in the heart of the Padania, the vast valley that takes its name from the Padus or Po, Italy's largest river. In the Padania, there are cities such as Pavia, Piacenza, Parma, Reggio Emilia, Mantua, Cremona, Ferrara, and Rovigo that have been the theaters of great events. The river, in its silent mobility, serves as the main artery of the Padania, mirroring every twist and turn of history, not only that written in the books but also that, much more tactile and warm, that has been lived year after year by the people of this vast plain. Everywhere, there is a great silence, one that is not due to any mere absence of noise. Life in the Padania has been assured and enriched through the efforts of men, who have ceaselessly battled the mighty river to keep it within its banks. There is no valley flatter than this sunny plain.

In all seasons, Mantua appears virtually deserted and silent, possessing a dreamlike quality. It offers a distinct impression of the fabulous, which can be sensed in the streets and the squares of the center. The city extends along the banks of the river Mincio, which, shaped like a fish hook, encloses it on three sides.

The city, of Etruscan origin, was later occupied by the Gauls and the Romans. The latter made it an agricultural center of modest importance, which was described by the poet Virgil, a native of the community. Between 1328 and 1627, Mantua was governed by the Gonzagas and became a humanistic center of major significance, attracting such artists as Brunelleschi, Leon Battista Alberti, Mantegna, who made it his home, and Giulio Romano, and the poet-scholar Poliziano (Politian). In the middle of the sixteenth century, the city reached the peak of its political and economic splendor, while on the borders of the duchy flourished autonomous Gonzaga lordships, including Sabbioneta,

the most famous, which was known as "little Athens."

Today, Mantua is the capital of a flourishing agricultural industry that is considered the richest and most remunerative in the world. But there are also light and heavy industrial plants of considerable dimensions as well. Still, the city abounds in splendid palaces and monuments and in important masterpieces of art of the fifteenth and sixteenth centuries. The Ristorante Il Cigno is immersed in that atmosphere of ancient sumptuousness and refinement, installed as it is in an imposing sixteenth-century palace named for Carlo D'Arco.

The ancient tradition that links Mantuan cuisine not only to the products of the area in which the city is situated but also to Oriental and Venetian experience can be discerned in the *tortelli di zucca* (large ravioli stuffed with pumpkin), which are rich, sweet, and aromatic, and in the *insalata di cappone* (capon salad), which is of Renaissance origin and abounds in contrasts, since the flavors are provided by vinegar, sugar, and sultanas. The ancient use of freshwater fish caught in the Mincio, the Po, and the ducal ponds has been renewed by Il Cigno with fillet of eel in *aceto balsamico* (vinegar aged in various types of wood on the Sherry system), and *luccio* (pike) in *salsa mantovana*. The rice dishes of this district have always been famous. The workers who cleaned the grains were known as *piloti* or *pilarini*, and they have lent their name to an extremely famous preparation, *risotto alla pilota*, in which the grain is served with a pork chop or a fish such as pike or carp. The method of cooking the rice is quite special. The grains are poured into the pan so that they form a cone, which is then covered with water and cooked without being stirred or disturbed. In that way, the grains remain separate.

The sixteenth-century palace in which Il Cigno is installed features friezes of the same period, lacunar ceilings (decorated with recessed panels), and antique furnishings. The restaurant's principal dining room is situated in a section of recent construction and laid out around an attractive garden. The room is divided into modular sections by a large planter. The atmosphere is calm and relaxing and during the day the dining room is illuminated by a suffused light that filters through the lush green plants. The principal room will accommodate about forty diners, while a smaller room provides space for about a dozen other diners. Another large room is used for conferences and large dinners.

The section of the D'Arco Palace now used by Il Cigno restaurant was occupied by an inn during the early years of the eighteenth century but the present restaurant was created in 1966 at the initiative of Countess Giovanni D'Arco, who entrusted the operation of the establishment to the Martini family. Il Cigno emphasizes the cuisine of the immediate territory through a reinterpretation of the recipes of

Piazza Carlo D'Arco 1 - 46100 Mantua. The restaurant is closed Mondays and Tuesday evenings and part of the month of August, depending upon the year. The Michelin one-star establishment is situated in the heart of the city, not far from the ancient Church of Sant'Andrea and the central railroad station.
AE and Diners cards accepted.
Tel. (0375) 327101

The restaurant's director is Gaetano Martini, an energetic, ambitious, proud, intelligent, and determined man, who has succeeded in giving the establishment a cultural dimension. With his personal magnetism and his capacity for analysis and immediacy, he has managed to give this refined "boutique" of inspired cuisine a particular appeal. In the kitchen, his wife, Alessandra, is a scrupulous interpreter of the original bourgeois recipes, producing dishes that are well balanced and refined. There is a great diversity of pastas, ranging from *tagliatelle* (noodles) to *anolini* (a type of ravioli). The numerous sausages are carefully chosen and Il Cigno's poultry is prepared in sumptuous style.

the bourgeois and, to some extent, popular cooking of the nineteenth and early twentieth centuries. It is a tradition derived from the magnificence of the Gonzaga court, which was witnessed and described between the fifteenth and seventeenth centuries by such outstanding writers on cuisine as Bartolomeo Sacchi, known as Il Platina, and Bartolomeo Stefani.

Hare in Salmis alla Mantovana

Lepre in salmì alla mantovana

Serves 4
1 hare, about 3 ¼ pounds (1.5 kilos)
2 cups (½ L) white wine
7 cloves
8 black peppercorns
3 bay leaves
Salt
Spices (pepper, nutmeg, clove, cinnamon, and mace)
1 onion
⅓ pound (150 g) bacon
6 tablespoons (100 g) butter
2 tablespoons white flour
Meat broth, if needed

Clean the hare and reserve the giblets. Cut the hare into pieces and marinate it for 10 hours in a marinade consisting of the wine, cloves, peppercorns, bay leaves, salt and pinch of spices.
Chop the onion, the giblets, bacon, and put them in a pan with the butter, and simmer. Add the pieces of hare, well dried, and brown them. Then pour over the marinade and cook over a low flame for one hour. When the hare is cooked, add the flour. If the sauce becomes too thick, add a bit of meat broth. When the sauce is ready, remove the meat, and pass the liquid through a fine sieve, and reheat. Serve the hare with the sauce.

Wine : Sassicaia (Tuscany), 7 years at least or Taurasi (Campania), 5 years and more

Rice and Pumpkin

Riso e zucca

Serves 4
1 medium-sized onion
1 carrot
1 celery stalk
1 slice fatty bacon, about 2 ounces (60 g)
2 tablespoons (30 g) butter
1 pound (500 g) pumpkin
Salt
4 cups (1 L) meat broth
1 ¼ cups (300 g) rice
1 scant cup (100 g) grated Parmesan

Chop the onion, carrot, celery, and bacon. Put those chopped ingredients into a pot in which the butter has been melted and brown over a low flame for 10 minutes. Pass the bacon mixture through a food mill.
Peel the pumpkin and cut into small cubes. Add the pieces of pumpkin to the bacon mixture and simmer for a time. Add salt and then the meat broth. Simmer over a low flame for 15 minutes. Add the rice and cook for about 15 minutes or until the rice is tender. Before serving, sprinkle with the Parmesan and stir vigorously.

Wine : Sauvignon del Collio (Friuli-Venezia Giulia), 1-3 years

Baked Boletus Mushrooms

Cappelle di funghi porcini al forno

Serves 4
4 boletus mushroom caps (about 1 ³/₄ pounds or 800 g)
Handful parsley
2 garlic cloves
1 cup (100 g) breadcrumbs, approximate
Salt and pepper
6 tablespoons (100 g) olive oil

Preheat the oven to 350 °F (180 °C).
Clean and wash the mushroom caps. Dry them carefully and then place them in the oven on a baking sheet for several minutes, turning them frequently so that they heat through.
Wash and dry the parsley and chop it along with the garlic. Put the breadcrumbs in the bottom of a baking dish, then place the mushroom caps in the dish and sprinkle the chopped parsley and garlic over them. Salt and pepper the mushrooms and sprinkle with oil. Bake for about 10 minutes then serve them hot.

Wine: Bardolino (the Veneto), 4-7 years

Pike in Mantuan Sauce

Luccio in salsa mantovana

Serves 4
1 pike, approx. 2 ¹/₂ - 3 ¹/₄ pounds (1.5 kilo)
1 onion, sliced
1 carrot, sliced
1 celery stalk, sliced
²/₃ cup white wine
Salt
4 bay leaves
1 garlic clove
²/₃ cup (150 g) capers
2 tablespoons chopped parsley
1 sweet red pepper
1 yellow pepper preserved in vinegar
6 tablespoons (100 g) olive oil
3 anchovies
2 tablespoons (25 g) vinegar
Peel of 1 lemon, grated
Chopped parsley for garnish

Poach the fish in water to which have been added onion, carrot, celery, wine, salt, and bay leaves.
Chop extremely finely the garlic, capers, parsley, and peppers, both the fresh and that preserved in vinegar. Put the oil in a pan along with the anchovies, which have been washed, boned, and chopped. Cook without allowing to come to a boil until the anchovies have dissolved. Add the chopped seasonings. Add salt and pepper to taste. In addition, add 2 tablespoons of vinegar, then cook slowly for 10 minutes.
Once the pike has cooled, break it into pieces and put them on a serving dish. Grate the lemon peel over the fish and pour over the sauce, making sure that it has entirely covered the fish. Sprinkle with chopped parsley. Allow the dish to "rest" for several hours, then serve the pike with its sauce. It is consumed cold, accompanied by slices of hot, toasted *polenta* (cornmeal mush).

Wine: Torre di Giane il Pino (Lungarotti, Umbria), 2-4 years

Breast of Capon Salad

Insalata di petti di cappone

Serves 4
2 capon breasts
1 carrot, sliced
1 celery stalk, sliced
1 onion, sliced
5 tablespoons (50 g) sultana raisins
¹/₂ cup sweetish white wine
1 tablespoons sugar
4 tablespoons (60 g) olive oil
3 tablespoons (35 g) vinegar
Peel of ¹/₂ lemon, grated
Salt and pepper

Poach the capon breasts in a little water along with the sliced carrot, celery, and onion. Allow the breasts to cool, then fillet them and put them in a terrine.
Soak the raisins in the wine, along with a tablespoon of warm water, and the sugar, dissolved. Blend in a bowl the oil, vinegar, grated lemon peel, raisins, wine, salt and pepper. Pour the sauce thus obtained over the capon fillets. Allow the dish to rest for several hours before serving.

Wine: Bianco di Pitigliano (Tuscany), 1-2 years

DAL PESCATORE

*Each member of the Santini family - Nadia, Giovanni,
Bruna and Antonio - makes a special contribution to
the success of Dal Pescatore , a comfortable and
appealing restaurant in the village of Runato near
Canneto sull'Oglio ; the area is close to Cremona in the
heart of the prosperous Po Valley.*

The Padania, the great plain created by the Po, is as rich in gastronomic traditions as it is fertile, abounding in products that ensure great culinary variety. It is the homeland of Parmesan cheese, the raw hams of Parma, the *culatello*, which is an even more refined type of raw ham, the salames of Feline and the Cremona area, which are famous, and, close to the river's delta, the *salama da sugo*, a sort of enriched and aged *cotechino*, a succulent and spicy sausage. The great plain, Italy's most important agricultural area, is particularly noted for its production of milk products and especially cheeses, as well as for the raising and slaughtering of swine.

The Ristorante Dal Pescatore is located in the very heart of this rich and fruitful lowland, in the village of Runato, which has no more than thirty-six inhabitants. It is not far from Gonzaga, the town from which the lords who dominated Mantua for centuries derived their name, or from Bozzolo, another village with a well-preserved sixteenth-century palace. Also in the vicinity is the Torre de' Picenardi, a small and appealing castle surrounded by a lake teeming with fish. Enormous progress has been made in this great "food valley" in developing agricultural production and the output is distinguished by its excellent quality and by the ancient traditions that link it to the daily habits of the people who live there. In this area, food and diet have always had an unusual importance, so much so that both have become the subject of research that has laid the foundations of current production activity. The deep roots of this research can be found in the household traditions of the plain and in the people's dietary behavior, so that Dal Pescatore has been able to synthesize, and benefit from, centuries of culinary research. Today, the restaurant represents a synopsis and a further elaboration

in a more modern key of what was once the noble cuisine of the princely families, then that of the peasants and, afterward, that of the townspeople.

The history of the restaurant and that of the Santini family are inseparably linked. There were Teresa and Antonio in the first decades of this century, then Bruna and Giovanni. Now Papa Giovanni sees to the breads and fish, Mamma Bruna to the first courses, and Nadia, their daughter-in-law, tends to the hors d'oeuvres, main-course preparations, and desserts. Antonio, their son, is, in a sense, the coordinator. Nadia and Antonio, the new generation, have transformed a family-style establishment, once an inn known as the Vino e Pesce (Wine and Fish), into one of Italy's leading restaurants. Its culinary philosophy is that of promoting to a wider public the living and generous soul of the Padania, while respecting tradition. Paying attention to the land and its products and interpreting them with refinement is a difficult synthesis, but one that has been successfully achieved. Even the structure of the restaurant is both elegant and rustic with small dining rooms and only a few places at table. The garden, bordered by a fine hedge, provides a relaxing setting for meals in the summer.

The restaurant has a wine list of great interest. In respect to Italian products, Antonio Santini provides outstanding quality, such as the La Versa brut Champagne-method sparkling wine and the Pergole Torte produced by Sergio Manetti, as well as the Solaia, the most recent gem of the House of Antinori, and the red produced by Maurizio Zanella of Cà del Bosco, which is one of Lombardy's most appealing wines. France is well represented with the wines of Burgundy, Bordeaux, and Champagne.

In the restaurant, there are echoes of the gastronomic insights and culture of the

The Po Valley is not a showy place. Among its inhabitants, who are noted for their industriousness, there is no place for opulence. Instead, solid comfort and abundance are prized, whether in daily life or in the daily diet. The Dal Pescatore restaurant faithfully reflects that predilection. It is a pleasant but unprepossessing establishment, where the feel and the decor of the dining rooms are restrained, comfortable, and informal. Service, as well, is efficient and professional but the staff is also as devoted to accommodating and anticipating the house's guests in a spirit of quiet, country hospitality, which is entirely compatible with the establishment and with the milieu. The restaurant's philosophy is that of promoting to a wider public the living and generous soul of the Padania, while respecting the valley's tradition.

Giovanni Santini, the second generation of his family to operate Dal Pescatore, is the establishment's baker, seeing to the making and baking of all the breads served in the restaurant. His son Antonio coordinates service in the house's many small dining rooms but he also dedicates

Località Runate - 46013 Canneto sull'Oglio (Mantua). The restaurant is closed Mondays and Tuesdays, as well as the first 15 days of January and the last 15 of August. Runate is 3 kilometers (2 miles) northwest of Canneto, toward Carzaghetto. Canneto is 4 kilometers (2 ½ miles) north of Piadena, between Mantua, 37 kilometers (23 miles) to the east, and Cremona, 30 kilometers (19 miles) to the west.
AE cards accepted.
Tel. (0375) 70304

Italian Renaissance. Among the first writers to compile a work of great value, the expression of his own intelligent style of living, was Bartelomeo Sacchi, known as Il Platina, who lived from 1421 to 1481. His treatise, *De honesta voluptate et valetudino* (On Honest Pleasure and Good Health), which drew on the work of an earlier expert, Maestro Martino, deals with the proper order of foods as indicated in the following brief extract, from the chapter titled "What Things Should Be Eaten First": "A certain order should be observed in taking foods, since at the beginning of a meal those things that put the stomach in movement and that provide light and measured nourishment are eaten, such as apples and some pears. I would add lettuces and all that can be consumed raw or cooked seasoned with oil and vinegar."

himself to the selection and preservation of the wines in the vast cellar. Antonio has assembled products from every region of Italy but there are also choice products of the vineyards of France as well. The Po Valley is a prolific producer of wines, especially the ubiquitous Lambrusco, which has been extremely popular in the United States for the last decade or so. Although the Lambrusco tribe of wines does go extremely well with the rich cuisine of the valley, no one, including the Padania's inhabitants, pretends that the wine is one of the world's most elegant beverages. However, hilly areas around the valley have recently begun to turn out impressive wines.

Goose Liver with Boletus Mushrooms

Fegato d'oca con funghi porcini

Serves 4
6 tablespoons (100 g) butter
4 slices of foie gras of goose
1 pound (500 g) of fresh boletus mushrooms
1 sprig of rosemary
4 tablespoons of white wine
Salt and pepper

Melt the butter in a copper pan. When the butter has turned a light golden color, add the slices of foie gras and cook them on both sides for 1 minute.
Remove the foie gras and put the mushrooms, cut into small pieces, in the pan. Add the rosemary, the white wine, and a pinch of salt and pepper. Cook over a moderate flame for 4 minutes or until the sauce is quite thick.
Return the foie gras to the pan for several minutes, then serve quite hot, accompanied by a green salad, small, boiled green beans, and some leaves of radicchio or red chicory (if available).

Wine: Müller Thurgau della Valle d'Isarco (Trentino-Alto Adige), 1-2 years

Boletus Mushrooms and Snails with Vegetables

Porcini e lumache alle verdure

Serves 4
1 pound (400 g) fresh boletus mushrooms
1 small celery stalk
1 carrot
1 scallion (or shallot)
$\frac{1}{2}$ cup chicken broth
3 tablespoons (50 g) of butter
1 clove of garlic
$\frac{1}{2}$ tablespoon of chopped parsley
Salt and pepper
For preparation of fresh snails*:
24 snails
2 ounces (50 g) coarse salt
5 quarts (5 liters) water
2 celery stalks
1 leek, cut in half lengthwise
1 carrot, cut in half lengthwise
1 onion, cut in half
2 bay leaves
3 garlic cloves

Purge, boil and clean the snails, if fresh ones are used. Chop the scallion quite fine, cut the celery and carrot into small cubes and crush the clove of garlic. Stew the vegetables in the butter. After several minutes, add the snails, broth, salt and pepper. Cook for 5 minutes. Wash and slice the mushrooms. Add to the casserole, and continue to cook for 3-4 minutes more, stirring with a wooden spoon. A moment before removing the pan from the fire, remove the garlic and sprinkle the dish with chopped parsley.
Put the snails in the boiling water with the bay leaves and the vegetables, including the garlic, tied together with kitchen string. Cook for 2 hours and leave the snails to cool in the water. Reserve the broth.

*To prepare fresh snails: purge the snails in the coarse salt for about 2 hours. Stir them around from time to time. Wash them under running water to remove the scum. Bring the water to a boil, add the snails, and cook for

2 minutes. Remove the snails from their shells and eliminate the intestine (the hard little black piece on one end of the body).
Wine : Bianco di Franciacorta (Cà del Bosco, Lombardy), 1-2 years

Pumpkin Tortelli

Tortelli di zucca

Serves 4
For the pasta :
2 cups (250 g) white flour
2 eggs
For the stuffing :
1 ³/₄ pounds (800 g) pumpkin or yellow squash
3 ¹/₂ ounces (100 g) *mostarda senapata* (fruit pickled in mustard ; mild chutney may be substituted)
2 ounces (60 g) *amaretti (*almond cookies)
2 tablespoons grated Parmesan
Nutmeg, Salt and pepper
For the sauce :
6 tablespoons (100 g) butter
3 tablespoons grated Parmesan
Salt

Prepare the pasta and cut it into squares of 4 inches (10 cm) per side.
Remove the seeds from the pumpkin or squash and cut into large pieces. Cook the pieces in a 350 °F (180 °C) oven for 20 minutes or until tender. Remove the skin and pass the pumpkin through a sieve.
Add to the puree the *mostarda* (or chutney) finely chopped, the *amaretti* crushed into a powder, the grated Parmesan, a pinch of nutmeg, salt and pepper. Blend well, making sure that the puree is quite consistent. Then form it into little balls.
Place a ball of filling on each square of pasta and fold over one corner of the dough diagonally. Press down on the edges to ensure that the pasta "envelope" is well sealed. Plunge the ravioli in boiling salted water and cook for 4-5 minutes. Remove the ravioli with a perforated spoon, one by one, working carefully to avoid breaking the pasta. Put the ravioli in heated dishes.

Melt the butter. Sprinkle grated Parmesan over the ravioli, then pour over the melted butter and serve.
Wine : Verduzzo dei Colli Orientali or dell Collio (Friuli-Venezia Giulia), 1-2 years

Rice with Dogfish and Chives

Risotto con pesce gatto e erba cipollina

Serves 4
1 dogfish, about 1 ³/₄ pounds (800 g)
Juice of ¹/₂ lemon
1 celery stalk
¹/₂ carrot
¹/₂ head of fennel
5 tablespoons (70 g) butter
1 *cipollotto* (a wild onion ; a regular onion may be substituted)
9 ounces (260 g) of rice
¹/₂ onion
4 ¹/₃ cups (1 L) fish or vegetable broth
2 tablespoons white wine
1 tablespoon chopped chives
Salt and pepper

Poach the dogfish in water with the lemon juice and the vegetables (celery, carrot, and fennel).
Stew some slices of *cipollotto* in 2 tablespoons (30 g) of butter. Add the flesh of the dogfish and stew for several minutes. Salt and pepper the fish and remove the pan from the heat.
Finely chop the onion and cook it for 5 minutes in a bit of butter, a pinch of salt, and several tablespoons of water. When the water has evaporated, add the rice and cook it for several minutes so that it absorbs the butter. Then cover the rice with broth. After 15 minutes, add the fish, the wine, and the chives. When the rice is cooked, add the rest of the butter and stir it in so that the preparation becomes creamy.

Wine : Soave Classico (the Veneto), 1-2 years

Fillet of Trout or Perch in White Wine

Filette di pesce persico-trota al vino bianco

Serves 4
1 ³/₄ pounds (800 g) trout or perch
¹/₂ cup white wine
3 tablespoons (40 g) butter
1 scallion (or shallot)
1 celery stalk
1 small carrot
1 small leek
1 tomato
Salt and white pepper

Poach the fish for 3-4 minutes in a court bouillon. Then fillet the fish.
Finely chop the scallion and cut the celery, carrot, and leek into small pieces. Put the butter in a pan, lightly brown the scallion, and then add the vegetables, sautéing for several minutes. Cover with white wine and add salt and pepper. Peel the tomato and cut into small pieces. Add them to the pan and cook for several minutes more.
Pass the sauce through a sieve and return it to the pan. Add the fish fillets and complete the cooking. Serve garnished with steamed vegetables.

Wine : Riesling Renano del Collio (Friuli-Venezia Giulia), 1-2 years

VECCHIA LUGANA

On the banks of Lake Garda on the boundary between the Veneto and Lombardy regions, Pierantonio Ambrosi has created a restaurant according to a new formula in keeping with the times and with the will to renovate without ignoring the tradition of the area, one of the most appealing in Italy.

Apple of islands, Sirmio, and bright peninsulas, set
in our soft-flowing lakes or in the folds of ocean,
with what delight delivered, safe and sound,
                              from Thynia
from Bithynia
    you flash incredibly upon the darling eye.
What happier thought
    than to dissolve
the mind of cares
    the limbs from sojourning,
and to accept the down of one's own bed
under one's own roof
    – held so long at heart...
and that one moment paying for all the rest.

So, Sirmio, with a woman's loveliness, gladly
    echoing Garda's rippling lake-laughter,
and, laughing there, Catullus' house
                catching the brilliant echoes !*

In some places, Lake Garda resembles the sea, a northward extension of the Mediterranean that reaches virtually into Austria, bringing with it the illusion of the south and the blue sky, a mirage that is abetted by the olive trees and lemons of the Lombardy and Veneto regions. The lake serves as the boundary between the Veneto and Lombardy, an extremely gentle and deep blue border, and there is no town or village along its shores that is not an inlet of calm and tranquillity.

In addition to the great natural beauty of the lake, there is history, a great deal of it. The verses of Catullus, the first-century (B.C.) Roman lyric poet, were cited for a reason. Situated on a slender peninsula jutting into the lake, the village of Sirmione (the Sirmio of the poem) was an important strategic and cultural center in the last centuries before the Christian era and for a short time afterward. The archaeological remains, which bear the erroneous but effective title of "Grotto of Catullus," are an impressive testimony of the existence there of a Roman villa in the early imperial period. It was beautifully sited, enjoying a superb view of the lake, the opposite shore, and the line of tall mountains beyond. If it were not, especially at certain times of the year, crowded with tourists, Sirmione would still be the "apple of islands... and bright peninsulas," as Catullus described it. However, it still remains an enchanted and enchanting place.

About two miles from Sirmione, in a hamlet anciently known as Silva Lucana and now called Lugana di Sirmione, is another gem of the Garda treasure chest, the Trattoria Vecchia Lugana. As early as Roman times, the site was a post station. The structure in which the restaurant is installed goes back to the eighteenth century and has always served as an inn. The building has been restructured and adapted to its current use, although its ancient characteristics have been retained. Pierantonio Ambrosi is the man who has brought the Trattoria Vecchia Lugana to its present eminence. His gifts are virtually in his blood, since the Ambrosi family has been traditionally involved in the operation of restaurants. Ambrosi is an expert sommelier and personally looks after the selection of the wines and liqueurs, as well as the composition of the menu. And the foods follow the seasons, so that the establishment is always able to offer its guests the best that is available on the market. He is aided by his mother, co-owner Alma Fumagalli Ambrosi, and his chef, Carmine Gazineo. Ambrosi has participated in various significant initiatives in the field of Italian gastronomy. One was the "Italian Line in Cuisine," which was created at Milan in

Fish from Lake Garda are one of the natural resources of the district tapped by the Vecchia Lugana. The establishment presents a cuisine that is an authentic expression of Italian culinary tradition, although one that has been further refined and modernized to appeal to contemporary tastes. Chef Carmine Gazineo is properly fastidious, not only in overseeing the preparation of the dishes issuing from the kitchen but also in selecting the materials that compose them. Gazineo fully realizes that the special qualities of Italian cuisine depend in great measure on the absolute freshness of the pro-

ducts used. In the restaurant's kitchen, the ancient fireplace still serves a practical purpose, for meats, poultry, and game are roasted on spits over a wood fire throughout the year but especially during the winter months. Garda is a popular resort, attracting throngs of tourists from the south as well as from the north. Lugana, where the Vecchia Lugana restaurant is situated, is only a couple of miles from the center of Sirmione, a village that was originally settled in pre-Roman days on a peninsula jutting into the sky-blue waters of the lake on its southern shore. The site was easily defended because of

the narrowness of the promontory and the depth of the surrounding waters, but nature was not enough for the della Scala family of Verona, who made Sirmione into an impressive fortress in the fourteenth century. The community possesses two fascinating churches, Santa Maria Maggiore, constructed in the fifteenth century and containing frescoes of the fifteenth-sixteenth centuries, and San Pietro in Mavino, which was built in the eighth century but remodeled in the eleventh, when the belltower was erected, and again in the sixteenth.

Piazzale Vecchia Lugana 1 - 25019 Sirmione (Brescia). The restaurant, with one star in the *Guide Michelin*, is closed Sunday evenings and Tuesdays, from November 1 to 10, and throughout January. Lugana is on the outskirts of Sirmione, about halfway between Milan, 126 kilometers (79 miles) to the west, and Venice, 149 kilometers (79 miles) to the west, and Venice, 149 kilometers (93 miles) to the east, close to Autostrada (Superhighway) A-4.
The restaurant does not accept any credit cards
Tel. (030) 919012

1978 and was dedicated, as it still is, to safeguarding the typicalness and the uniqueness of Italian cuisine. The effort was perhaps undertaken to combat some tendencies that were in vogue several years ago. Another initiative was the "Golden Apple Club," a name that might seem slightly dubious. However, the organization has an extremely serious purpose, creating a close union among a very few but highly qualified Italian restaurateurs, journalists, and experts in the field and with their American counterparts. The intention, again, is to protect the name and the image of Italian cuisine abroad.

* *The Poems of Catullus*, 31, translated by Peter Whigham (Penguin Books, 1966) p. 88

Fillet of Beef *al Pesto*

Filetto al pesto

Serves 4
4 walnuts
1 tablespoon (10 g) pinenuts
20 basil leaves
1 tablespoon chopped parsley
Salt and pepper
$^{1}/_{4}$ cup (50 g) olive oil
4 fillets of beef, each weighing $^{1}/_{3}$ pound
  (150 g)
2 tablespoons (30 g) butter
$^{1}/_{2}$ cup (1 dl) red wine
1 cup ($^{1}/_{4}$ L) meat sauce

Prepare the *pesto* by pounding the walnuts, pinenuts, basil, parsley, and salt and pepper in a mortar until a well-blended paste is obtained. Add the oil and blend well. Sauté the fillets in the butter over a high flame. Remove the fillets and keep them warm. Pour off the fat, add the wine and the meat sauce, and cook slowly until the sauce becomes quite thick. Serve the fillets on individual dishes, pouring over the sauce and garnishing with the *pesto*.

Wine: Bricco Manzoni (Piedmont), 4-8 years

Trout Mousse on a Bed of Rocket (Mustard Greens)

Spuma di pesce su letto di rucola

Serves 4
2 trout, about 1 $^{3}/_{4}$ pounds altogether
  (800 g)
6 tablespoons (100 g) butter
1 cup ($^{1}/_{4}$ L) fish stock
$^{1}/_{2}$ cup (1 dl) white wine
$^{1}/_{3}$ teaspoon powdered gelatin
  (or 1 sheet fish glue)
Rocket (or mustard greens or lettuce)
Salt and pepper

Preheat oven to 350 °F (180 °C).
Fillet the trout and put them in a buttered ovenproof dish. Salt them and baste with the white wine and fish broth. Dot with the remaining butter and cook in the oven for about 15 minutes.
Puree the fish in a blender and strain the cooking liquid. Put the fish puree in a bowl and blend in the cooking liquid a little at a time.
Mix in the gelatin previously softened in cold water. The resulting mixture should not be too thick or too soft. Add salt and pepper to taste and pour the puree in a mold. Refrigerate for at least 12 hours.
Serve on individual plates on a bed of rocket, mustard greens, or lettuce.

Wine: Bianco di Custoza (the Veneto), 1-2 years

Fillets of Coregone with Basil

Filetto di coregone al basilico

Serves 4
2 *coregoni* weighing 2 ¼ pounds altogether (1 K) (a sweet, firm-fleshed
  freshwater fish may be substituted)
20 basil leaves
1 garlic clove, minced
½ tablespoon (10 g) mustard
2 egg yolks
1 cup (200 g) olive oil, approximate
Juice of ½ lemon
4 lettuce leaves
Salt

Clean and fillet the fish. Salt the fillets and
cook them in a steamer.
Finely chop the basil and put in a bowl with
the garlic, mustard, and egg yolks. Blend the
ingredients, using a whisk.
Add the oil a little at a time, whisking throughout the process until a soft mayonnaise-like
cream is obtained. Add salt and lemon juice
and blend in well.
Scald the lettuce leaves in boiling water,
then lay them out on dishes. Put the fillets of
fish atop the lettuce and pour the sauce over
them.

Wine : Lugana (Lombardy-the Veneto), 2-
3 years

Fine Noodles with Wild Waterfowl Sauce

Tagliatelle al salmi di uccelli d'acqua dolce

Serves 4
For the pasta :
2 cups (300 g) white flour
3 eggs
Salt
For the sauce :
1 small coot
1 wild duck
1 cup (¼ L) red wine
1 carrot, chopped
1 onion, chopped
1 celery stalk, chopped
2 bay leaves
½ cup (1 dl) olive oil
Cloves
Salt and pepper

Bone the coot and the duck and cut into
small pieces. Put the meat in the red wine
along with the chopped carrot, onion, and
celery, and the bay leaves and cloves. Marinate for 24 hours.
Combine the flour, eggs, and a pinch of salt
and work energetically for 15 minutes until a
smooth dough is obtained. Roll out into an
extremely thin sheet. Roll it into a tube and,
using a sharp knife, cut the pasta into strips
½ inch (1 cm) in thickness. Unroll the strips
and scatter them around the doughboard so
that they do not stick together.
Remove the meat from the wine and strain
the liquid through a sieve. Put the oil in a
pan, add the vegetables from the marinade,
and brown lightly. Add the meat, wine, salt
and pepper and cook over a slow fire for
about 2 hours.
Pass all the ingredients, including the meat,
through a food mill after removing the bay
leaves.
Cook the noodles in boiling salt for 8 minutes,
drain them, and serve with the sauce.

Wine : Valpolicella (Capitel Lucchine, the
Veneto), 1-3 years

Honey Ice Cream with Poppy Seeds

Gelato al miele con semi di papavero

Serves 4
1 egg
5 egg yolks
1 ¼ cups (250 g) sugar
1 teaspoon (5 g) vanilla
4 cups (1 L) milk
¾ cup (175 g) honey
5 tablespoons (75 g) poppy seeds

Beat the whole egg and the egg yolks with the
sugar and vanilla in a bowl. Scald the milk,
and add it to the egg mixture. Pass through a
fine sieve. Stir in the honey and poppy seeds,
blend well, and freeze in an ice cream maker.

Wine : Malvasia delle Lipari Passito (Sicily)

ANDREA

Geographically, the town of Merano is well within Italy but in mentality it is Middle European. This ambiguity of character is reflected in the ambience and cuisine of the Restaurant Andrea, which owes its name and its inspiration to Andreas Hellrigl, the proprietor, and to Walter Oberrauch, his chef.

Via Galilei 44 - 39012 Merano (Bolzano). The Michelin one-star restaurant is closed Mondays and from January 5 to March 15. Merano is 28 kilometers (17 ½ miles) northwest of Bolzano from which it is reached by SS (Highway) 38. Bolzano is 154 kilometers (96 miles) north of Verona and can be reached by Autostrada (Superhighway) A-22.
No credit cards accepted
Tel. (0473) 37400

The "architecture" of Andreas Hellrigl's cuisine, as it has been described because of its aesthetic vigor, is the highest expression of the mediation between creativity and technical accomplishment. Andreas Hellrigl is the most methodical and precise of contemporary Italian cooks. He is also one of the most accomplished, for his choices bear the imprint of unequaled dedication to quality. With Walter Oberrauch, his chef, Hellrigl has succeeded in balancing intuition and academic awareness to achieve an absolute harmony, creating without falling into the absurd, the trite, or the experimental.

Hellrigl is also something of a "repository" of the Middle European tradition of gastronomy, for he is without doubt the interpreter of what has remained or what he has been able to revive of this cuisine, which from the middle of the nineteenth century to the early decades of the twentieth drew its inspiration from the cultural milieu of central Europe. This tradition was formed around Austria during the time of the Habsburg empire and flourished in Germany as well as Austria and in the northeastern part of Italy, extending as far to the south as Lombardy. Naturally, it influenced the Trentino-Alto Adige. The Trentino-Alto Adige is an extraordinary region. It is necessary, if difficult, to ignore the ethnic conflicts afflicting that region, which periodically erupt in a manner that attracts wide attention. That factor aside, it is easy for the casual visitor to become very fond of this district. It is an appealing part of Italy. In the winter, it is a severe landscape, in which stories of gnomes and elves are still recounted under the fir trees. In the summer, the fields are brilliant with the whites, reds, greens, blues, and yellows of the blossoms and plants, so many that the eye is dazzled. Alto Adige is not the inheri-

tance of a few but an abundance of wealth to be shared by all with a refinement and style that blend the best of "happy" Austria and of the once proud republic of Venice.

The town of Merano has a great deal of history behind it, for it was an ancient and, especially, a medieval urban nucleus. At the turn of the century, it was a vacation site favored by many artists, writers, and musicians. It is a grande dame, still well groomed, of obvious nobility. Merano is a discreet place that does not blatantly advertise its fine villas and parks. There is a closeness to nature, a softness and restraint, that is pleasant and relaxing. It is a style that captivates in understated fashion. Yet that style is cultivated with a certain stubbornness and with constant application of insight and experience, which is typical, as well, of Hellrigl's approach.

Hellrigl's dedication has placed him at the apex of European gastronomy. His restaurant, Andrea, is a testimony to that as, for that matter, is the nearby Villa Mozart, the beautifully stylish small hotel that he has also created. Andrea, which opened in 1958, is situated in the center of the town, across from the Castello Principesco. The atmosphere, which has a solemn aspect, is warmed by a particular charm and by the impeccable service of the staff, overseen with special sensitivity by Signora Emy.

It is an establishment of great refinement and discretion: no superfluous frills but pure elegance. And the stubbornness is there as well in Hellrigl's continuous search for the best. For he is dedicated to perfection and has never ceased to seek it.

The restaurant is rather small and intimate, for it can accommodate no more than 25 guests. It is superbly furnished and well orchestrated to ensure privacy and intimacy, so that it has come to be regarded as perhaps the most refined and elegant restaurant in Italy. It is situated in the heart of Merano, facing the historic Castello Principesco, which was constructed in 1480 by Archduke Sigismond of Habsburg. The castle is extremely well preserved, for even its original decor and furnishings are intact. Nearby is the Duomo, a church in the Gothic style that was erected in the fourteenth and fifteenth centuries. Merano is a popular resort in the summer but it really enters into its own in the winter when the slopes of the surrounding mountains are crowded with skiers from virtually every country in Europe.

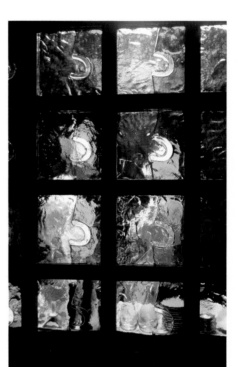

Veal Tongue with Potatoes and Cress

Lingua di vitello con patate e crescione

Serves 4
1 veal tongue
½ onion
2 carrots
2 celery stalks
1 leek
5 peppercorns
2 bay leaves
4 medium-size potatoes
2 teaspoons (10 g) butter
4 tablespoons (60 g) olive oil
1 tablespoon (15 g) red-wine vinegar
1 teaspoon (5 g) Sherry vinegar
2 teaspoons (20 g) red onion, sliced fine
1 tablespoon (7 g) finely chopped chives
1 ounce (30 g) watercress
Salt and pepper

Cook the tongue in 3 quarts (3 L) of salted water along with the onion, carrots, celery, leek, peppercorns, and bay leaves. Keep the tongue hot.
Peel the potatoes and cut them into slices ¹⁄₁₆ inch (3 mm) thick and cook slowly in a bit of salted water to which the butter has been added.
Prepare a sauce by mixing the oil, vinegars, red onion, chives, and a pinch of salt and pepper.
Skin the warm tongue and cut it into slices about ⅛ inch (5 mm) thick. Arrange the tongue slices and the potatoes in a circle on the plate. Baste with the sauce and garnish the potatoes with the cress.

Wine: Veltliner della Valle d'Isarco or Eisacktaler (Trentino-Alto Adige), 1-2 years

Lasagna with Snail and *Fines Herbes* Sauce

Lasagne con ragù di lumache e erbe fini

Serves 4

40 fresh or prepared snails*

For the pasta:
1 beaten egg
Salt
PLAIN: 3 cups (400 g) white flour
4 eggs
3 tablespoons (50 g) olive oil
RED: ¾ cup (100 g) white flour
1 egg
1 tablespoon (15 g) olive oil
1 cooked turnip, pureed
GREEN: ¾ cup (100 g) white flour
1 egg
1 tablespoon (10 g) white flour
2 tablespoons (20 g) cooked pureed spinach
For the sauce:
2 scallions (or shallots)
4 tablespoons (60 g) butter
⅓ cup (8 cl) white wine
¾ cup (200 g) cream, whipped
4 teaspoons (20 g) cold butter
1 tablespoon whipped cream
1 garlic clove
1 tablespoon tarragon
1 tablespoon chervil
1 tablespoon chives
1 tablespoon watercress
1 tablespoon red chicory (if available)
1 tablespoon pickles
Salt and pepper

For each kind of pasta, pour the flour onto a board, make a well, and break the egg(s) into it. Add a pinch of salt. Add the turnip puree to one small batch, the spinach puree to the other. For each batch, combine the ingredients and knead for 10 minutes to make smooth dough.
Roll each out into a thin leaf. Cut the red and the green into fine noodles. Brush the plain pasta with 1 beaten egg. Lay the red noodles atop the egg pasta. Then, at right angles, place the green noodles atop the red so that a grid or plaid pattern is formed. Pass the pasta through a machine to press the three layers together or force together with a rolling pin. Cut into lasagna shapes.
For the sauce, brown the sliced scallions in 2 tablespoons of butter. Baste with white wine, add the cream, and reduce by half. Cut the snails in half and quickly brown them in 2 tablespoons of butter. Salt and pepper them. Add 1½ cups (3 dl) of the snail broth or the liquid in which the snails were packed. Bind with the 4 teaspoons of cold butter and whipped cream. Flavor with the garlic clove, removing it after a few minutes. At the last moment, add all the herbs, finely chopped, and the pickles.
Cook the lasagna in abundant water to which a tablespoon of oil has been added to keep the pasta from sticking together. Drain.
Place one piece of lasagna on a plate. Cover with the snail sauce. Add another lasagna and serve.

*Instructions on preparation of fresh snails are given on page 80.

Wine: Kreutzbichle Bianco (Joseph Brigl, Trentino-Alto Adige), 2-3 years or Müller Thurgau (Trentino-Alto Adige), 1-2 years

Sweet Ricotta Dumplings with Pureed Mixed Fruits

Canederli di ricotta con purea di frutta mista

Serves 4
For the canederli:
7 tablespoons (100 g) butter
3 eggs, separated
2 tablespoons (30 g) sugar
Peel of ½ lemon, grated
Pinch of cinnamon

Pinch vanilla sugar, or $\frac{1}{8}$ teaspoon
   vanilla extract
Pinch of salt
1 pound (500 g) ricotta cheese
1 tablespoon (15 g) powdered sugar
5 tablespoons (50 g) raisins soaked for a
   day
1 $\frac{1}{4}$ cups (120 g) breadcrumbs

For the coating:
7 tablespoons (100 g) butter
$\frac{1}{2}$ cup (50 g) breadcrumbs
3 tablespoons (50 g) sugar
1 teaspoon (5 g) cinnamon

For the puree of fruit:
$\frac{1}{2}$ pound (200 g) raspberries
$\frac{1}{2}$ pound (200 g) kiwis
$\frac{1}{2}$ pound (200 g) Williams pears
2 tablespoons (30 g) powdered sugar
$\frac{1}{2}$ tablespoon (8 g) sugar

To prepare the *canederli*, cream the butter
with the egg yolks and sugar. Add the grated
lemon peel, cinnamon, vanilla-flavored
sugar, salt, and ricotta, which has been
passed through a sieve. Blend well.
Beat the egg whites with the powdered sugar
until they are stiff and fold them carefully
into the ricotta mixture. Drain and dry the
raisins. Add them and the breadcrumbs.
Allow the batter to rest for 2 hours.
Form the batter into small, round lumps and
boil them in salted water over low heat for 10
minutes. Drain.
Melt 7 tablespoons of butter in a pan. Add $\frac{1}{2}$
cup (50 g) of breadcrumbs, 3 tablespoons (50
g) of sugar, and the cinnamon, and blend.
Dredge the *canederli* in this mixture, making sure that they are thoroughly coated.
Blend the raspberries with 1 tablespoon of
powdered sugar. Peel the kiwis and blend
with 1 tablespoon of powdered sugar. Peel
and core the pears, cut them into slices, and
cook them in a little water with $\frac{1}{2}$ tablespoon
of sugar. Blend the pears and pass them
through a sieve. Put the three purees on
dishes and place the canederli atop the
purees.

Wine: Moscato Giallo or Goldmuskateller
(Trentino-Alto Adige), 1 year

Fillet of Trout in Red Wine with Scallions (or Shallots)

Filetti di trota al vino rosso con scalogno

Serves 4
2 trout, about 1/2 pound (200 g) each
7 scallions (or shallots)
2 mushrooms
1 carrot
1 celery stalk
1 leek
9 tablespoons (130 g) butter
1 cup ($\frac{1}{4}$ L) water
1 cup ($\frac{1}{4}$ L) Champagne
3 tablespoons Port
1 cup ($\frac{1}{4}$ L) red wine
1 tablespoon olive oil
2 bay leaves
Salt and pepper

Clean and fillet the trout, cutting the fillets
extremely fine.
Dice one scallion, the mushrooms, carrot,
celery, and leek and brown them in 4 teaspoons (20 g) of butter. Add the fish carcasses, water, Champagne, salt and pepper,
and cook for 20 minutes. Pass the sauce
through a fine sieve and keep it hot.
Put the red wine and Port in a pan along with
1 scallion chopped fine. Reduce as much as
possible and blend in 7 tablespoons (120 g)
of butter.
Brown 5 scallions, cut in half lengthwise, in 2
teaspoons (10 g) of butter and 1 tablespoon
(15 g) of oil. Add the bay leaves and cook for
15 minutes. Salt and pepper lightly and keep
warm.
Salt and pepper the trout fillets. Put them in
the hot but not boiling fish broth and allow
them to absorb the flavor for 3 minutes on
each side. Pour the wine sauce on the plates
and arrange the fillets on it. Decorate with
the scallions laid out in the shape of stars.

Wine: Santa Maddalena or St. Magdalener
(Trentino-Alto Adige), 2-3 years

Medallion of Roebuck in Juniper Sauce

Medaglioni di capriolo in salsa ginepre

Serves 4
1 saddle of roebuck (or venison), about
   2 $\frac{1}{2}$-3 pounds (1.2 K)
$\frac{1}{2}$ cup (1 dl) grape-seed oil (or vegetable
   oil)
$\frac{1}{2}$ cup (100 g) *mirepoix* (diced vegetables - onion, celery, leek and carrot)
1 bay leaf
15 juniper berries
10 white peppercorns
3-4 tablespoons (50 g) tomato concentrate
2 cups ($\frac{1}{2}$ L) red wine
2 quarts (2 L) water
$\frac{1}{4}$ cup ($\frac{1}{2}$ dl) red wine
1 tablespoon Port wine
1 $\frac{1}{2}$ tablespoons (20 g) cold butter
1 teaspoon gin
Salt and pepper

Bone the saddle of roebuck or venison. Cut
the bones into small pieces and put them in a
425 °F (220 °C) oven with $\frac{1}{4}$ cup of the grape-
seed oil and *mirepoix* and brown. Remove the
pan from the oven and skim off the grease.
Add the bay leaf, 10 juniper berries, the white
peppercorns, the tomato concentrate, and
2 cups ($\frac{1}{2}$ L) of red wine. Reduce. Add 2 quarts
(2 L) of hot water and cook slowly over low heat
for 2 hours. Remove and discard the bones,
then pass the sauce through a sieve and reduce
until only 1 cup ($\frac{1}{4}$ L) of liquid remains.
Cut the boned saddle into medallions. Salt
them and brown them in $\frac{1}{4}$ cup ($\frac{1}{2}$ dl) of very
hot oil for about 3 minutes. Remove the
medallions from the pan and keep them warm.
Pour off the oil and, in the same pan, add 5
crushed juniper berries, $\frac{1}{4}$ cup red wine, and
1 tablespoon of Port. Reduce the liquid by
two thirds. Add the sauce to the pan. Reduce
further and blend in the cold butter. Cook
for several minutes more, then add the gin.
Place the medallions on plates and pour over
the sauce.
Wine: Lagrein Scuro.

IL DESCO

In the heart of ancient Verona, Elia Rizzo, chef, and Natale Spinelli, sommelier, have established an enviable reputation for Il Desco, a restaurant that succeeds in satisfying the somewhat traditional inclinations of the Veronese, while taking new paths in the preparation and preservation of foods.

Via Dietro San Sebastiano 7 - 37121 Verona. The restaurant is closed Sundays but open throughout the year without interruption. Il Desco, which has one Michelin star, is fairly close to the Piazza delle Erbe and only a few blocks from the House of Juliet at Via Cappello 23. From the restaurant it is a relatively short walk along the Via Stella and Anfiteatro to the ancient Roman arena.
Diners, AE, Visa, Eurocard cards honored
Tel. (045) 595358

Verona, a fascinating and sober city of an ancient model, seems an incongruous locale for a modern, easygoing restaurant like Il Desco. However, the contradiction is more apparent than real. Although Verona, a point of exchange where Italy confronts the rest of Europe as well as a center of important economic currents, is also deeply devoted to tradition, a restaurant of a European tone was bound to flourish sooner or later. Verona is an historical city with deep roots, where a walk in the Piazza Brà still has a certain significance and where every gesture still has an extremely provincial cadence. Yet, quite slowly, a more "continental" mode of behavior is gaining strength.

Il Desco represents for the city a focus of innovation in gastronomy. The restaurant is itself a spectacle, and a meal there is a presentation, for a couple of young restaurateurs have succeeded in achieving a balance between the ancient and the modern requirements of the city, between tradition and contemporary creativity.

Verona's slightly drowsy atmosphere should not mislead those who wish to know the city's discreet beauty. It may seem that nothing has ever happened there, but in reality Verona has been the theater of many events, public and private. Behind the open, public conflict of two Veronese families, the Montagues and Capulets of Shakespeare's Romeo and Juliet, are the Montecchi and Capuleti of history. Founded by the Gauls in the sixth or fifth century B.C., Verona was first the capital of the Ostrogoth King Theodoric and then of the Lombard King Alboin. It became a free commune but was later subjected to the rule of the della Scala (Scaliger) family and then the Viscontis of Milan before passing to Venice. At the end of the eighteenth century, Austria occupied Verona

and held it until 1866. Verona boasts a well-preserved Roman arena as well as a theater and the Arco dei Gavi (a Roman triumphal arch). The relics of the past, of the medieval and other periods, are scattered throughout the urban center.

The rare delectability and harmony of the city's monuments and sites, such as the Piazza delle Erbe, are characteristic, too, of the palace in which Il Desco is installed, a sixteenth-century building that was recently restored. It was once the dormitory of the monks of the Church of St. Sebastian only a short distance away. It is also close to what is supposed to have been the house of Juliet (at Via Cappello 23, near the Piazza delle Erbe) - an enchanting structure, no matter who once lived there. The interior of the Desco palace is as delightful as the exterior, for it is furnished with antiques and everything is elegant and extremely inviting. Even the cellar, where aperitifs are often served, is appealing, with its great vaulted ceilings and its antique furnishings.

The establishment was founded in 1981. Elia Rizzo and Natale Spinelli, the cook and the sommelier, had already had considerable experience : Rizzo in the restaurant field and Spinelli first in managing hotels and then restaurants. For a year, they traveled together, visiting restaurants and gathering recipes, in Italy and France. They then returned to Verona to open Il Desco.

Rizzo now tends exclusively to the cuisine. All the dishes are prepared the moment they are ordered, including the sauces. Rizzo emphasizes a light cuisine stripped of most fat or grease. And on a daily basis he selects the raw materials with meticulous care. It is a traditional cuisine but one that has been personalized, elaborated, and re-created, the fruit of steady dedication and attention.

Il Desco is installed in an ancient building – actually, there are few "new" structures in the heart of Verona, which was one of the leading cities of the Roman Empire – and its atmosphere is due in considerable measure to the fascination of old stones worn by weather and use. However, it has all the efficiency of a modern, although highly refined, installation. It is a spacious establishment but, at the same time, one that is warm and inviting.

TRATTORIA DALL'AMELIA

*Dall'Amelia has always specialized in
seafood, which is natural for a
restaurant only a few miles from the
Venetian Lagoon. The wine list is also
quite special since owner Dino
Boscarato is president of the Italian
Association of Sommeliers.*

Via Miranese 113 - 30171 Mestre. The restaurant, which has been accorded one star in the *Guide Michelin*, is closed Wednesdays from October to June and is open every day during the summer season. Mestre is an industrial city, which has preserved few monuments of interest, the most outstanding of which is a church in classical style with a Romanesque belltower, the church San Lorenzo. Visa, AE, Diners, Eurocard, cards accepted.
Tel. (041) 913951, 913952

A stop at the Amelia is tantamount to a plunge into the fantastical world of Venetian gastronomy, although there are also some dishes resulting from a modern intuition. The special character of the fish and shellfish, combined with the sensitive preparation of the dishes, makes the Amelia the finest interpreter of Venetian cuisine, which is certain to arouse the enthusiasm of every lover of seafood. The menu emphasizes small shell-less crabs, their larger brethren, octopus, *capelunghe* (a shellfish), scallops, prawns, shrimp, and squid, all prepared with great care and dedication so that the dishes reflect the gaiety and the luxury of the Venetians themselves. There is a delicate seductiveness in the *risotti* or rice dishes, whether they are composed with fish or shellfish or with vegetables and greens. The tonalities of flavor are even more varied in the main dishes, such as turbot, sea bass, and *baccalà* (dried, salted cod) or in the alternative dishes in which game is balanced with a traditional dish, the *fegato* (calf's liver) *alla veneta*, rounded off with the *castraore* (small wild artichokes) from such islands in the lagoon as Pallestrina and Sant'Erasme.

Maestre is the last important community of the mainland before Venice. It, too, was once fragmented by canals. Today, there remain only two waterways and each year even they shrink as the town expands. It was there that Dino Boscarato founded his establishment in 1961 in quarters once occupied by an inn, including stalls for travelers' horses, which was built in 1926. And it immediately became the goal of Venetians who wanted to escape the city for a time to enjoy themselves amid the greenery of the mainland fields.

It was there, too, that Boscarato founded an association in 1965 to award the Amelia Prize each year to an outstanding personality in the world of art or culture. Boscarato's vivacity has led him to undertake various initiatives that parallel his activity as a host. He is, for example, president of the Italian Association of Sommeliers, which, with its approximately five thousand members, is the largest society of professional wine stewards in the world. As a consequence, the restaurant's cellar is well stocked. There is a wide selection of wines from the area surrounding Venice but also of products from the entire peninsula.

The cuisine prepared by the Amelia's chefs is in general closely linked with the Venetian tradition, which excels in freshness and features foods that have all the bright transparency of a sky in a Tiepolo painting. There is, as well, an alternation of colors, somewhat on the order of a mosaic, and a crescendo of aromas and flavors. It is a cuisine that fascinates because of the abundance of seafood and the sensitive treatment of garden greens and vegetables. Boscarato has managed to combine this ancient culinary tradition of Venice and the Veneto with modern innovations that are full of fantasy and vitality.

The establishment is spacious, with vast windows facing toward the south and overlooking a small garden. The ambience is not intimate but rather bucolically festive, a place for lively and enjoyable gatherings. Both the environment and the foods are the expression of the spontaneity and joviality to be found in the best of Italian restaurants. At the Amelia, this warm and lively atmosphere is assured by each waiter, sommelier, and maître d', and by Dino Boscarato himself and his wife, Mara.

The Dall'Amelia restaurant is located in an area that was, not so long ago, open countryside in the immediate vicinity of Venice. It is now ensnarled in the mesh of superhighways and approach roads that bounds the town of Mestre, an industrial community that confronts the lagoon with a surrealistic industrial complex of depressing dimensions. Across the water, Venice glitters in the intense light that floods its pinnacles, palaces, and canals, a fantastical atmosphere in which it lives on as a city unique, a place of fable, in clear distinction to the reality of Mestre.

The considerable spaciousness of Dino Boscarato's Dall'Amelia restaurant is diminished in appearance because of the diffused light entering the large windows facing the small garden. Immediately inside the main entrance is the section reserved for those who want to eat only seafood, which is abundant in the Adriatic. The remaining space is divided into more intimate and inviting angles. In the background is a large frame in which are displayed the portraits of all the winners of the Amelia Prize. The menu offers rustic and honest foods of the Venetian tradi-

tion combined with modern creations, a juxtaposition that is at times rather daring but, in reality, harmonious and extremely pleasing. The establishment can accommodate as many as 200 diners.

Fish "Pie"

Pasticcio di pesce

Serves 4
<u>For the pasta:</u>
1 ¹/₂ cups (200 g) white flour
1 egg
Salt
<u>For the filling:</u>
¹/₃ pound (150 g) rose crayfish
1 pound (500 g) sole
¹/₂ scallion
Juice of 1 lemon
¹/₂ bay leaf
Handful of parsley
Salt
6 tablespoons (50 g) white flour
6 tablespoons (100 g) butter
³/₄ cup (170 g) cream
¹/₂ hot red pepper
1 egg yolk
1 tablespoon (20 g) olive oil
²/₃ cup (80 g) grated Parmesan

Make a dough with the flour, egg, and salt, adding a bit of warm water if necessary, and roll it out into a thin sheet. Cut the dough into lasagna shapes or to a size sufficient for the dough to fit a baking pan.
Boil the crayfish in salted water and shell them. Fillet the sole and poach it in the wine, along with the scallion, half of the lemon juice, bay leaf, parsley, and salt.
Separately, boil the fish and shellfish carcasses in water to cover. Pass the resulting broth through a fine sieve and make a sauce with it by blending in, over the heat, the flour, butter, cream, the remaining lemon juice, and hot red pepper. Cook for several minutes, then remove the red pepper. Remove the pan from the heat and whisk in the egg yolk.
Meanwhile, cook the pasta in salted water to which a tablespoon of olive oil has been added so that the lasagna pieces will not stick together. Drain the pasta and put the pieces on a moist towel to cool.
Preheat the oven to 350 °F (180 °C).
Arrange the ingredients in a baking pan, alternating layers of pasta with crayfish, sole, and sauce until all have been used. Sprinkle with grated Parmesan and bake until lightly browned.

Wine : Pinot Bianco dei colli Orientali or del Collio (Friuli-Venezia Giulia), 1-3 years

Cockle and Boletus Mushroom Salad

Insalata di capesante e funghi porcini

Serves 4
1 ripe tomato
¹/₄ pound (100 g) boletus or other mush-rooms that are in season
3 tablespoons (60 g) olive oil
Salt and pepper
Balsamic vinegar (or another highly aromatic vinegar can be used)
¹/₄ pound (100 g) green beans
¹/₄ pound (100 g) rocket (mustard greens may be substituted
12 large cockles
¹/₂ tablespoon chopped parsley

Preheat the oven to 400 °F (200 °C).
Peel and seed the tomato and cut into small pieces. Cut the mushrooms into thin slices. Put the tomato and the mushrooms in an ovenproof dish. Add olive oil, salt, and pepper and mix well. Bake in the oven for 10 minutes. Remove the dish from the oven, add some drops of balsamic vinegar, and stir well.
Cut the green beans into small pieces, and briefly boil or steam them al dente (when they still have a bite). Arrange on each dish the rocket (or other greens) and the green beans. Pour over the cockles and mushrooms and sprinkle with chopped parsley.

Wine : Ribolla dei Colli Orientali (Friuli-Venezia Giulia), 1-3 years

Squid alla Veneziana

Seppie alla Veneziana

Serves 4
2 ½ pounds (1.2 K) small squid
6 tablespoons (100 g) olive oil
½ onion
1 garlic clove, chopped
Salt and pepper
1 cup (¼ L) white wine
½ pound (200 g) fresh tomatoes,
   chopped
1 tablespoon chopped parsley

Clean the squid, removing the bone and the ink sacs. Reserve two of the ink sacs. Heat the oil and fry the onion and garlic until the onion has browned lightly. Add the squid and brown them. Salt and pepper to taste, then add the wine and the tomatoes.
After 15-20 minutes, when the squid are about half cooked, add the two ink sacs. When the squid are tender, sprinkle with chopped parsley. Serve with hot polenta (cornmeal mush).

Wine : Merlot delle Grave (Friuli-Venezia Giulia), 1-3 years

Scallops of Seabass with Nettles

Scaloppe di branzino alle ortiche

Serves 4
¾ pound (400 g) fresh nettles (sorrel or
   watercress may be substituted)
1 scallion
3 tablespoons (40 g) butter
6 tablespoons (1 dl) white wine
3 tablespoons cream
2 ½ pounds (1.2 K) seabass
Salt

Wash and boil the nettles in a little water. Squeeze them dry and chop them. Brown the scallion in 4 teaspoons (20 g) of butter, then add the chopped nettles, 3 tablespoons of white wine, and the cream. Simmer to reduce the liquid and pass it through a fine sieve.
Wash, clean, and fillet the seabass, cutting out four steaks from which the skin should be removed. Brown the steaks on both sides in 4 teaspoons (20 g) of butter, and pour off the fat. Baste with the remaining white wine and salt the fish. Add the purée of nettles, finish simmering until done, about 5 minutes, and serve on heated plates.

Wine : Sauvignon del Collio (Friuli-Venezia Giulia), 1-3 years

Caramelized fruit and Ring Cookies

"Golosezzi" Veneziani e Bussolai

Yields approx. 6 dozen cookies
3 ¾ cups (500 g) white flour
1 ¼ cups (300 g) sugar
6 egg yolks
10 tablespoons (150 g) butter
½ cup water
1 teaspoon vanilla extract
Salt
Peel of 1 lemon, grated

Preheat oven to 325 °F (160-170 °C).
Pour the flour in a cone onto a doughboard. Add the sugar, the egg yolks, and the butter cut into small pieces. Work into a smooth mixture without kneading excessively. Add ½ cup water, the vanilla, a pinch of salt, and the grated lemon peel. The mixture should not be overly kneaded and the dough should be smooth and soft.
Form the dough into small oblong shapes that are about the circumference of the small finger and about 4 inches (10 cm) in length. Twist the two ends around and press them together so that they do not separate. Bake for 15 minutes or until golden brown.
Cool the cookies and store in a covered container overnight to soften them slightly. However, they are usually dipped in sweet dessert wine, which flavors and softens them.
Mix fresh and dried fruits and nuts, such as : plums, roasted chestnuts, dates, dried figs, slices of dried peaches or apricots, walnuts, peanuts, hazelnuts, almonds, Muscat or other raisins. Sugar, oil (almond or flavorless).
Put various kinds of fruit and nuts on a wooden skewer. Immerse the spits with the fruit, which should be quite dry, in a pan of caramelized sugar that is blond in color. Place the skewers on a hard surface, marble if possible, that has been rubbed with almond oil and allow the caramel to harden.

Wine : Recioto di Soave (the Veneto), 4-5 years or more

HARRY'S BAR

Taking up where his legendary father, Giuseppe, left off, Arrigo Cipriani has made Harry's Bar in Venice a name known to millions of people throughout the world. It is the "drawing room" of the city's most elegant visitors.

San Marco 1323 Calle Vallaresso - 30124 Venice. The restaurant, which is on the Grand Canal, is closed Mondays and throughout January. The establishment functions as a bar as well as a restaurant. However, there is no interruption in service, the tables being set and converted from bar to restaurant use with the smoothness of long experience.
AE, Mastercard, Visa, Diners cards accepted.
Tel. (041) 5236797, 5285331

Although it is situated in the very heart of Venice, at the point where the Grand Canal begins its majestic sweep past the Piazza San Marco, Harry's Bar has more in common with the islands of the Venetian Lagoon. The lagoon, rather than the sea, is Venice's natural environment, forming an incomparable framework for the city and at the same time affecting its life. Without the lagoon and the tides that cleanse it, Venice's physical existence would be impossible. A journey around the islands provides an insight into Venice's rapport with its lagoon. One approach is from Chioggia on its small island linked to the mainland by bridges. Afterward, moving toward the east and Venice, comes Palestrina, a long and narrow strip of sand that ends as the island of the Lido begins. Across from the Lido, in the center of the lagoon, rises the city.

Embraced by the water, the city is a cosmos of its own, unique and eternal. It is built of air and water rather than of stone, for it is those two elements that give the city its attractive power. And the light that bathes it alters hour by hour and season by season. The city has a thousand faces. The wind, blowing strong, alters the tints, brilliance, and transparency of the water. The city then assumes an epic cast, its marble pillars and façades illuminated by violent contrasts of light and shade. When the sky is bright and limpid, the canals take on an intense and tormented hue and the water becomes an almost obsessive presence.

A visit to Harry's Bar is as essential as a tour of the Doges' Palace. The atmosphere, personalities, and food and drink combine to make the establishment unique. Giuseppe Cipriani welcomed and served the ordinary client as warmly as he did the great and famous, and his son Arrigo carries on in that spirit. It is the approach of men who love their profes-

sion. There is no doubt that Arrigo Cipriani knows his profession supremely well. He is not simply an exceptional restaurateur but much, much more, which was also true of his late father. He is additionally an expert in public relations. That assertion, so baldly stated, might be considered a reason for suspicion rather than a compliment. But it is absolutely accurate if public relations is taken as meaning human relations, close contact with and sensitive appreciation of human nature and human needs.

Two famous recipes were launched by Harry's Bar, both linked to great artists, Bellini and Carpaccio. The first is an aperitif and the second a meat dish. Both are now famous throughout the world.

The excellent cuisine at Harry's Bar, of an extreme refinement that can come only from great simplicity, and the wines served are a basis, a foundation or a starting point. For they provide a steady and unfailing accompaniment to discussion and gossip, glances and laughter and the daily clatter of dishes, cutlery, and goblets – in short, all that makes for conviviality. Giuseppe first and now Arrigo have been the masters of this tradition of hospitality. The Ciprianis, father and son, have had in superabundance a capacity to know humanity and serve it. At the same time, they have had the professional skill and knowledge to provide a selection of wines and gastronomical creations of the same high level of competence and imagination. Their hospitality and culinary substance together represent a tradition that must be experienced to be fully appreciated. And then it will be quite clear to those who have known it why this tradition should never be abandoned or permitted to lapse.

Arrigo Cipriani is a dynamic and eclectic restaurateur, writer and personality, whose friends are scattered throughout the world. Entering his establishment is tantamount to a plunge into a world far removed from pedestrian reality, one that has severed all links with contemporary existence, or even with Venice, although it, too, is a place of fable and dream. Inside, there is a cosmopolitan universe. It is no longer Venice but, perhaps, some place in the heart of London or New York. But then the welcome, a drink and a dish immediately bring the guest back to Venice. However, it is the Venice of the Ciprianis, an elite cosmos populated by the beautiful people, visitors and residents alike.

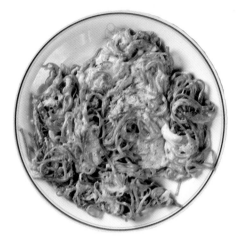

Green Noodles

Taglierini verdi

Serves 4
For the pasta:
2 ¼ cups (300 g) semolina flour
3 eggs
12 ounces (300 g) raw spinach
Salt

For the sauce:
4 tablespoons (60 g) butter
4 tablespoons grated Parmesan

Clean and wash the spinach. Cook it in a little salted water. Press the moisture out of the spinach, chop it fine and pass it through a sieve.
Prepare the pasta by combining the flour, eggs, a pinch of salt, and the pureed spinach. Work into a dough and knead it for about 15 minutes. Roll out the dough into a thin sheet. Roll the pasta into a tube and, using a sharp knife, cut the roll into extremely thin disks. Unroll the strips and scatter them about the board so that they do not stick to each other. Allow them to dry.
Cook the *taglierini* in abundant salted boiling water for 2 minutes. Drain.
Sprinkle the grated Parmesan on the noodles, melt the butter and pour over the cheese, mix well, and serve.

Wine: Soave Classico (Veneto), 1-2 years

Carpaccio

Carpaccio alla Cipriani

Serves 4
14 ounces (400 g) fillet of beef
¼ cup (60 g) mayonnaise
1 teaspoon Cognac
Worcestershire sauce

Cut the fillet of beef into slices of about ¹/₃₂ of an inch (1 mm) in thickness. Put the slices on a serving dish. Add the Cognac and several drops of Worcestershire sauce to the mayonnaise, blending well. Pour it over the beef and serve.

Mayonnaise/*Maionese*
3 egg yolks
2 cups (½ L) mild olive oil
2 teaspoons lemon juice
1 teaspoon mustard
Salt

Beat the 3 egg yolks, then incorporate the oil drop by drop. At the end, add the lemon juice, mustard, and salt to taste.

Wine: Sauvignon del Collio (Friuli-Venezia Giulia), 1-3 years

Pasta and Bean Soup

Pasta e fagioli

Serves 4
1 cup (200 g) small dried white beans
1 carrot
1 celery stalk
2 onions
3 medium-size potatoes
2 ripe tomatoes
8 tablespoons (100 g) olive oil
3 ¹/₂ ounces (100 g) noodles (a large handful)
Salt and pepper

Soak the beans for 12 hours in cold water. Cut the carrot, celery, onions, potatoes, and tomatoes into small pieces. Put the chopped vegetables, the beans, and oil in a pot with 3 quarts (3 L) of cold water. Add salt and pepper. Cook over a high heat for about 2 hours. Pass the beans and vegetables through a sieve. Add the noodles broken into small pieces and cook for another 10 minutes.

Wine : Valpolicella (Veneto), 2-3 years

Hunter's Style Chicken

Pollo alla cacciatora

Serves 4
1 chicken, about 2 ¹/₄-2 ¹/₂ pounds (1.2 K)
2 tablespoons (30 g) butter
¹/₂ cup white wine
1 ¹/₂ cups (150 g) onion, thinly sliced
1 cup (100 g) carrot, cut in rounds
1 celery stalk, finely chopped
¹/₃ pound (150 g) cultivated mushrooms
1 pound (400 g) tomatoes
1 cup (¹/₄ L) chicken broth
¹/₂ cup (50 g) white flour
Salt and pepper

Cut the chicken into pieces. Lightly dredge the pieces in flour and brown them in the butter. Baste with the white wine and cook until the liquid has virtually evaporated. Put the chicken in another pot with the onion, carrot, celery, and the mushrooms cut into thin slices. Add the tomatoes, which have been peeled, seeded, and cut into pieces, and the broth. Add salt and pepper. Cook over moderate heat for about 40 minutes. Garnish with a slice of toasted *polenta* (cornmeal mush).

Wine : Cabernet dei Colli Berici (Veneto), 3-7 years

Rice with Spring Vegetables

Risotto alla primavera

Serves 4
2 cups (300 g) spring vegetables, such as zuccini, artichokes, eggplant, peppers, mushrooms or spinach, cut in small cubes or shredded
1 ¹/₂ cups (300 g) rice
2 quarts (2 L) unsalted chicken broth
3 generous tablespoons tomato puree
7 tablespoons (100 g) butter
¹/₂ cup (50 g) grated Parmesan
1 tablespoon chopped parsley
Salt and pepper

Cook the vegetables, each separately, in boiling salted water. They should not be overcooked but firm. Drain and keep warm.
Put the rice in a deep pan and warm it over moderate heat.
When the rice is warm, add boiling chicken broth. The volume of broth should be double that of the rice. Stir in the tomato puree.
Cook slowly, stirring the rice frequently with a wooden spoon. After 5 minutes, stir in the vegetables. If necessary, add more broth, for the rice should always be covered with liquid.
Eighteen minutes after beginning the cooking, remove the pan from the heat. Stir. The rice should be virtually dry. Mix in the butter and grated Parmesan. Salt and pepper to taste. Serve immediately.

Wine : Sauvignon del Collio (Friuli-Venezia Giulia), 1-2 years

BOSCHETTI

*The Boschetti is an old inn in the Friuli-Venezia
Giulia region, a border district where Italy confronts
Eastern and Central Europe. Giorgio Trentin
has perfected its ancient tradition of hospitality
and breathed new life into its cuisine.*

Piazza Mazzini 10 – 33019 Tricesimo
(Udine). The restaurant is closed Mondays and during the first 15 days of
August. Attached to the restaurant is a
hotel with 32 rooms. Tricesimo is 12
kilometers (7 ½ miles) north of Udine, a
couple of miles from Autostrada (Superhighway) A-23. Udine is 127 kilometers
(80 miles) east of Venice and can be
reached by Autostrada A-4.
AE, Visa, Diners cards accepted
Tel. (0432) 851230, 851531

Boschetti was historically a well-known
inn where coaches paused during their
journeys to Vienna. Today, it still attracts
travelers passing through as well as many
clients who go there purposefully to
savor the cuisine. It seems an arduous
undertaking and it is – mediating between a regional cuisine and one that is
contemporary or otherwise creative.
However, the Boschetti has succeeded in
the enterprise. The regional cuisine of
Friuli-Venezia-Giulia, in Italy's northeast corner, is quintessentially rustic,
involving components and condiments
that are coarse or extremely simple. The
greatest difficulty consists in renovating
the local recipes, putting them forward
in a new way that is compatible with an
establishment as elegant and refined as
the Boschetti. One way of achieving that
compromise is by adopting wholeheartedly the path of contemporary experimentation. And that is the route that
Giorgio Trentin, along with his nephews
Rinaldo and Roberto Krcivoj and chef
Vinicio Dovier, has emphasized.
Entering the restaurant, which is linked
to the hotel, the guest is immediately
aware of a Middle European rigor and
spirit of perfection, which are as apparent in the establishment's general
appearance as in its mode of operation.
Both are the result of Trentin's refined
sensibility. In Friuli, the atmosphere is
a complex of many elements but there
is above all a sense of the intimate, a
conversational and easy-going attitude
among people. The Boschetti fully
reflects that environment just as its
menu arises from the same spirit.
Although the restaurant structurally is
partly modern, there lingers on the
memory of a greater Austria, a vast
empire that has left a particular mark on
this part of Italy. The Boschetti began
250 years ago as a posting station. Tricesimo is on the road leading to Austria.

The inn was, therefore, virtually an obligatory halting place for those who were
heading for Vienna from the Veneto and
Trieste to pay homage to the current
Habsburg ruler or to waltz away a few
nights at the imperial court. A fire was
always going in the inn's fireplace, roasting game and birds loaded on huge spits.
And the name was well known to travelers.
That excellent reputation was there to be
exploited further when Germino Trentin, father of the current owner, bought
the establishment in 1954. He transformed it into a restaurant and hotel.
And he began an effort to establish levels
of quality and prestige commensurate
with the ancient reputation, a program
that continues today. The same quality
can also be found in the house's pastries,
its *grissini* (breadsticks), its salted butters and special sausages. The hearth fire
that was so essential to the spit-roasted
meats is the center of the dining room in
the winter, creating a friendly and welcoming atmosphere. In the summer, a
large terrace permits full appreciation of
the surrounding greenery and fresh
mountain air.
The restaurant's cellar is well stocked.
There is an abundance of Italian and
French products but there is also a wide
range of the wines of Friuli, the home
of the most famous of Italian whites:
Sauvignon, Tocai, Riesling and Cabernet
di Russiz Superiore, Schiopetto, the
Abbazia di Rosazzo and Volpe Pasini.
Guests are greeted and advised in their
choices by Giorgio Trentin and also by
his nephews, who represent the innovative element, the link between the present and the future.

During the winter, the Boschetti can accommodate 50 guests in a cozy, wood-paneled dining room, but during the summer when the terrace and garden are in use, there is space for 100 diners. The restaurant's winter dining room is especially warm and inviting, since it is laid out around a Friulian fireplace, a type that was once found in the central halls of old inns and lordly mansions of the region. The Boschetti has achieved a sort of fusion of the traditional cuisine of Friuli, which is rustic, and that arising from contemporary creative impulses. There is also a sense of rigor and perfection that is due to the influence of Middle European culture, which is strongly felt in this border district.

Scallops of Roebuck

Nocette di capriolo con purea di bledine e di mele

Serves 4
Roebuck (or venison) bones
3 tablespoons (45 g) oil
7 tablespoons (100 g) butter
2 cups (¹/₂ L) white wine
1 tablespoon (15 g) mustard
¹/₂ onion, chopped
¹/₂ celery stalk, chopped
1 small carrot, and 1 leek, chopped
Pinch each of sage, thyme, and rosemary
¹/₄ pound (100 g) venison liver
¹/₄ pound (100 g) chicken livers
1 cup (¹/₄ L) red wine
¹/₄ cup (¹/₂ dl) cream, approximate
1 pound (500 g) saddle of roebuck (or venison), cleaned and boned
¹/₄ cup flour - 2 sour apples
¹/₂ pound (200 g) fresh spinach
6 tablespoons (100 g) myrtle-berry jelly

Brown the bones in the oven in the oil and 4 teaspoons (20 g) of butter. Add 1 ¹/₂ cups of white wine and the mustard. Roast for several minutes more and then pass the juice through a fine sieve, and reserve the liquid. Chop the onion, celery, carrot and leek, add the sage, thyme, and rosemary, and brown in 2 tablespoons (30 g) of butter along with the venison liver and chicken liver both cut into thin slices. Salt and add the red wine. Cook down until there is little liquid, then add the cream. Blend well, reduce slightly, and pass the liquid through a fine sieve. Combine both sauces.
Cut scallops of about 1 ³/₄ ounces each from the saddle of venison. Dredge them in the flour, and brown lightly in 2 tablespoons (30 g) of butter until they are three-quarters cooked. Add the sauce and finish the cooking. Peel and core the apples and cook in the remaining white wine. Mash into a puree. Scald the spinach in hot water, then sauté it in butter and reduce to a puree.
Serve the scallops of venison with the sauce, the two purees, and red myrtle-berry jelly.

Wine: Schioppettino dei Colli Orientali (Friuli-Venezia Giulia), 5-6 years

Breast of Pheasant in Liver and Black Truffle Sauce

Petto di fagiano alla salsa di fegato e tartufo nero

Serves 4
1 pheasant about 2 ¹/₂-3 pounds (1.2 K)
1 cup (¹/₄ L) Cognac
1 cup (¹/₄ L) dry Marsala wine
1 cup (¹/₄ L) white wine
4 sage leaves
4 tablespoons (60 g) butter
¹/₂ onion, chopped
¹/₂ celery stalk, chopped
¹/₂ carrot, chopped
1 cup (¹/₄ L) cream, approximate
1 black truffle
Salt

Remove the breast from the pheasant and set aside the liver. Put the carcass and the legs of the pheasant in a pot along with the Cognac, Marsala, white wine, and sage leaves. Cook over a moderate flame for about 2 hours or until a dark, thick sauce is obtained. Pass it through a fine sieve.
Brown the pheasant liver in 2 tablespoons (30 g) of butter along with the onion, celery, and carrot. Cook for 15 minutes, then pass through a sieve and combine with the wine sauce. Blend in the cream and some slivers of black truffle.
Meanwhile, poach the pheasant breast in the remaining butter. Salt the meat, then add the sauce and cook for 20 minutes, or until dense. Cut the breast into thin slices. Spread the slices in the shape of a fan on the serving dish. Half cover the slices with the sauce. Garnish with greens, steamed fennel slices, and cherries.

Wine: Ronco dei Roseti (Abbazia di Rosazzo, Friuli-Venezia Giulia), 4-7 years

Barley, Bean and Tripe Soup

Zuppa di orzo, fagioli e trippe

Serves 4
2/3 cup (150 g) dried white beans
1/3 cup (70 g) pearl barley
2 potatoes
6 tablespoons (90 g) olive oil
2 strips (100 g) fatty bacon
1 onion
2 garlic cloves
1 celery stalk
4 ripe tomatoes
Pinch each of sage, basil, rosemary, marjoram, and oregano
1 tablespoon chopped parsley
1/3 pound veal tripe
4 teaspoons (20 g) butter
1 cup (1/4 L) white wine
Salt and white pepper

Soak the beans for 12 hours in cold water. Separately soak the pearl barley for 12 hours in cold water. Simmer the barley in 10 cups water for 2 hours.
Peel and chop the potatoes. Cook the beans in 2 quarts (2 L) water along with 2 tablespoons oil for about 1 hour or until they are fairly tender. Add the potatoes about 40 minutes after starting the beans. Pour off some of the water if there is too much.
Finely chop 1 strip of bacon, half the onion, a clove of garlic, the celery, and 2 peeled and seeded tomatoes. Stew in 2 tablespoons of oil, and add the sage and rosemary. Cook for 5 minutes, then add to the beans a pinch of salt. Continue cooking over a low flame until the beans are done. Put half the beans and potatoes through a sieve or puree in the blender. Return the puree to the pot.
Wash the tripe well and cut into small strips. Finely chop the remainder of the bacon and onion and another garlic clove. Add to a pan with 2 tablespoons of oil, the butter, basil, marjoram, oregano, and parsley. Stew for 5 minutes, then add the remaining tomatoes, peeled and seeded, and the tripe. Add the white wine and continue to simmer.

Add the pearl barley to the bean soup. Add the tripe mixture to the soup. Serve hot, pouring in a few drops olive oil and a pinch of white pepper.

Wine: Pinot Nero di Oleis (Livio Felluga, Friuli-Venezia Giulia), 1-4 years, or Pinot Nero del Collio (Friuli-Venezia Giulia), 1-4 years

Pumpkin Gnocchi with Butter and Smoked Ricotta Cheese

Gnocchi di zucca al burro e ricotta affumicata

Serves 4
1 pound (500 g) pumpkin or other winter squash
2 eggs
1 1/2 cups (200 g) flour
2 1/2 tablespoons (40 g) butter
4 sage leaves
2 ounces (60 g) smoked (or plain) ricotta cheese, grated
Salt

Peel the pumpkin or squash, seed and chop. Steam or bake until tender, then pass it through a sieve. Allow it to cool.
Add to the pumpkin puree the eggs, flour, and a pinch of salt. Mix energetically and thoroughly. If the resulting dough should be too soft, add a bit more flour.
Using a spoon, form lumps of dough, dropping them in boiling salted water. When the gnocchi come to the surface, skim them from the water with a slotted spoon. Then drop them in a pan of cold water.
Stew the sage leaves in a pan in the butter. Dip the gnocchi a second time in boiling salted water. Drain them and put them in the pan with the butter. Serve the gnocchi with the grated smoked ricotta sprinkled over.

Wine: Traminer dell Collio (Friuli-Venezia Giulia), 1-2 years

Soufflé Cake of Walnuts and Almonds with Coffee Cream

Torta soffiata di noci e mandorle alla crema di caffè

Serves 12-16
8 eggs, separated
1 cup (250 g) sugar
2 tablespoons (10 g) breadcrumbs
2 tablespoons (30 g) rum
1 cup (4 1/3 ounces; 125 g) finely ground walnuts
1 cup (4 1/3 ounces; 125 g) finely ground almonds
Whole nuts or confectioner's sugar (optional)
For the coffee cream:
7 tablespoons (100 g) butter
7 tablespoons (100 g) sugar
1 egg yolk
1-2 tablespoons very strong coffee
1 teaspoon instant espresso powder

Preheat oven to 350°F (180°C).
Beat the egg yolks with the sugar. Add the breadcrumbs soaked in rum, the ground walnuts and almonds, and the whites beaten until they are stiff. Pour the batter into a buttered and lightly floured spring-form pan and bake for 50 minutes to an hour.
To make the coffee cream, beat the butter until it is creamy along with the sugar. Add the egg yolk and blend well. Then add the black coffee, which should be tepid, and the espresso powder.
When the cake has cooled, cut it in half horizontally and fill it with the coffee cream. Some of the cream may be used to decorate the top of the cake.
To serve, pour some crème anglaise onto a dish and place a slice of cake atop the sauce. Create a design with melted chocolate on the cream and serve.

Wine: Verduzzo di Ramandolo (Friuli-Venezia Giulia), 5-7 years

ANTICA OSTERIA DEL TEATRO

Two nations, Italy and France, have joined forces at the Antica Osteria in the heart of Piacenza, about fifty miles south of Milan. Franco Ilari, who is responsible for the fine selection of wines, is Italian and chef Georges Cogny is French.

Via Verdi 16 – 29100 Piacenza. The restaurant, with one Michelin star, is closed Sundays and throughout August. Piacenza is 64 kilometers (40 miles) southeast of Milan. The Antica Osteria is a few blocks from the attractive Piazza dei Cavalli and the Gothic structure of the Palazzo del Comune (City Hall). The square contains fine equestrian statues of Alessandro Farnese and his son Ranuccio.
AE, Diners cards accepted.
Tel. (0523) 23777

The history of European gastronomy abounds in exchanges and fusions that have conditioned tastes and comportment. A minute example of that integration of cuisines and gastronomic philosophies is the achievement of the Antica Osteria del Teatro. There, Georges Cogny, a cook of French origin and training, has succeeded in blending the gastronomic traditions and trends of his country with some usages and intuitions of an Italian nature, drawing upon the raw materials of the district and responding to the requirements of a Mediterranean clientele. Cogny, under the direction of Franco Ilari, has in a sense opened a new school, a sort of ancient craftsman's shop or, better, the studio of an artist in which new forms of cuisine are elaborated. The "school" arises from new culinary insights. But it has also found disciples who, acting in a rather independent fashion, are spreading the message of the new cuisine.

The establishment is installed in a palatial building that has accumulated five centuries of history. It is an interesting ensemble with an American bar, an attractive wine cellar, a welcoming dining room, and a comfortable anteroom. The arrangement is so perfect that the careful attention given foods and wines can be discerned simply from appearances.

Piacenza was settled in prehistoric times. It then became a Roman colony and was later incorporated in the kingdom of the Goths. The Franks held it before it became a free commune and, as such, resisted the claims of Frederick Barbarossa. The city later came under the sway of the Visconti dukes of Milan and their successors, the Sforzas. At the beginning of the nineteenth century, the peace treaty arranged at the Congress of Vienna assigned the duchy to Marie Louise, who ruled with great wisdom and accomplished many works of great utility to the community, including the establishment of a university.

There are at least three good reasons for making the journey to the Antica Osteria del Teatro at Piacenza. The first is the cuisine. Piacenza is in Emilia-Romagna, a region of impressive traditions that have served as the basis of Cogny's art. He has succeeded admirably in grafting a splendid tree to the roots already existing in Piacenza and in endowing it with the attributes of his native culture. It is a complementary cuisine that has exalted local regional specialties, drawing upon native herbs, cheeses, sausages, fish, and initial courses, integrating them, renovating them, and making them more personal. The second great attraction at Antica Osteria del Teatro is the cellar, which guests may visit. Here, Ilari is in charge. It is exemplary for its quality and vast range, with Italian and French, Californian and South African wines. Not many establishments can provide such a wide spectrum.

Finally, the establishment itself and its location are worthy of notice. Bounded by the Po, Piacenza is a city of medieval palaces with an atmosphere softened by humanism and a discreet and elegant beauty of the past that does not overpower but rather enfolds the visitor. The Antica Osteria del Teatro is installed in a fifteenth-century *palazzo* in the very heart of the city and it deserves its name. It is truly *antica*, or ancient, and it was an osteria, or hostel, serving for many years as a shop where wines could be bought by the bottle or the glass. And it is at the theater *(del teatro)*, since the Teatro Municipale di Piacenza is nearby.

The architect, retained by Franco Ilari and Georges Cogny to restructure their restaurant has carried out a sensitive program of restoration. He has exalted the original structure, which is severe, rational, and formidable, even if it is softened in places with graceful curves. The restaurant functions smoothly within this envelope of Renaissance rationality and guests automatically sense this orderliness. For the restaurant's owners have been able to mesh the architectural strength of the past with the efficiency required of a modern restaurant: inside, the guest feels himself far removed from the present, under the vaulted ceilings and enclosed by the mellow, exposed-brick walls. Eye and palate are both delighted by the triumphant orchestrations of a splendid kitchen. Ilari and Cogny opened the Antica Osteria del Teatro in 1977. Their choice of setting was quite appropriate since the old inn had also served as a wineshop. The house offers a double menu. One is inspired by the culinary tradition of Piacenza and of the Apennines nearby. The other is an expression of a search for a more contemporary and creative cuisine.

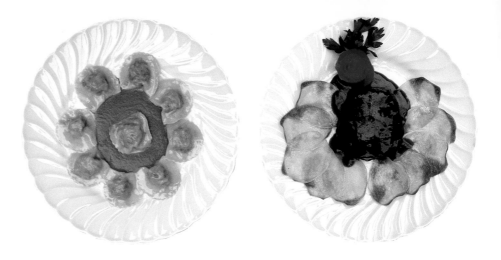

Ravioli Filled with Duck in Sweet-Pepper Butter

Ravioli d'anatra al burro di peperone

Serves 4
For the pasta:
Scant 2 cups (250 g) white flour
2 eggs
Salt
For the filling:
12 ounces (300 g) breast of duck, with
    the skin
2 ounces (40 g) spinach
¹/₂ slice of bread, crust removed
¹/₂ cup (1 dl) milk
2 scallions (or shallots)
1 ounce (25 g) mushrooms
2 teaspoons (10 g) butter
³/₄ ounce (20 g) beef marrow, chopped
2 tablespoons (10 g) chopped parsley
3 tablespoons (40 g) cream
Salt and pepper
For the sauce:
3 tablespoons cream
6 tablespoons (80 g) butter
1 sweet red pepper, cooked and pureed

Prepare the pasta by pouring the flour onto a board, making a well in it and putting the eggs in the well. Combine all the ingredients and knead the dough for about 10 minutes. Roll out into a sheet.
Prepare the filling by finely chopping the duck breast, along with the skin. Boil the spinach, drain it, squeeze it dry, and chop it fine. Soak the bread in the milk. Press out the moisture with the fingers and add to the spinach.
Chop the scallions and the mushrooms and brown lightly in 2 teaspoons (10 g) of butter. Add the duck breast and cook for several minutes, stirring constantly. Remove the pan from the flame, add the spinach, the beef marrow, the chopped parsley, and the cream. Blend and add salt and pepper. Cook for an additional 3-4 minutes.
Put the filling in small dollops on half of the pasta sheet. Fold over and press down all around the lumps of filling to ensure that each pasta "envelope" is securely sealed. Cut out the ravioli with a toothed roller. Cook them in boiling salted water for 5 minutes, then drain them.
Make the sauce by reducing the cream and then fluffing it up by incorporating the butter. When the sauce is quite fluffy, add 3 tablespoons of pepper puree. Blend well. Arrange the ravioli on individual plates. Pour out a ring of pepper sauce on each dish and serve hot.

Wine: Soave (the Veneto), 1-2 years

Fillet of Beef with Gorgonzola

Filetto di manzo al Gorgonzola

Serves 4
4 beef fillets, about ¹/₂ pound (200 g) each
3 tablespoons (40 g) butter
1 scallion (or shallot), chopped
2 tablespoons white wine
4 teaspoons (20 g) Dijon mustard
4 tablespoons (60 g) strong meat broth
4 ounces (100 g) Gorgonzola cheese
Salt and pepper

Cook the fillets in 2 tablespoons (20 g) of butter. Salt and pepper them.
Remove the fillets and add the chopped scallion to the same pan. Brown the scallion for a minute or two, then add the white wine, mustard, broth, and Gorgonzola. Reduce the liquid and bind with the remaining butter. Arrange the fillets on plates and pour over the sauce. Serve with potatoes thinly sliced and sautéd in butter.

Wine: Rubesco (Umbria), 6-7 years, or Tignanello (Tuscany) 7-10 years

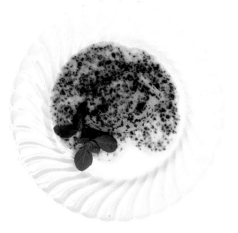

Stuffed Potatoes in Beurre Blanc with Truffles

Patate ripiene al burro bianco e tartufo

Serves 4
4 medium-size potatoes
2 celery stalks
2 zucchini
2 carrots
7 ounces (200 g) butter
2 scallions (or shallots), finely chopped
1 cup (¼ L) white wine
1 tablespoon cream
2 black truffles
Salt

Peel and wash the potatoes, then create a large cavity in each. Cut the celery in small pieces and slice the zucchini and carrots. Braise them in 7 tablespoons (100 g) of butter. Salt.
Fill the potatoes with the braised vegetables and wrap them in buttered aluminum foil. Put them in a shallow pan and bake them in a moderate oven 350°F (180°C) for 30 minutes. Put the finely chopped scallions in a pan with the white wine and reduce the liquid by two thirds. Add the cream and the remaining butter, a little at a time, whisking energetically. Cut the truffles into fine pieces and add them to the cream. Salt to taste. Remove the foil from the potatoes and serve with the truffle sauce poured over.

Wine: Greco di Tufo or Fiano di Avellino (Campania), 3-4 years

Scallops in Pastry

Tortino di capesante

Serves 4
For the short pastry:
2 ⅛ cups (300 g) white flour
9 tablespoons (150 g) butter
1 teaspoon (7 g) salt
1 teaspoon (7 g) sugar
5 tablespoons (75 g) water

16 scallops, including beards and coral
1 celery stalk
1 carrot
2 small onions
1 leek
3 tablespoons (50 g) butter
3 small zucchini
2 tablespoons olive oil
½ cup (1 dl) cream
1 ripe tomato
Salt

Prepare the short pastry by delicately combining the flour, butter, salt, and sugar with the fingers. Make a well in the mixture, pour in the water, and quickly stir with the fingers. Allow the dough, in a bowl covered with a damp cloth, to "rest" in the refrigerator for 3 hours.
Preheat the oven to 450°F (235°C).
Roll out the dough and cut out 4 thin disks of about 3-3 ½ inches (8-9 cm) in diameter. Bake them in the oven for 10 to 12 minutes or until lightly browned.
Clean the scallops, removing the "beard" and the corals. Prepare the essence of scallops, simmering the "beards," the celery, 1 carrot, and 1 onion in 1 cup water. Reduce until only ½ cup is left.
Cut the leek and the other onion in slices and braise them in the butter. Spread them on the pastry disks. Cut the meat of the scallops in small rounds. Briefly steam the zucchini. Cut the zucchini into thin slices. Place the scallops on the disks in an overlapping circle pattern, alternating them with the zucchini. Sprinkle over some drops of oil, salt lightly, and place the disks in the oven for 4 minutes.
Prepare the sauce by combining, in a blend-er, the corals, cream, and scallop essence. Pour into a pan, bring to a boil, and cook for 2-3 minutes, stirring constantly. Pass the sauce through a fine sieve.
Pour the sauce into plates, forming a circle. Put the pastries atop the sauce. Garnish the center of the pastries with some pieces of tomato previously peeled and seeded.

Wine: Sauvignon or Pinot Grigio del Collio (Friuli-Venezia Giulia), 1-2 years

Pears Cortigny

Pera Cortigny

Serves 4
4 Williams pears
6 tablespoons (100 g) sugar
2 tablespoons (30 g) honey
2 cups (½ L) water
1 bay leaf
1 clove
1 black peppercorn
4 ounces (100 g) piquant Gorgonzola cheese
2 teaspoons thinly sliced white truffle
For the zabaione:
2 egg yolks
⅔ cup (1 ½ dl) Sauterne
¼ cup (60 g) sugar

Wash and peel the pears. Prepare a syrup by combining and heating the sugar, honey, water, bay leaf, clove, and peppercorn.
Cook the pears in the syrup for 15 minutes. Remove the pears from the syrup and allow them to cool.
Prepare the zabaione by whisking the egg yolks with the wine in a double boiler for 10 minutes. Add the sugar and blend well. Remove from the heat and whisk it for an additional 5 minutes.
Core the pears and fill them with the Gorgonzola. Arrange them on a dish, pour over the zabaione, and garnish with the slices of truffle.

Wine: Torcolato di Breganze (the Veneto), 2-4 years, or Verduzzo di Ramandolo (Friuli-Venezia Giulia), 3-5 years

DANTE

Dante Casari of Bologna's Dante restaurant confronted a considerable challenge, one he triumphantly met, when he opened his establishment in 1973, for the city has an ancient tradition of dining and drinking well and in gargantuan quantity.

Via Belvedere 2 – 40100 Bologna. The restaurant, which has one star in the Guide Michelin, is closed Mondays and for lunch on Tuesdays as well as the last week of December and the first week of January. It is located a few blocks northwest of the Piazza Maggiore and the Cathedral of San Petronio in the heart of the city.
AE, Visa, Diners cards accepted.
Tel. (051) 224464, 239510

Culinary tradition is a powerful force at Bologna, not so much for the quantities stipulated in the recipes or in the meals actually consumed as for the emphasis given to pasta. It is the territory of *tagliatelle, lasagne, tortellini, tortelli, agnolotti, ravioli,* and *cappelletti,* as well as many others. All those preparations are made with fresh pasta, which has, as it has always had, a vital role to play in the diet in every part of Emilia. The stuffed pastas such as *tortellini, cappelletti,* and ravioli are little treasure chests that contain the finest meats prepared in combinations that vary from district to district, town to town. The formulas express the tastes and the evolution of cuisine in the different areas and are derived without doubt from a time when the princely houses were the scenes of extraordinary banquets.

Pasta first "scaled the heights" in the sixteenth century and, at that time, the capital of Emilian gastronomy was Ferrara, the realm of the Este family. The Este court was served in that period by one of Italy's most noted *scalchi.* A *scalco* was not just a cook but the master of a kitchen of many cooks and the overseer of the dining room staffed by numerous butlers and waiters. The *scalco* was not only perfectly trained in the techniques of cooking and presenting foods but was also a man of considerable direct experience in courtly life. He knew how to create a complete entertainment of which food and wine were only one element, although an extremely important one. There must be pauses as well for dances and songs, plays and concerts in the course of a princely banquet. This extremely competent *scalco,* a native of Flanders, was Cristofore di Messisbugo, who died at Ferrara in 1548. He left to posterity an extremely interesting book, *Banchetti, composizione di vivande ed apparecchio generale* (Banquets, Compositions of Dishes and General Applications).

This incomparable inheritance has without any doubt stimulated Dante Casari, who greets his guests with an amiable smile and a lively visage. The eyes above the luxuriant mustache are watchful at first but then become good-natured and friendly with acquaintance. His restaurant is a spacious lead-gray cube, illuminated by streaks of tenuous light softened by the curtains arranged somewhat in the fashion of those in the wings of a theater's stage. The lamps on the tables bring out the rose tints of the tablecloths, making each an island to itself against the brown background of the carpet. The paintings on the walls are changed at the beginning of each season, and include works by such contemporary artists as Del Pezzo, D'Orazio, and Ceroli.

Dante Casari, who had already had considerable experience at other restaurants, opened his establishment in 1973 and immediately revolutionized the city's gastronomic substratum. He did not jettison the history and age-old quality of the Bolognese culinary tradition, for it would have been absurd to abandon such a treasure. Instead, he has provided a personal reinterpretation of the dishes of the Bolognese canon. It must be said to his credit that he has provided even the most demanding gourmet an opportunity that was difficult or even rare to find in Bologna in the past. It is a gastronomy that achieves the level of art, a feast for the five senses and a compendium of history and culture.

Dante is close to Bologna's main square, the Piazza Maggiore, which is bounded by the Via delle Pescherie Vecchie. In that street there is a rich and fascinating market of food products, the bounty of which is an effective testimony to the city's delight in food and in eating. The visitor should walk through the center of Bologna, a city of mellow brick and faded roof tiles, in early winter, when the sky is gray and the city is wrapped in fog. It is easy then to understand why Lucio Dalla, a popular singer and songwriter, has said that it is impossible for even a baby to get lost in the center of Bologna. It is difficult to go astray in the midst of so much communicativeness, which finds expression in a lively and explosive dialect. At the side of the restaurant is the Mercato delle Erbe (vegetable market).

Rabbit Terrine in Gelatin

Composta di coniglio alla prugna

Serves 4
1 rabbit, about 2 ¹/₂-3 pounds (1.2 K)
2 chicken necks
4 carrots
4 onions
Herb bouquet consisting of celery, parsley and rosemary
Pinch of thyme
¹/₂ pound (200 g) fatty bacon, cut in slices
1 cup (¹/₄ L) plum brandy
1 bay leaf
4 juniper berries
³/₄ envelope (3 sheets) powdered gelatin
Salt and pepper

Bone the rabbit and cut the meat into pieces of about 2 ounces (60 g) each. Salt and pepper the pieces. Bring 2 quarts (2 L) of water to a boil and add the rabbit bones and 2 chicken necks. Skim and add 2 carrots and 2 onions cut into large pieces, the herb bouquet, tied, and a pinch of thyme. Reduce to about 2 cups (¹/₂ L) of broth. Pour the broth through a cloth and set aside.
Line a terrine with half the strips of fatty bacon cut in slices. Cut the remaining 2 onions and 2 carrots in rounds. Place the rounds of carrot and onion in a layer atop the bacon in the terrine. Add the pieces of rabbit. Pour in the plum brandy. Cover the terrine with the remaining strips of bacon and garnish with the bay leaf and the juniper berries. Cover the terrine with a sheet of buttered paper and put it in a larger pan partly filled with hot water. Bake in a 325°F (170°C) oven for about 2 hours. Remove the terrine from the oven. Let it cool.
Dissolve the gelatin in a little water and

add to the broth. Stir until the gelatin has entirely blended with the broth.
Remove the paper, the bay leaf, and juniper berries and pour in the gelatin. Leave the terrine in the refrigerator for 2 hours. Serve in slices, decorating the plates with cherries or other fruits and greens.

Wine: Torre di Giano il Pino (Lungarotti, Umbria), 2-4 years

Sea-Bass Fillets in Vinegar and Pepper

Filetti di branzino all'aceto e pepe

Serves 4
1 sea-bass, about 2 ¹/₂-3 pounds (1 K)
2 tablespoons (30 g) pounded white peppercorns
²/₃ cup (150 g) olive oil
2 garlic cloves, crushed
²/₃ cup (150 g) vinegar
3 tablespoons (50 g) tomato puree
2 tablespoons (30 g) mustard
2 cups (¹/₂ L) white wine
Cinnamon
4 tablespoons (60 g) butter
¹/₄ cup (¹/₂ dl) cream
Salt and pepper

Clean the sea-bass and fillet it. Salt the fillets and dredge them in the pounded pepper.
Stew the head and bones of the sea-bass in oil along with any remaining pepper and the 2 cloves of crushed garlic. Pour in the vinegar and blend in the tomato puree, mustard, white wine and a pinch of cinnamon. Stir with a whisk and simmer for 10 minutes. Pass through a fine sieve.
Brown the fish fillets on both sides in the butter. Remove the fillets and put them on hot plates.
Add the sauce to the pan in which the fillets

were browned. Bring to a boil, reduce the sauce, and add the cream. Reduce for a few minutes more. Pass the sauce through a sieve and pour it over the fillets. Serve with steamed vegetables.

Wine: Chardonnay (Gaja, Piedmont), 2-5 years

Scallops in Pastry with Broccoli Sauce

Sfogliata di capesante, salsa ai broccoli

Serves 4
For the pastry:
2 cups (200 g) white flour
2 eggs
Salt
For the broccoli sauce:
1 ¹/₄ cups (300 g) broccoli
1 scallion (or shallot)
2 tablespoons (30 g) butter
1 cup (¹/₄ L) concentrated fish broth
Salt and pepper
3 tablespoons (50 g) cream
12 scallops removed from their shells
For the fish broth:
The heads of several mild fish
1 onion, chopped
1 celery stalk, chopped
1 carrot, chopped
1 cup white wine
1 cup water
Salt and white pepper

Make the fish broth by combining all the ingredients in a nonferrous pan and simmering until 1 cup of liquid remains. Strain through several layers of cheese cloth.
Pour the flour onto a board and make a well in it. Put the eggs and salt in the well and combine to make a dough. Work it well so that the dough becomes smooth and compact. Roll out a thin leaf of dough and cut it into 8 pieces, each about 1 ¹/₂ by 6 inches (4 by 15 cm). Cook the pastry pieces for

5 minutes in boiling salted water to which a tablespoon of oil should be added to keep the pasta from sticking.

Drain the pasta. Press 4 pieces of pasta, while still hot, onto the top sides of 4 scallops shells and allow them to cool. The pasta pieces should develop creases and ridges so that they resemble scallop shells.

Wash and roughly chop the broccoli. Chop the scallion (or shallot) and brown it lightly in 2 tablespoons (30 g) of butter for about 5 minutes. Add the broccoli and cook for 15 minutes. Pour in the fish stock and cook until the broccoli is tender.

Reserve some broccoli flowerets for garnish, and puree the rest of the broccoli in a blender. Return the puree to the pan. Salt and pepper, add the cream and thicken the sauce slightly by cooking slowly over an extremely low flame. Butter an oven dish. Cut the scallops in half and put them in the dish. Cover with aluminum foil and cook in a 350°F (180°C) oven for 5 minutes. Pour some broccoli sauce into each plate, add a piece of plain pasta, then the scallops and a bit of the cooking juices, and cover with a piece of pasta pressed into a shell shape. Dot the pasta with butter and sprinkle over some grated Parmesan. Put the dishes under a hot grill for a few minutes to gratiné.

Garnish the dishes with broccoli flowerets that have been steamed and lightly poached in butter. Serve hot.

Wine: Regaleali (Sicily), 1-3 years

Rice of a Thousand and One Nights

Risotto mille e una notte

Serves 4
1 cup (240 g) fine-grained rice
¹/₂ onion, chopped
4 teaspoons (20 g) butter
¹/₂ cup (1 dl) white wine
4 cups (1 L) meat or vegetable broth
1 carrot, boiled and cut into small cubes
1 celery stalk, boiled and cut into cubes

¹/₄ cup (50 g) cooked peas
4 ounces (100 g) cooked spinach
4 ounces (100 g) boletus mushrooms, thinly sliced
8 tablespoons (40 g) raw ham cut into small cubes
¹/₂ cup (1 dl) cream
¹/₃ cup (40 g) grated Parmesan
Salt and pepper

Cook the rice and chopped onion in the butter until the grains become translucent. Add the white wine and cook until the wine evaporates. Add the broth a little at a time and continue cooking until the rice is half done, about 10 minutes.

Add all the vegetables, the mushrooms, the raw ham, the cream, and a pinch of pepper. Continue the cooking, adding broth as needed until the rice is done. Add the Parmesan, stir vigorously so that the rice becomes creamy, and serve.

Wine: Lagrein Rosato or Kretzer (Trentine-Alto Adige), 1-2 years

Lasagne with Meat Sauce and Mushrooms

Lasagne gialle al ragù antico e funghi

Serves 4
For the pasta:
2 cups (200 g) white flour
2 eggs
Salt
For the sauce:
¹/₃ carrot, chopped
¹/₃ white onion, chopped
¹/₂ celery stalk, chopped
3 tablespoons (40 g) butter
3 tablespoons olive oil
1 bay leaf
¹/₃ pound (150 g) ground veal
¹/₃ pound (150 g) ground pork loin
Salt and pepper
3 tablespoons brandy
1 garlic clove

¹/₂ tablespoon chopped parsley
4 cups (400 g) sliced boletus mushrooms
1 hard-boiled egg
2 tablespoons (20 g) grated Parmesan
4 tablespoons (50 g) *stracchino* (or another soft, cow's milk cheese)
For the béchamel:
2 tablespoons (25 g) butter
2 tablespoons (30 g) white flour
2 cups (¹/₂ L) milk
2 tablespoons (20 g) grated Parmesan
3 tablespoons (50 g) *stracchino*
Salt and pepper

Pour the flour onto a board, make a well in the center, break in the eggs, and add the salt. Combine the ingredients by hand. Knead for about 10 minutes until the dough is smooth and well blended. Roll out the dough into a thin sheet and cut the pasta into rectangles the size of your oven dish.

Sauté the chopped carrot, onion, and celery in 3 tablespoons (40 g) of butter and 1 tablespoon of oil. Add the bay leaf and the ground veal and pork. Salt and pepper, then allow to brown for about 15 minutes. Baste with 3 tablespoons of brandy. Burn off the alcohol. Remove the bay leaf and put the pan in a 350°F (180°C) oven. Leave for 10 minutes. Separately, put 2 tablespoons of oil in a pan and cook the garlic, parsley, and thinly sliced boletus mushrooms. To prepare the béchamel, bring the milk just to a boil. Melt the butter in a pan. Add the flour, then the milk, and cook for 10 minutes, stirring with a whisk. At the end add the Parmesan, *stracchino* or other soft cheese, and a pinch each of salt and pepper. Blend well.

Cook the pasta rectangles in lightly salted boiling water. Remove the pieces of pasta as they float to the surface and place them on a towel to dry and cool.

Butter an oven dish. Lay in the bottom a layer of pasta. Pour in enough béchamel to form a thin layer, then add a bit of meat, some mushrooms, a bit of the crumbled yolk of the hard-boiled egg, some grated Parmesan, a tablespoon of béchamel sprinkled over in dollops, then another layer of pasta. Continue layering until all the ingredients have been used up. Dot the surface with flakes of butter and put the dish in a 400°F (200°C) oven for 25 minutes.

SAN DOMENICO

*The San Domenico of Imola has a slightly
regal touch, for founder Gianluigi Morini was
inspired by Nino Bergene, former cook
to the King Vittorio Emanuelle III, while chef
Valentino Marcattilii was formed in the same
tradition of refined but innovative cuisine.*

Via Gaspare Sacchi 1 – 40026 Imola
(Bologna). The restaurant, which has
been awarded two Michelin stars, is
closed Mondays. Otherwise, it is open
throughout the year. Imola is 33 kilometers (20 miles) southeast of Bologna on
the Via Emilia, SS (Highway) 9, or Autostrada (Superhighway) A-14.
AE, Visa, Diners cards accepted.
Tel. (0542) 29000

The building in which the San Domenico is installed has been marked by
some of the historical events of the Imola
area of Emilia-Romagna. The structure
was the house of the steward of the
Dominican order, who served both the
adjoining Romanesque residence for
friars and the neighboring convent for
nuns. The complex was reconstructed in
the fifteenth century by Mastro Giorgio
Fiorentino and his son Checco, under
the patronage of the Sforzas. During the
same period, the two architects also
altered the face of Imola, renewing it.
The steward's house consists of two
floors. The ground floor was used for
administrative purposes. The upper
floor served as a guesthouse. The cellar,
in which the restaurant now keeps its
large treasury of wines, was once a store-
house where the produce grown on the
farms owned by the Dominicans was
stored.

During the Cisapline Republic, Napoleon requisitioned the entire complex.
After the restoration, when confiscated
ecclesiastical property was restored to
the Papal States, the buildings passed
into the hands of the diocese of Imola.
The convent was transformed first into a
barracks and then into a school. The
building was acquired early in this century by Gianluigi Morini's grandfather.
The residence of the friars was only
recently converted into a picture gallery,
and the name San Domenico has passed
to the former steward's house and now to
the restaurant.

In glancing through Morini's biography,
it is impossible not to be impressed by
the many projects he has undertaken.
As a youth, he wanted to be an actor. Evi-
dently, his passion for the stage
remained, for with a group of friends he
organized a society that has awarded
prizes and served as a point of encounter
for much of the Italian film world. But
his perfectionism has found its release
and its ideal expression in the restaurant
he founded, for he is a restaurateur par
excellence. It may be that he inherited
his fascination with cuisine from his
father and grand-father, both of whom
were deeply involved with food.

Gianluigi Morini took the family house,
restored and renovated it, adapting it to his
purpose with an absolutely extraordinary
attention to detail, the results of which are
quite impressive. The style is evident in
the William Morris prints on the walls and
Thonet chairs, while the same taste
appears in every aspect, from the heavy
linen tablecloths and napkins to the classical music in the background, as well as the
paintings that decorate the restaurant.

The San Domenico opened its doors on
March 7, 1970, and at first it offered a
menu divided into two "mainstreams."
On one side, there was the traditional
regional cuisine and on the other the
"cuisine of the house," preparations that
were as carefully composed, as refined,
and as delicate as anyone could wish. It
was obvious that Morini would even-
tually opt for the second line of cooking.
And in doing so, he sought and obtained
the collaboration of a "monarch of gastronomy," Nino Bergese, who was once
cook to the royal house of Italy. Bergese,
who was the greatest Italian chef of this
century, has left behind him a sort of
breviary in his invaluable recipe book,
Mangiare da re (To Eat Like a King).
The current chef of the San Domenico,
Valentino Marcattilii, is a product of the
Bergese school of cuisine.

Morini's idea, which he has fully realized, was to found an establishment that
treated its guests as if they were close
friends. Brillat-Savarin wrote that "to
invite someone to dinner means to
dedicate yourself to his happiness while
he is under your roof." There is no other
rule more important at the San Domenico.

Morini's father was a banker, a profession that he, too, as things usually turn out in Italy, should have entered. However, he refused to follow precisely in his father's footsteps and, after numerous and varied experiences, he finally reached the safe harbor of his current profession. The establishment he created, which is intimate and unforgettable because of the taste of its furnishings, the suffused music, the smoothness of its service, and the style of every accessory, can accommodate about fifty guests.

Salad of Botargo and Black Olives

Insalata con bottarga e olive nere

Serves 4
1 small head (300 g) lettuce
20 slices of *botargo* (or dried tuna roe)
Juice of 1 lemon
Salt and white pepper
2 tablespoons (30 g) *extra-vergine* olive oil
2 tablespoons (30 g) walnut oil
15 pitted black olives
4 walnut meats

Separate the lettuce leaves, wash and dry them, and put them in the center of individual dishes. Arrange the slices of botargo atop the lettuce in the form of stars.
Put the lemon juice in a bowl, add the salt, pepper, olive oil and walnut oil, and blend well.
Pound the black olives and walnuts in a mortar and distribute over the salad. Pour over the sauce. Serve with hot buttered toast.

Wine: Gavi dei Gavi (Piedmont), 1-3 years

Egg and Truffle Ravioli

Uovo ai tartufi

Serves 4
For the pasta:
1 1/2 cups (200 g) white flour
2 eggs
Salt
For the filling and sauce:
1/4 cup (50 g) cooked spinach
3 1/2 tablespoons (50 g) ricotta cheese
3/4 cup (100 g) grated Parmesan
5 eggs
Nutmeg
Salt and white pepper
1 3/4 ounces (50 g) white truffle, cut in thin rounds
7 tablespoons (100 g) butter

Combine the flour, eggs, and a pinch of salt and knead into a smooth dough. Roll out a thin sheet of pasta and cut out 8 disks, each about 6 inches (15 cm) in diameter.
Finely chop the spinach and blend it with the ricotta, half of the grated Parmesan, 1 egg, a pinch of nutmeg, and salt and pepper. Work the mixture until all the ingredients are well blended.
Place 4 pasta disks on individual circles of buttered brown paper. Divide the filling into 4 equal parts and put a portion on the center of each pasta disk. Hollow out the center of the filling and place in it 1 egg yolk with half of the white. Salt and pepper lightly. Using a brush, moisten the rim of the pasta disks with cold water and place the remaining 4 disks atop the filling. Press down lightly to eliminate all air from the interiors and seal the ravioli.
Cook the ravioli in boiling salted water for 2 minutes. Using a skimmer, remove the ravioli from the water and drain well.
Put the ravioli in hot pasta dishes and sprinkle them with the thinly sliced truffle and the remaining Parmesan. Put the butter in a pan and melt it over a high flame. When the butter has turned nut brown, pour it over the ravioli and serve.

Wine: Vintage Tunina (Jermann, Friuli-Venezia Giulia), 3-5 years

Spiny Lobster with Artichokes

Astice ai carciofi

Serves 4
4 spiny lobsters (crawfish), about 2/3 pound (300 g) each
1 1/3 cup (300 g) butter
3 tablespoons (50 g) bacon or ham fat
16 artichoke hearts
2 carrots, cut into thin rounds
1 large onion, cut into thin slices
1/2 lemon
1 cup (1/4 L) water
1 tablespoon chopped parsley
1 tablespoon tarragon leaves
Salt and white pepper
Parsley sprigs (for garnish)

Plunge the lobsters into boiling water and leave them for 8 minutes. Let them cool.
Melt 4 tablespoons (50 g) of butter in a deep pot and sauté the bacon or ham fat for 2 minutes. Remove the ham fat and add the carrots, onion, artichoke hearts, and 1/2 lemon. Stew over a low flame for about 10 minutes, then remove the 1/2 lemon.
Add the water and continue the cooking over moderate heat for a further 10 minutes. Remove the vegetables from the water and reserve. Allow the water to stand for at least 10 minutes or until the fat has risen to the surface. Skim off the fat and discard. Put the water in a pan and reduce by half.
Meanwhile, cut the lobsters in half lengthwise. Extract the meat and cut it into small cubes. Cut the artichoke hearts in small cubes. Add to the reduced cooking liquid the remaining butter and whip with a whisk over a low heat until the butter becomes creamy. Add the lobster and artichoke pieces, the carrots, onion, chopped parsley, and tarragon leaves. Salt and pepper. Mix well and cook for 3-4 minutes.
Put 2 lobster shell halves in the center of each of 4 heated plates. Fill the shell halves with the lobster meat and artichoke heart mixture. Garnish with some sprigs of parsley and serve.

Wine: Bolgheri Rosato (Antinori, Tuscany), 1-2 years

Guinea Fowl with Savoy Cabbage and Boletus Mushrooms

Faraona alle verze con funghi porcini

Serves 4
1 guinea fowl, about 3-3 1/2 pounds (1.5 K)
1/2 cup (1 dl) *extra-vergine* olive oil
4 tablespoons (50 g) butter
5 garlic cloves
1 sprig rosemary
2/3 pound (300 g) fresh boletus mushrooms, cut into large cubes
2 heads Savoy cabbage
4 cups (1 L) meat broth
Salt and white pepper

Preheat the oven to 300°F (150°C).
Clean the guinea fowl, salt and pepper the interior, and truss with kitchen string. Put it in a roasting pan along with the butter and 2 tablespoons of oil. Put the pot in the oven and roast for about an hour, turning the bird at frequent intervals.
Separately, in a dutch oven, sauté the garlic and rosemary in the remaining oil. Take care that the garlic does not brown. Allow the oil to cool slightly and remove the garlic and rosemary. Pour the mushroom cubes into the same pan and sauté them over high heat for about 2 minutes.
Cut the leaves from the main stalk of the cabbages, wash them, and chop them coarsely. Add the mushrooms. Add the broth and salt and pepper, if necessary, and cook over low heat for 30 minutes.
Take the guinea fowl from the oven, remove it from the roasting pan, and put it in the pot with the cabbage and mushrooms. Cover and put the pot in the oven for about 10 minutes.
Cut the guinea fowl in slices and arrange them on individual dishes. Garnish with the cabbage and mushrooms and serve.

Wine : Barbaresco (Piedmont), 4-8 years

Pear Mousse

Spuma alle pere

Serves 4
1/3 Genoese biscuit (or a sponge cake), cut horizontally (the recipe appears below)
1 1/4 cups (250 g) sugar
1 1/2 cups (3 dl) water
2 tablespoons kirsch
2 cups (1/2 L) cream
1 pound (500 g) pears, pureed
1 tablespoon of gelatin powder (or 15 g of fish glue in sheets)
2 egg whites
2 cooked pears (for decorating the plates)
3 pears, pureed

Place a ring mold without its bottom on a sheet of pastry cardboard and arrange the Genoese biscuit or sponge cake in the middle of the ring. Boil 1/4 cup (50 g) of sugar with 1 cup of water. When the water has boiled and the sugar is completely dissolved, allow the syrup to cool and add the kirsch. Using a brush, moisten the sponge cake with the syrup.
Whip the cream and add 1 pound of pureed pears. Put the mixture in the refrigerator.
Boil 1 cup (200 g) of sugar in 1/2 cup of water for about 5 minutes.
Dissolve the gelatin in a little cold water; dissolve completely by placing the bowl in a pot of tepid water and stirring energetically. Beat the egg whites until they are stiff and add the sugar syrup by letting it run down the side of the bowl.
Rapidly beat the whites with a whisk to incorporate the sugar syrup. Add the gelatin and continue to whisk, but more slowly, until the mixture becomes tepid. Add the whipped cream and pear mixture and blend in rapidly. Pour the mixture onto the sponge cake in the mold.
Garnish with the cooked pears cut in slices. Put the mold in the refrigerator for at least 4 hours. Remove the mousse and cake from the mold. Pour some pear puree onto the plates, slice the mousse, and put the slices on the plates.

Wine : Torcolato di Breganze (Veneto), 2-4 years

Sponge Cake

Biscotto Genoese (pan di Spagna)

1 cup (150 g) white flour
2 tablespoons (30 g) potato starch (or cornstarch)
4 eggs
3/4 cup (150 g) sugar
4 teaspoons (20 g) butter

Preheat the oven to 350°F (180°).
Butter and lightly flour a cake pan. Mix the starch with the flour and sift.
Combine the eggs and the sugar and beat the mixture over a low heat until it becomes quite hot. Remove from the stove and continue beating the mixture until it has cooled. Add the flour-starch and blend with the spatula. Pour into the pan until it is three-quarters full and bake for 20 minutes. Take the cake from the oven and remove it from the pan. Place it on a rack to cool.
Wait until it is quite cold before using it with the pear mousse.

LA FRASCA

*Fine wines, carefully chosen by owner
Gianfranco Bolognesi, and superb cuisine,
carefully prepared by chef Marco Cavallucci
are the two essential pillars of strength of
La Frasca, which is located in the small
thermal resort of Castrocaro.*

Via Matteotti 38 – 47011 Castrocaro
Terme (Forlì). The Michelin two-star
restaurant is closed Tuesdays and from
January 2 to 20. The town is 11 kilometers (7 miles) southwest of Forli, with
which it is linked by SS (Highway) 67.
Forli, which is 63 kilometers (39 miles)
southeast of Bologna, can be reached
from that city by taking Autostrada
(Superhighway) A-14.
AE, Diners cards accepted.
Tel. (0543) 767471

Gianfranco Bolognesi, creator and director of La Frasca, offers the two complementary elements that make a fine table:
all the best wines of Italy and France and
foods that have been sensitively refined
and perfected. Bolognesi's absolute passion for wine and his knowledge of the
subject bring to mind the figure of Sante
Lancerio, who was among the first to describe Italian wines scientifically.

Sante Lancerio was cellarmaster to Pope
Paul III, and the letter that he sent to Cardinal Guido Ascanio Sforza in respect to
the nature and quality of wines was written four-and-a-half centuries ago. It can
be considered the commencement of
Italian oenological literature. Two
extracts from Lancerio's text will show
his depth of knowledge about the tastes
of that Farnese pontiff and his capacity
to describe wines. About Malvasia, or
Malvagia as he calls it, he wrote: "If you
want to savor the best, you should be sure
that it is not cloudy or turbid with sediment but that it is of a golden color. If it
should be otherwise, it will be dense and
the repeated drinking of it will affect the
liver." In respect to Trebbiano, he said,
among other things: "Such wines and
such goodness led Messer Bindo Altoviti
(brother of the bishop of Florence) to
come to Rome and give them to His Holiness, who drank them willingly in the
autumn, between the old and the new
season." In the text can be found evaluations of individual wines as well as organoleptic analyses of the appearance, the
aroma and the flavor of each in addition
to comments on the suitability of each as
an accompaniment for specific foods.
There is, therefore, no separation
between foods and wines.

Bolognesi, the soul, the creator, the
director and the moving force behind La
Frasca, is a concrete example of a man
who takes both food and wine seriously.
In 1974, he was adjudged Italy's top som-

melier. Now he belongs to the limited
circle of outstanding Italian restaurateurs. Bolognesi opened his establishment in 1971. The name, La Frasca, is
significant. In many parts of Italy, the inn
or wineshop that ties a shrub *(frasca)* to
its doorframe or sign is telling the world
at large that the new wine is ready to be
drunk. This practice has given rise to the
saying that "a good wine needs no bush."
Wine in Bolognesi's restaurant is the
keystone of the entire structure. That
concept, on which the establishment was
founded, has never been abandoned or
modified. Wine is always given a leading
role, although it now shares the spotlight
with foods of similar repute. Bolognesi
deeply loves his native region of Emilia-Romagna, and this affection has led him
to boost and reinvigorate public knowledge and appreciation of the wines of the
Romagna, which are not synonymous
with Sangiovese. Bolognesi himself
tends personally to the selection of the
wines. He looks after them and selects
them as if they were rare blossoms or
objets d'art.

The care devoted to the wines can be
sensed in every detail of the restaurant
and its cellar. Dishes, tablecloths, goblets, and furnishings are of the regional
tradition.

Among the fittings are attractive ceramics of Faenza made especially for the
house by a craftsman and tablecloths
typical of the Romagna, which are made
with stencils cut in time-honored
designs and then tinted with colored
inks.

But tradition is continuously reinterpreted, reexamined and reinvented, as it
should be. The dishes offered by Bolognesi, who is ably assisted by his wife,
Bruna, do not fail to equal and better the
region's great tradition.

La Frasca, occupying a fine old building in a little Romagna town below a steep hill topped by the ruins of an ancient castle, has a small garden between the road and the main building and in one corner of it is a huge stack of empty bottles. They are the relics of tastings and form a sort of multicolored mosaic. Their labels are those of the most prestigious crus of Italy and France. That stack also serves as an advertisement of the great importance that wine enjoys at La Frasca, for the cellar contains an imposing collection from which withdrawals can be made, not only in the three appealing dining rooms, but also in the attached bar and wineshop.

The Romagna, the region in which La Frasca is situated, is noted for its cuisine and for its tradition of open and generous hospitality. It was the native land of Pellegrino Artusi, a leading gastronome and culinary writer of the nineteenth century. Artusi has left many texts that are, in his native district, regarded as virtually sacred and to which reference must constantly be made when matters culinary are being discussed. However, while Artusi's injunctions must be and are respected, not even the most adamant of local boosters believes that they must be literally applied. Artusi's writings must be interpreted with intelligence and an appreciation of the times in which we live with new modes of cooking and new preparations. In that, La Frasca has succeeded admirably.

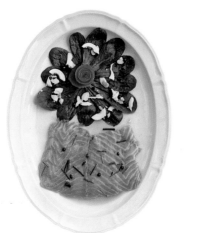

Marinated Fresh Salmon

Salmone fresco marinato

Serves 4
Fresh salmon, about 1 pound (500 g)
2 ¼ cups (500 g) coarse salt
6 tablespoons (100 g) *extra-vergine* olive oil
3 teaspoons green peppercorns
1 teaspoon raspberry vinegar
Chopped chives
Basil
Thyme
Mentuccia (a member of the mint family; omit if not available)

Cut 2 fillets from the salmon. Put half of the coarse salt on a plate. Lay the salmon fillets atop the salt. Cover the fish with the remaining salt, along with half the green peppercorns. Allow to infuse for 10 hours.
Wash the fillets in running water, then slice them lengthwise into extremely thin strips. Put the strips in a bowl and add the vinegar, remaining green peppercorns, and herbs. Allow to marinate for several hours. Garnish with raw mushrooms, greens, and a curl of raw carrot and serve with hot toast.

Wine: Gavi dei Gavi (Piedmont), 1-3 years, or Fiano di Avellino (Campania), 3-5 years

Ravioli with Eggplant and Zucchini Flavored with Thyme

Mezzelune con melanzane e zucchine al timo

Serves 4
For the pasta:
2 cups (300 g) white flour
3 eggs
Salt
6 ½ tablespoons boiled pureed spinach
For the filling and sauce:
4 eggplants
4 zucchini
7 tablespoons (100 g) butter
½ cup (1 dl) white wine
1 ⅓ cups (3 dl) cream
1 sprig of thyme
1 ⅔ cups (400 g) ricotta cheese
1 scant cup (100 g) grated Parmesan
Salt

Combine the flour and eggs and a pinch of salt and knead into a smooth dough. Divide the dough in half. One half of the pasta should be flavored and tinted with the pureed spinach.
Cut 3 eggplants and 3 zucchini into small pieces and put them in a pan with 2 tablespoons (30 g) of butter. Cook, then salt and baste with the white wine.
Add the cream and a little thyme. Reduce by half. Remove the vegetables, pass the sauce through a sieve, and set aside. Puree the vegetables. Combine three-quarters of the puree with the ricotta cheese and a scant ½ cup (50 g) of Parmesan. Salt lightly and blend well.
Cut the pasta into circles about 3 inches (7-8 cm) across. Place filling on each circle, fold over, and press down the edges.
Put the remainder of the blended vegetables in the sauce and keep warm. Dice the remaining eggplant and zucchini. Sprinkle with a bit of salt. Add some thyme and stew in 4 teaspoons (20 g) of butter.
Cook the ravioli in abundant salted water. Drain them and flavor with the remaining butter and Parmesan.

Pour some sauce into each plate. In the center of each plate put the diced vegetables and arrange around them the ravioli, alternating the yellow and the green.
Wine : Soave Classico (the Veneto), 1-12 years

Stuffed Rabbit

Coniglio farcito agli aromi

Serves 4
1 rabbit, about 2 ²/₃ pounds (1.2 K)
¹/₄ pound (120 g) ground veal
¹/₄ pound (120 g) ground pork
5 tablespoons (80 g) mortadella (bologna may be substituted), chopped
2 eggs
3 tablespoons grated Parmesan
1 ounce (30 g) bacon, chopped
1 hard-boiled egg
6 pitted green olives
2 tablespoons (30 g) butter
1 cup (¹/₄ L) white wine
¹/₂ cup (1 dl) olive oil
3 tablespoons white-wine vinegar flavored with a scallion or shallot
Pitted black olives, basil, salt and pepper

Bone the rabbit. Salt and pepper the interior. Prepare a stuffing consisting of the chopped rabbit giblets, the ground veal and pork, the mortadella (or bologna), 2 eggs, and the Parmesan. Blend well. Chop the bacon, hardboiled egg, and green olives and add those ingredients to the stuffing. Spread the stuffing on the boned rabbit. Roll up the rabbit and tie it with string.
Brown the rabbit roll in the butter and then cook it over low heat for about an hour, basting it from time to time with the white wine. When the rabbit is cooked, place it under a weight for 4 to 5 hours so that the stuffing becomes quite compact. Mix the oil, whitewine vinegar flavored with scallion (or shallot), pitted black olives cut into small pieces and chopped basil.
Serve the rolled rabbit, cut in slices, cold or tepid, with small cheese soufflés or quiches.

Wine : Sangiovese di Romagna (Ronco dei Ciliegi, Emilia-Romagna), 4-5 years

Saddle of Hare with Cabernet Sauvignon

Sella di lepre al Cabernet Sauvignon

Serves 4
2 saddles of hare (or rabbit), each about 1 ³/₄ pounds (800 g)
¹/₂ cup (1 dl) olive oil
¹/₂ cup (1 dl) strong meat broth
7 tablespoons (100 g) butter
For the marinade :
6 cups (¹/₂ L) Cabernet Sauvignon
2 carrots, coarsely chopped
1 celery stalk, coarsely chopped
¹/₂ onion, sliced
1 small scallion (or shallot)
1 bay leaf
Handful of parsley
1 sprig thyme
2 teaspoons (10 g) black peppercorns
1 sprig rosemary
Salt and pepper

Bone the saddles of hare (or rabbit) and put the meat in a large bowl with all the ingredients for the marinade. Allow to marinate for 24 hours. Preheat the oven to 350°F (180°C).
Remove the hare from the marinade. Strain off the liquid, reserving the vegetables.
Chop the bones of the hare into small pieces, and brown them in the oil. Add the vegetables from the marinade and cook for a few minutes over low heat. Degrease the liquid. Baste with the marinade wine, reduce, and add the meat broth. Reduce again. Pass the liquid through a sieve and blend in 4 teaspoons (20 g) of butter. Keep the sauce warm. Salt and pepper the meat and brown it over high heat in 5 tablespoons (80 g) of butter. Then roast the meat in the oven for 12-15 minutes. Remove the meat from the oven and cut it into slices.
Pour some of the sauce onto heated plates and arrange the slices of meat in a fan shape. Garnish with pureed chestnuts or onions.

Wine : Torgiano Rosso (Umbria), 2-5 years, or Sassicaia (Tuscany), 5 years and more

Hazelnut Semifreddo

Semifreddo alle nocciole salsa profiteroles

Serves 4
For the semifreddo :
1 ¹/₃ cups (7 ounces ; 200 g) hazelnuts
2 eggs, separated
²/₃ cup (150 g) vanilla-flavored sugar
5 teaspoons (25 g) chopped hazelnuts
1 egg white
7 tablespoons (100 g) cream
For the chocolate sauce :
2 cups (¹/₄ L) water
3 ¹/₂ tablespoons (50 g) sugar
3 ¹/₂ ounces (100 g) semisweet chocolate
7 tablespoons (100 g) cream
For the honey zabaione :
1 egg yolk
10 teaspoons (50 g) Acacia honey
¹/₄-¹/₂ cup Armagnac
7 tablespoons (100 g) cream

Make a hazelnut paste by crushing 1 ¹/₃ cups of hazelnuts in a mortar, then blending with 2 egg whites beaten stiff. Separately beat the egg yolks and sugar until creamy. Add the hazelnut paste and the chopped hazelnuts, and stir. Beat the egg white until stiff and whip the cream. Gently fold each into the hazelnut mixture.
Pour the semifreddo into individual molds and put them in the freezer for several hours. For the chocolate sauce, bring the water to a boil and pour over the sugar in a bowl. Roughly chop the chocolate and stir into the hot water until it melts. Allow the sauce to cool. Whip the cream and fold gently into the chocolate sauce. For the zabaione, beat the egg yolk with the honey and the Armagnac in a double boiler. Remove from the heat and add cream, whipped, folding in carefully.
Pour the chocolate sauce onto half of each plate. Pour the zabaione onto the other half. Drizzle thin stripes of the chocolate sauce across the zabaione, and vice-versa. Draw a knife across the stripes, first in one direction, then the other. Unmold a semifreddo in the middle of each plate. Garnish with chopped hazelnuts and tiny pieces of chocolate.
Wine : Moscato d'Asti (Piedmont), 1 year or Verduzzo di Ramandolo (Friuli-Venezia Giulia)

ENOTECA PINCHIORRI

Annie Féolde was born a cook, of a family of cooks, while her husband, Giorgio Pinchiorri, is an avid collector and connoisseur of wines. Together, they have created a restaurant that is the finest in Florence and one of the most outstanding in Italy.

An invitation to dinner at the Enoteca Pinchiorri is the prelude to the discovery of the immense fascination of wine, of innovation in foods, and of the richness of human communication. Here the recipes, as they are interpreted, are creative and refined. A new type of observation can be sensed in the cuisine, for Annie Féolde has succeeded in giving her "art" an immediate and pure character. She does not struggle with the formulas of her craft, for she knows how to interpret in creative terms, fully expressing an orientation that is richly stimulating and that can be fully appreciated in all the dishes served. Annie Féolde gives her cuisine its own image of freshness and immediacy, of reflection and communicativeness. The foods from her kitchen always appear new and wholesome, and they still have the perfume of nature, since their preparation is shrewdly achieved without any trace of academicism.

Giorgio Pinchiorri, her husband, has an obsession that is apparent to all: his cellar. Those who dine in the restaurant must without fail visit the cellar, since it is the most important in Italy and without doubt one of the most prestigious in the world. Wine is Pinchiorri's vocation. He loves to seek it out and discover all that it has to offer. Further, he has the extraordinary capacity of transmitting his zeal to others. He knows how to startle and please his guests with his novel recommendations. He conjures up a succession of wines with complete disregard for frontiers, taking products from Italy and France, America and South Africa, although French wines are his abiding passion. His cellar is a cathedral of wine but it is not a reliquary. Visitors are perennially surprised by the great quantity of wines and impressed, too, by the astuteness of his selection. The cellar harbors many magnums, and among them the crème de la crème of the world's wines.

The establishment, founded and molded by Pinchiorri and his wife, Annie, has been constructed gradually, by stages, each of which was carefully meditated. They have proceeded one step at a time, and they have reached the peak of the Italian restaurant world. Thanks to sheer willpower and to a ferocious determination to succeed, as well as to an unfailing love for their chosen profession, to study and to a steady quest for the best, the Pinchiorris have seen their creation recognized as one of the finest restaurants in Italy.

The Enoteca Pinchiorri's setting, a sixteenth-century palace in the ancient center of Florence, is entirely appropriate. For it fits snugly into that framework of civilization and art. Even a brief and rapid excursion in Florence would require thirty or fifty pages to describe. It is sufficient to say that the city's fame is universal because of its beauty and its artistic treasures and because of its contribution to Italian civilization, since it was the cradle of the country's language and literature. It remains a great cultural center and the home of flourishing and expert crafts. Those who walk along the Via Ghibellina, where the Enoteca is located, should not and cannot forget that they are only a few steps from the Uffizi Gallery, the Piazza della Signoria, and the Duomo and Baptistry. Enoteca, Duomo, Uffizi. The level is the same, as is the will to succeed and abundant human ingenuity.

Giorgio Pinchiorri has assembled an enormous collection of superb wines from countries throughout the world in the cellar of the sixteenth-century palace, in which his restaurant is installed on the ground floor. Italian wines are well represented but there may well be more bottles from France. When the Pinchiorris first opened their enoteca (wineshop), the emphasis was almost entirely upon wine. Pinchiorri no longer sells directly to the public but, instead, offers the fine products so zealously gathered and carefully preserved in the cellar almost exclusively to diners in the restaurant. It is not therefore difficult to find appropriate beverages to accompany the dishes issuing from the kitchen. The real problem is narrowing the choice to only two or three. The Enoteca Pinchiorri's main dining room is elegant and in sober good taste. But it is not large and altogether only about sixty guests can be accommodated inside. During good weather, however, tables and chairs are set up in the building's courtyard, where a further forty guests can be served. On summer evenings, especially, the courtyard is a cool refuge from the heat and noise of the center of Florence.

Via Ghibellina 87 – 50122 Florence. The restaurant, which is given two stars in the Guide Michelin, is closed Sundays, at noon Mondays, and throughout August. AE cards accepted.
Tel. (055) 242777, 242757

Shrimp Tails with Fresh Shelled Beans, Basil-flavored Oil and Lemon

Code di scampi con fagioli sgranati, olio al basilico e limone

Serves 4
16 jumbo shrimp
1 quart (1 L) water
2 ½ cups (500 g) fresh, shelled white
  beans
Salt and pepper
1 cup (¼ L) *extra-vergine* olive oil
8 fresh sage leaves
1 sprig rosemary
10 basil leaves
Juice of ½ lemon

Shell the shrimp and remove the heads. Put the tails in the refrigerator.

Bring the water to a boil and add the fresh, shelled white beans. When the water comes to the boil again, add salt and pepper, and about ¼ cup of olive oil.

At the same time, heat ¾ cup olive oil in another large pan. Add the sage leaves and rosemary sprig, both carefully washed, and salt and pepper.

Boil the beans for about 5-8 minutes. If canned beans are used, cook only for about 2 minutes. Drain the beans and add them to the pan with the oil, sage, and rosemary. Remove the pan from the heat and allow the beans to cool after stirring them so that they are fully coated with oil.

Chop the basil leaves. Remove the shrimp tails from the refrigerator, salt and pepper them, and sauté them in a pan with 1 tablespoon of olive oil, cooking them for 2 minutes on each side. At the last moment, add the lemon juice and chopped basil.

Place a spoonful of the beans on each plate. Arrange 2 shrimp tails atop the beans, decorate with basil leaves, and serve.

Wine: Sauvignon del Collio (Friuli-Venezia Giulia), 1-2 years

Maltagliati Pasta in Duck Sauce with Black Olives

Maltagliati al ragù di anatra e olive nere

Serves 4
For the pasta:
2 ⅛ cups (300 g) white flour
1 ½ eggs
Water, as needed
Salt
For the sauce:
Bones of the duck
1 carrot, chopped
1 onion, chopped
1 celery stalk, chopped
1 tablespoon chopped parsley
1 cup (¼ L) red wine
1 duck liver
Salt and pepper
For the meat sauce:
½ cup (100 g) zucchini, cut into strips
  the size of matches
½ cup (100 g) carrots, cut into strips the
  size of matches
1 duck breast
1 tablespoon olive oil
3 tablespoons (50 g) butter
16 pitted black olives, cut into thin
  rounds
Salt and pepper

Prepare the pasta by combining the flour, egg, salt and water as needed. Knead until a smooth, well-blended dough is obtained. Roll out into a sheet that is not too thin. Using the point of a knife, cut the dough into small triangles.

For the sauce, put the duck bones, the carrot, onion, celery, and parsley in a pot. Add the red wine and simmer until the liquid has been reduced to ½ cup (1 dl). Strain, add salt and pepper, if necessary, and add the raw, finely chopped duck liver. Cook for several minutes.

Scald the strips of zucchini and carrot in boiling salted water.

Brown the whole breast of duck in a tablespoon of olive oil. Salt and pepper the meat and cook it lightly so that the meat is still quite pink. Allow the breast to cool, then cut it into strips the size of matches.

Cook the pasta in abundant boiling water so that it is *al dente* (still with a bite).

Drain the pasta and put it in a frying pan. Add the sauce, the butter, the vegetables (carrots and zucchini), the duck breast strips, and the olives. Check the seasoning, adding salt and pepper if needed. When the ingredients are hot, serve immediately.

Wine: Merlot del Collio (Friuli-Venezia Giulia), 1-3 years

Fillet of Veal with Yellow-Squash "Pearls" and Black Truffles

Filetto di vitella alle perle di zucca e tartufo nero

Serves 4
1 pint (½ L) meat broth
1 cup (100 g) tiny balls of yellow squash (or pumpkin)
5 tablespoons (100 g) butter
¼ cup (½ dl) olive oil
2 veal fillets cut into 8 pieces, total weight 1 pound (400 g)
1 ounce (30 g) black truffle
12 green asparagus tips
Salt and pepper

Put the broth in a pot over low heat and reduce by half.
Pour in the squash balls and remove the pot from the heat.
Melt 1 ½ tablespoons of butter in another pan and brown the veal pieces, cooking them about 5 minutes on each side. Keep them warm.
Degrease the pan and add the broth and squash balls.
When the broth is hot, lower the heat to moderate. Cut the truffle in julienne slices and add them along with 1 tablespoon of butter to the broth, which should be quite dense. Shake the pan to amalgamate the butter. Keep hot.
Cook the asparagus tips in a pan with 2 ½ tablespoons of butter. Salt and pepper to taste. The asparagus should be stirred frequently and cooked for about 10 minutes.
Place the asparagus tips on heated plates. Put the pieces of veal atop the asparagus and pour over the sauce and the balls of squash.

Wine: Carmignano (Tuscany), 4-6 years

Pigeons in Honey and Sherry Vinegar

Piccioni al miele e aceto di Xeres

Serves 4
4 pigeons (young cockerels can be substituted)
1 garlic clove, finely chopped
2 tablespoons (40 g) butter
Salt
1 tablespoon of chestnut honey
1 tablespoon of Sherry vinegar
½ pound (200 g) raw spinach
<u>For the meat broth:</u>
2 carrots, chopped
1 onion, chopped
1 celery stalk, chopped
1 sprig of thyme
½ bay leaf
1 clove
2 cups (½ L) red wine
Salt

Clean and bone the pigeons. Fillet the breasts and remove the legs, and liver.
Prepare the broth by browning the pigeon bones and all the other ingredients in a little butter and oil, then adding the wine. Cook until the liquid is reduced by three-quarters. Pass through a fine sieve and add more salt, if needed.
Boil the spinach, then sauté it briefly in a pan with 4 teaspoons (20 g) of butter and the finely chopped garlic. Salt lightly.
With the remaining butter, sauté the legs, livers, and fillets, which should be cooked only until the meat is rare. Keep the meat warm.
Pour off the fat from the pan in which the meat was sautéed, add the broth, the honey, and the vinegar and blend thoroughly. Reduce slightly.
Place a bed of spinach on each plate, then the fillets cut in half, the legs, and the livers. Pour the sauce through a fine sieve over the meat, and serve.

Wine: Barbaresco (Piedmont), 4-8 years

Chesnut Cream Mold

Semifreddo di marroni

Serves 4
20 ounces (600 g) cleaned chestnuts
18 tablespoons (250 g) granulated sugar
Scant ¼ cup (1 dl) thick cream
1 tablespoon rum or Armagnac
4 egg whites
2 tablespoons (20 g) powdered sugar

Cook the chestnuts in water. Drain them, add granulated sugar, and pass through a sieve. Reserve 1 cup of puree.
Whip the cream and delicately blend in the rum or Armagnac.
Beat the egg whites until they are stiff. Fold in the powdered sugar.
Fold the whipped cream and the stiff egg whites into the chestnut puree. Working cautiously, form the puree into 4 balls or 4 cones.
Put the reserved puree atop the cones or balls and shape it in the form of flakes or scales.
Put the semifreddo in the refrigerator for at least 2 hours.
Pour a little thick cream into each dish. Pour over some chocolate sauce and place the semifreddo atop it. Dust with powdered sugar and serve.

Wine: Moscato d'Asti (Piedmont), 1 year

VILLA SAN MICHELE

Francesco Forlano is the director of the Villa San Michele, a luxurious hotel and restaurant perched on the side of a mountain at Fiesole overlooking the center of Florence. The buildings, in Renaissance style, may have been designed in part by Michelangelo.

Via Doccia 4 – 50014 Fiesole (near Florence). The restaurant and hotel are open from March 1 to November 30. During that period, both function every day without interruption. From Piazza della Libertà on the northern edge of the center of Florence, take Via Minzoni and then Via Alessandro Volta toward Fiesole.
AE, Eurocard, Diners cards accepted.
Tel. (055)59451

The restaurant is reached by one of the most appealing and scenic roads in all of Tuscany. The route itself is an authentic advertisement of the refinement that awaits the guest at the restaurant. Fiesole is an enchanted spot. Of Etruscan origin, the town still preserves a stretch of wall from that period but it also offers numerous relics of Roman civilization, including the theater, which was built in 80 B.C. Fiesole is also one of the Florentines' favorite excursions. Only five miles from Florence, Fiesole is perched on a hill that overlooks the entire valley in which Florence is situated and enjoys a splendid panorama that extends as far as the hills on the other side of the Arno River. The town abounds in gems of medieval art, beginning with the Duomo, which was built on a Roman foundation and contains sixteenth-century and Renaissance frescoes. There is also the fifteenth-century church of San Domenico, which offers paintings by Fra Angelico, and the Gothic chapel of San Francesco, on the summit of the hill, which is reached by a route featuring astounding views of Florence and its monuments far below. There is today an air of profound humanism at Fiesole, a perfect symbiosis of human and natural elements in which ancient construction is compatibly inserted in the environment, almost as if the builders meant to complete a mosaic that would lack something without this particular tessera.

The Villa San Michele attains the same level of fulfillment, the fruit of the efforts of many centuries. And it appears to all who visit it that it, too, serves to complete a refined mosaic. The restaurant and hotel Villa San Michele are installed in what was once a small chapel and residence that were constructed in the fifteenth-century and occupied by Franciscan friars. Structurally it still reveals sixteenth – and seventeenth-cen-

The Villa San Michele is now owned by a company headquartered in London but it is in style and practice fundamentally Italian. The director, Francesco Forlano, zealously preserves the spirit of hospitality and refined ease habitual to noble families of a gentler day. For the hotel and restaurant are installed in a superbly restored and maintained villa that was acquired from the Franciscans, who had used it as a residence, by the patrician Davanzati family of Florence and made into a palatial country home. The same commitment to preservation and regard for the tradition of the

tury elements. The building was expanded and remodeled in the seventeenth-century by the Davanzati family, whose coat of arms is displayed in the courtyard and on the façade. The convent remained the property of the Franciscan order until 1817, when it was converted to lay use as a villa. Since then, it has undergone many alterations at the hands of its various proprietors.

The Villa San Michele is now owned by a company headquartered in London, although its direction and inspiration are entirely Italian or, rather, Tuscan. That means that internal modernization has gone hand in hand with preservation. There has even been a successful effort to bring to light the structure's Renaissance elements. During the summer months, meals are served on the *loggia* or roofed terrace inspired by Michelangelo's architectual vision, from which diners enjoy a splendid view of Florence. During other periods of the year, meals are taken in an intimate dining room in what was once the refectory. Even the cuisine takes its inspiration from the structure, for it is based on traditional, regional gastronomy, although it has been delicately reworked to match the modern mood. It is a reflection of a culture of immense breadth.

Tuscan cuisine emphasizes the essential, the primary flavors and scents of the foods themselves. When the raw materials are excellent, elaboration is not only unnecessary but also undesirable. The region's culinary tradition stresses soups, often involving the use of large quantities of bread, beans, Tuscan black cabbage, green and fruity olive oil, and roasted and grilled meats. The Villa San Michele respects that tradition and the result is a cuisine that is as wholesome as it is delectable.

past can be detected in the establishment's cuisine, the preparation of which is directed by chef Giuseppe Dalla Rosa.
Parts of Italy are as flat as the Great Salt Lake desert; some are as craggy as the Rockies, while others are nearly as lush as Florida. Despite that enormous variety, nearly everyone, when he or she thinks of Italy, conjures up in the mind's eye a vision of gentle hills covered with cypresses, umbrella pines, olives, acacias, vines, and oaks. That is really a picture of Tuscany, although for most people it is also the quintessence of Italy. Whether

they know it by words or by paints, people all over the world know Tuscany, although they may never have visited the region or its capital, Florence. The panaroma from the windows and terraces of the Villa San Michele are familiar, then, to everyone everywhere.

Beef Fillet Gratinéed with Herbs and Barbaresco Sauce

Filetto gratinato alle erbe con salsa Barbaresco

Serves 4
Rosemary, thyme, and tarragon
1 ⅓ cups (300 g) butter
4 fillets of beef, each about ½ pound (200 g)
1 cup (1 dl) Barbaresco wine
Salt and pepper

Finely chop the herbs and work them into 1 cup (200 g) of butter, using the fingers. Form the butter into a cylinder and put it in the refrigerator.
Put the remaining butter in a frying pan. Cook the fillets, salted and peppered, on both sides. Remove the fillets from the pan, add the wine, and reduce.
Cut the chilled cylinder of butter flavored with the herbs into rounds. Place a round of butter on each fillet and gratiné briefly under a grill. Pour over the sauce and serve, garnishing the plate with potatoes pureed with cream.

Wine: Barbaresco (Piedmont), 4-8 years

Gilt-head Bream with Herbs

Orata alle erbe aromatiche

Serves 4
4 gilt-head bream, each about ¾ pound (350 g) (porgy may be substituted)
½ cup flour
8 tablespoons (120 g) olive oil
½ cup (1 dl) white wine
½ cup (1 dl) fish stock
Rosemary, sage, thyme, tarragon, parsley
Salt and pepper

Preheat the oven to 350°F (180°C).
Wash, clean, and scale the bream. Salt and pepper the fish, then dredge it in flour. Heat the oil in a frying pan and brown the bream on each side.
Finish the cooking, which will require about 10 minutes, in the oven. Then remove the bream from the pan. Pour off the cooking oil. Add the white wine and the fish stock and reduce by cooking rapidly over high heat. Chop the herbs and sprinkle over the bream. Serve with the wine sauce.

Wine: Montecarlo Bianco (Tuscany), 1-2 years

Strisce Pasta and Chick-pea Soup

Strisce e ceci

Serves 4
For the pasta:
1 ½ cups (200 g) white flour
Water
Salt

¾ cup (200 g) dried chick-peas
2 garlic cloves
1 sprig of rosemary
2 ripe tomatoes
6 tablespoons (100 g) olive oil
Salt and pepper

Soak the chick-peas in cold water for 2 days. Combine the flour with a pinch of salt and sufficient water. Knead to obtain a soft, smooth dough. Roll out the pasta into a thin sheet, then roll it up into a tube. Using a sharp knife, cut the pasta into rather wide noodles. Unroll the noodles and scatter them around the doughboard so that they do not stick together.
Cook the chick-peas over moderate heat for at least 3 hours. Pass half of the chick-peas through a sieve.
Stew the garlic, rosemary, and tomatoes, which have been peeled, seeded, and cut into small pieces, in the olive oil. Add the chick-peas and the water in which they were cooked. Boil for 15 minutes. Remove the garlic and rosemary. Add salt and pepper as well as the noodles and cook for 10 minutes. The soup should be rather thick. Serve hot or warm with a bit of olive oil poured over.

Wine: Chianti Classico (Tuscany), 3-5 years

Vegetable Soup

Carabaccia

Serves 4
3 large onions
2 carrots
2 celery stalks
5 tablespoons olive oil
4 cups (1 L) meat broth
7 ounces (200 g) homemade bread
⅓ cup (40 g) grated Parmesan
Salt and pepper

Cut the onions into julienne slices and the carrots and celery into small cubes. Stew the carrots, onions, and celery in the oil for about 10 minutes. Add the broth and simmer for 20 minutes. Add salt and pepper. Cut the bread into round slices and toast the slices. Put the toasted bread in a soup tureen and pour in the boiling soup. Sprinkle with the Parmesan and serve piping hot.

Wine: Chianti dei Colli Senesi (Tuscany), 3-4 years

Rice in Cuttlefish Ink

Risotto al nero di seppie

Serves 4
14 ounces (400 g) cuttlefish (squid may be substituted)
1 onion, thinly sliced
1 garlic clove
1 cup (¼ L) white wine
1 cup (250 g) rice
4 cups (1 L) fish broth
4 tablespoons (60 g) olive oil
4 teaspoons (20 g) butter
Salt and pepper

Clean the cuttlefish, setting aside the ink sacs. Cut the cuttlefish into thin strips. Sauté the onion and garlic in the oil. Add the cuttlefish and stew them for a few minutes, then add the ink, and white wine as needed. Simmer slowly.
Add the rice and allow it to stew for a few minutes. Add the broth a little at a time during the subsequent cooking. Cook for about 20 minutes.
At the end, stir in the butter and continue stirring until the dish is creamy. Add a pinch of salt and pepper and serve.

Wine: Pomino Bianco (Tuscany), 4-6 years

La Mora

*Sauro Brunicardi and his wife, Angela,
who along with Bruno Ercoli is in charge
of the kitchen, have made La Mora,
a shrine of Tuscan cuisine, one that
retains the best of the past while keeping
in step with contemporary trends.*

Via Sesto di Moriano 104 – 55029 Ponte a Moriano (near Lucca). The restaurant is closed Wednesday nights and all day Tuesday, as well as during the first 15 days of July. Ponte a Moriano, which is 9 kilometers (5 miles) north of Lucca, can be reached by taking SS (Highway) 12. AE, Eurocard, Diners, Visa cards accepted. Tel. (0583) 57109

La Mora is located in a part of Tuscany that is completely unknown to most foreigners and even to many Italians, an area that is in places gentle and in others wild; both aspects can be found as well in the cuisine of this district. Sauro Brunicardi is a tireless investigator of matters culinary, as can be seen in the quality of the foods offered in his restaurant.

At La Mora, the recipes, securely anchored in the tradition of Tuscany, have all been reinterpreted by Brunicardi's wife, Angela, who applies her own feminine sensibility to the preparation of each dish. Bruno Ercoli is co-chef.

The restaurant is situated in a small village, although it is relatively close to Lucca, a major community of the region. Of Roman origin, Lucca enjoyed extraordinary prosperity and growth in the twelfth and thirteenth centuries because of the production and sale of silk and extensive banking operations. It was an age of gold as well in the community's artistic life, and the city's growth coincided with the flowering of the Romanesque style. Lucca's walls are still intact, a tree-lined circuit enclosing the center of the community that was constructed in the late sixteenth and early seventeenth centuries. It is one of the most significant examples of urban military construction in Tuscany, with eleven bastions that are now used for expositions, and various other cultural events.

In the civic center, Lucca has preserved the appearance of an ancient city-state, a perfectly maintained medieval urban layout with extremely narrow streets and alleys above which soar numerous stone towers. The cramped thoroughfares open up at irregular intervals into small squares on one side of which, almost inevitably, there is a church in the Romanesque style. Those churches are among the most attractive buildings in Lucca,

equaled only by the palatial buildings of the sixteenth and seventeenth centuries. Lucca was also the home of four great Italian composers and musicians, Francesco Geminiani, Luigi Boccherini, Alfredo Catalani, and Giacomo Puccini.

At La Mora, only a few miles outside Lucca, the Tuscan tradition stands revealed as a gastronomic heritage of great importance. It is a place that, as the name itself indicates, is of ancient origin. Mora is derived from the Latin *morare*, which means to stop over or stay. That would indicate that there was an inn or hostel on the site in the time of the ancient Romans. The place's tradition of hospitality can be more definitely attested to in recent times, for La Mora was a *trattoria* or small family-run restaurant beginning in 1867 and continuing to the present day. Since 1867, the purest, most unadulterated dishes of Tuscan cuisine have been dispensed in this restaurant on the banks of the Serchio River. Brunicardi's father, Pellegrino, purchased the establishment in 1946. At that time, it was primarily offering its clients wine, bread, and fried fish from the Serchio. Extensive modifications of the establishment were carried out, although a country tone has always been maintained. It is the same sort of approach that has been proudly preserved in the restaurant's cuisine. In 1970, Sauro Brunicardi succeeded his father, and the gastronomic line altered according to a natural evolution and a well-conceived and steady program of modernization. La Mora today offers the traditional preparations of the Lucca district and of the Garfagnana, a mountainous area to the northeast of the city, dishes such as the spelt soup *(zuppa di farro).* However, the cuisine has been reconsidered and rendered more appealing.

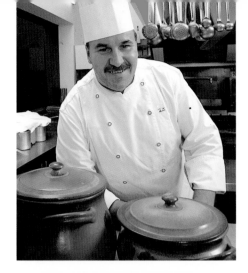

La Mora is perched on the banks of a small stream, the Serchio, which has always provided, in the form of fish and eels, some of the raw materials for its kitchen. However, the restaurant owes as much or more to the soil of the Lucca district and especially its olive trees, which provide an oil much touted by the inhabitants of the district and much exported – the United States is one of its biggest markets. Tradition is an important factor of life in the Lucca area, for the city was one of the last independent city states of Italy, losing its freedom only in the nineteenth century. The Brunicardis, while respecting that commitment to the past, have still managed to perfect a cuisine that is modern and totally in keeping with contemporary tastes.

Tacconi Pasta, Luccan Style

Tacconi alla lucchese

Serves 4
For the pasta:
2 ⅛ cups (300 g) white flour
3 eggs
1 tablespoon water
1 tablespoon olive oil
Salt
For the sauce:
½ rabbit, the haunch, about 24 ounces (600 g)
2 cups (½ L) red wine
2 small onions
2 small carrots
2 celery stalks
2 garlic cloves
2 cloves
Pinch of cinnamon
3 ounces (80 g) bacon
2 bay leaves
4 tablespoons (60 g) *extra-vergine* olive oil
1 ⅓ cups (300 g) ripe tomatoes
Salt and pepper
4 tablespoons (20 g) grated Parmesan

Cut the rabbit into pieces. Combine the wine with the onion, carrot, and celery stalk cut into small pieces. Add 1 clove of garlic, 1 clove, and the cinnamon, and marinate the rabbit for 12 hours in it.
Prepare the pasta by combining all the ingredients listed above and kneading until the dough is smooth. Roll out into a leaf about ¹⁄₁₆ inch (3 mm) thick.
Remove the pieces of rabbit from the marinade. Pass the marinade through a sieve, reserving the liquid.
Chop 1 onion, 1 carrot, 1 stalk of celery, 1 clove of garlic, the bacon and 2 bay leaves into fine pieces and sauté them in the oil. Add the pieces of rabbit, baste with the marinade, and cook until virtually all the liquid has evaporated. Add the tomatoes, salt, and pepper and simmer slowly for about 1 ½ hours.

Remove the pieces of rabbit from the pan, extract the bones, and cut the meat into small pieces. Pass the sauce through a sieve, and return the meat to the pan.
Cut small squares *(tacconi)* of ⅛ inch (5 mm) per side from the leaf of pasta and cook them in abundant boiling salted water for 4-5 minutes. Drain.
Arrange a layer of *tacconi* in pasta plates, then pour in the rabbit sauce, which should be quite hot. Continue with more layers until all the ingredients are used up. Sprinkle with grated Parmesan and serve.

Wine : Carmignano (Tuscany), 5-8 years

Guinea Fowl with Boletus Mushrooms

Faraona ai funghi porcini

Serves 6
5 tablespoons (75 g) olive oil
1 onion, sliced
1 celery stalk, cut in small cubes
1 carrot, cut in rounds
2 garlic cloves
4 sage leaves
1 guinea fowl (or chicken), about 2 ½-3 pounds (1.2 K)
14 ounces (400 g) fresh boletus mushrooms
2 ripe tomatoes, peeled, seeded, and chopped
1 sprig of *mentuccia* (calamint may be substituted)
Salt and pepper

Preheat the oven to 400°F (200°C).
Put 2 tablespoons of oil, the onion slices, celery pieces, carrot rounds, 1 clove of garlic, and the sage leaves in a roasting pan. Arrange the guinea fowl in the pan and roast for 30 minutes. Remove the bird from the pan and keep it warm.
Cut the mushrooms into thin slices. Brown 1 clove of garlic in the remaining oil, then add the mushrooms, the tomatoes, and the *mentuccia*. Salt and pepper. Sauté for about 10 minutes.
Cut the guinea fowl into 6 pieces and put them in the sauce with the mushrooms. Cook over moderate heat for 15 minutes and serve.

Wine : Morellino di Scansano (Tuscany), 3-5 years

Spelt Soup

Gran Farro

Serves 4
2 cups (500 g) fresh (or canned) red
  (kidney) beans
½ onion, chopped
1 garlic clove
½ celery stalk, chopped
2 sage leaves
1 sprig of marjoram
3 tablespoons (50 g) *extra-vergine* olive
  oil
4 ounces (100 g) ham rind
⅔ cup (150 g) tomatoes
Salt and pepper
1 ½ cups (150 g) spelt (or pearl barley)

Boil the beans and drain them. Set aside the
water in which they were cooked. Puree the
beans and pass them through a sieve.
Chop the garlic, onion, celery, sage leaves,
and marjoram and sauté them in the oil
along with the ham rind cut into small
pieces. Salt and pepper.
Add the tomatoes and cook for 15 minutes.
Pass through a sieve and add the puree to the
beans along with 1 cup (¼ L) of the water in
which they cooked. Mix well and add the
spelt or pearl barley.
Cook for 35-40 minutes, adding a bit of the
water in which the beans were cooked from
time to time. The soup should be rather
thick. Sprinkle with some drops of olive oil
and serve.

Wine: Chianti Classico (Tuscany), 2-4 years

Eels in Zimino (Tomatoes and Vegetables)

Anguille del Serchio in zimino

Serves 4
2 small onions
2 celery stalks
1 garlic clove
Peel of ½ lemon
Handful of parsley
1 sprig rosemary
4 tablespoons (60 g) olive oil
1 ⅓ cups (300 g) tomatoes
½ cup (1 dl) white wine
2 pounds (about 1 K) eels
2 tablespoons (10 g) white flour
Salt and pepper

Chop the onions, celery, and garlic. Mince
the lemon peel into tiny pieces. Chop the
parsley and the rosemary. Put all these
ingredients in a pan and sauté in the oil.
Add the tomatoes, which have been peeled,
seeded, and cut into small pieces, and the
white wine. Stir, and cook for 5 minutes.
Cut the eels into small pieces, each about
3-4 inches (7-10 cm) in length. Dredge the
pieces in flour and put them in the pan with
the sauce. Cook for a further 10 minutes.
The sauce should be quite thick. Add more
salt and pepper, if necessary. Serve hot.

Wine: Vernaccia di San Gimignano Riserva
(Tuscany), 2-3 years

Traditional Luccan Dessert

Antico dolce Lucchese

Serves 4
½ cup (100 g) sugar
½ cup (1 dl) water
1 ½ cups (350 g) strawberry puree
½ cup (1 dl) strawberry liqueur
1 tablespoon lemon juice
10 ounces (300 g) pan di Spagna
  (sponge cake)
6 tablespoons dry Marsala
⅔ cup (150 g) cream, whipped

Prepare the strawberry sauce by combining
the water and sugar and cooking until the
syrup caramelizes. Add the strawberry puree
and blend well. Stir in the strawberry
liqueur and lemon juice.
Cut the sponge cake into thin slices and
baste with the Marsala.
Place the slices of cake on dessert plates, garnish with the whipped cream, and pour over
the strawberry sauce.

Wine: Vin Santo (Tuscany), 5-8 years or
Moscato d'Asti (Piedmont), 1 year

La Chiusa

*La Chiusa's owners, Dania and Umberto Lucherini,
are committed body and soul to the pleasure
and the wholesomeness of life in
the Tuscan countryside. Their restaurant's
cuisine is a real and elegantly simple
expression of their commitment.*

Via della Madonnina 88 – 53040 Montefollonico (near Siena). The restaurant is
closed on Tuesdays in the winter but open
every day in summer. It also closes from
January 8 to March 10. Montefollonico is
approached from the Sinalunga-Perugia exit
of the Autostrada del Sole (Superhighway
A-1) at Bettolle, 100 kilometers (62 miles)
southeast of Florence. From Bettolle, it is
only a few miles to Montefollonico.
AE, Diners cards accepted.
Tel. (0577) 669668

Dania Lucherini is one of the few women
securely established in the firmament of
famous Italian chefs. And the restaurant
she directs clearly shows a woman's
touch, with a traditional oven for baking
breads, a press for the extraction of olive
oil, and jams and preserves made in the
house. That sensibility also finds expression in the foods she offers, which always
represent a marriage of the regional cuisine with a new intuition that is never
haphazard. For her, creativity is not an
end in itself but the application of imagination with the intention of breathing new
life into ancient formulas.

This establishment, located among the
vineyards in the heart of Tuscany, recalls
the "Dithyramb of Bacchus in Tuscany"
(Ditirambo di Bacco in Toscana), written
by Francesco Redi (1626-1698), a native of
Arezzo. Redi was a naturalist and doctor as
well as a poet. The text of the "Dithyramb"
was the gospel of the sommelier and oenol-
ogist, as the following brief extract shows:

Of the gracefulness
of the divine
Moscadelletto
di Montalcino
occasionally as a jest
I request a goblet
but I will not run the risk
of drinking a third.
It is an entirely charming wine
but, still, too much of it and I am sated.
Such a wine
I assign
to the excesses and pleasures
of those severe virgins
who, confined to the sacred place,
are invested with the task of tending the
flame.
Such wine
I consign
to the women of Paris
and to the gratification of those
so beautiful
who dwell beside the Thames.

The panorama offered by La Chiusa is one
of indescribable beauty, a landscape that is
miraculously intact. At Montefollonico,
the traveler is halfway between Florence
and Siena. On one side is Montepulciano
and on the other Pienza, both small gems
of astounding beauty. In this district, air
and art penetrate the skin and leave a mark
on the soul, as if made by a firebrand. It is
impossible, having visited these places, to
shake the impression they have created.
They remain a light weight on the shoul-
der, like guardian angels. Such places have
their own reasons to exist. A journey
among these hills, which remain as the
great Sienese artists depicted them in the
greens and blues of their paintings and
frescoes, provides memories for a lifetime.
If the traveler's intention is to savor a
beauty created by nature and man in fruitful partnership, he will be happy to come
at last to the small village of Montefollonico, an island that time has left untouched.
Amid the splendid relics of bygone centuries there is La Chiusa. It is an old Tuscan
farm, owned since the nineteenth century
by the family of the couple who now operate it as a small, intimate restaurant, Dania
and Umberto Lucherini. They have
earned the voyager's gratitude for they
have rebuilt the old farm with great insight
and skill. Where grain was once stored,
there is now the restaurant. An ancient
olive press still functions perfectly, below
the dining room, and the smell of baking
bread wafts from wood-burning ovens.
"Self-sufficiency from the eggs to the ice
cream" is the way the two patrons describe
their approach to cuisine. The farmers of
the district harvest some of the best produce in Italy, and they furnish the restaurant with all of its meats, fruits, and vegetables. La Chiusa relies completely on
local provisions. In this area, agriculture
respects the wisdom of the earth, and tradition is loved and wisely held in esteem.
Those who dine at La Chiusa will realize
how fortunate are those who live in this
environment, and enjoy its heritage.

Visitors, who must necessarily come a considerable distance to sample the rustic but refined cuisine of La Chiusa, breathe the air of an old farm with the scent of freshly baked bread, the oil of the great press, and many other good things of the Tuscan fields and forests. The menu abounds in vegetables, meats, and game of a country goodness and represents a gastronomic tradition that is austere, essential, and lean, while the components and methods of preparation are simple and essential as well. The excellence of the raw materials can be clearly seen and appreciated in every dish. Dania has succeeded in combining the essentiality of Tuscan cuisine with a wider vision that extends far beyond the borders of the region.

Large Ravioli Filled with Ricotta

Raviolo grande di ricotta

Serves 4
For the pasta:
2 ½ cups (250 g) flour
1 egg
1 tablespoon olive oil
Salt
For the stuffing:
1 cup (200 g) fresh ricotta
1 egg
1 tablespoon chopped parsley
1 tablespoon grated Parmesan
Salt and pepper
For the sauce:
2 tablespoons (40 g) melted butter
2 tablespoons (40 g) grated Parmesan

Combine the flour, egg, olive oil, and a pinch of salt. Knead energetically until a smooth dough is obtained. Roll out into a thin sheet and cut into squares 3 ½ inches (8 cm) per side.
Whip the ricotta with a beater and blend in the egg, chopped parsley, grated Parmesan, and a pinch each of salt and pepper. Put a dollop of filling in the center of half of the pasta squares. Place the remaining squares atop the filling and press down along the edges with a fork to seal the two pieces of pasta together.
Cook the ravioli in abundant salted water for about 5 minutes. Remove them from the pot with a slotted spoon and place 2 ravioli on each of 4 heated dishes. Melt the butter over moderate heat and pour over the pasta. Sprinkle with coarsely grated Parmesan and serve hot. Decorate with pieces of skinned fresh tomato and a few leaves of fresh rosemary.

Wine: Bianco della Valdichiana (Tuscany), 1-2 years

Pumpkin Flowers

Fiore di zucca

Serves 4
½ cup (100 g) ricotta cheese
1 tablespoon chopped parsley
1 egg
4 pumpkin flowers
1 tablespoon (20 g) butter
10 ripe tomatoes
Salt and pepper

Blend the ricotta cheese with the egg, parsley, salt, and pepper.
Lightly wash the pumpkin flowers, which must be quite fresh, and remove the pistils. Fill the flowers with the cheese mixture and pinch them shut at the open end.
Melt the butter in a pan. Add the peeled and seeded tomatoes, cut into pieces, and cook for 5 minutes. Add the stuffed pumpkin flowers, acting delicately to avoid breaking the "containers," and cook for a further 5 minutes.
Place a couple of the flowers on each dish and decorate by brushing with tomato sauce. Put a celery leaf or two on each plate as well.

Wine: Pinot Bianco del Collio (Friuli-Venezia Giulia), 1-3 years

Coffee Custard

Pan di caffè

Serves 4
5 eggs
9 tablespoons (125 g) sugar
2 cups (½ L) strong tepid coffee
1 teaspoon rum
For the sauce:
1 demitasse cup strong espresso-type coffee
½ demitasse cup thick cream
1 tablespoon sugar

Preheat the oven to 350°F (180°C).
Beat the eggs with 5 tablespoons of sugar. Add the coffee and rum. Blend well. Make a caramel with the remaining 4 tablespoons of sugar.
Coat the sides and bottoms of 4 small round molds, with the caramel. Let the caramel cool. Pour the egg mixture into the molds. Set the molds in a pan partly filled with water and cook in the oven for 20 minutes. Let the custards cool, then place them in the refrigerator for an hour or so before serving. Dissolve the sugar in the hot coffee. Allow to cool. Blend in the cream. Pour some of the mixture into dishes and place the custards atop it. Sprinkle over small pieces of chocolate and serve.

Wine: Torcolate di Braganze (Maculan, the Venete), 2-4 years

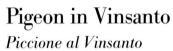

Large Noodles with Vegetables

Pappardelle alle verdure

Serves 4
For the pasta:
2 ½ cups (250 g) flour
1 egg
1 tablespoon olive oil
Salt
For the sauce and garnish:
2 small zucchini
2 small carrots
4 ounces (100 g) extremely fine green
  beans
2 ½ tablespoons (50 g) butter
2 fresh garlic cloves
10 fresh basil leaves
Salt and pepper

Combine the flour, egg, olive oil, and a pinch of salt, knead well, and roll the dough into a ball. Roll out the dough into a sheet that is not too thin. Roll up the sheet and, using a sharp knife, cut the dough into noodles that are fairly long and about 1 ¼ inches (3 cm) wide.
Cut the zucchini lengthwise into thin strips and slice the carrots in rounds. Parboil the carrots and drain them. Remove the tips of the green beans but leave them whole.
Melt the butter in a pan and lightly brown the garlic cloves. Remove the garlic and discard it. Put the zucchini, the carrots, the green beans, and the basil leaves in the pan. Add a couple of tablespoons of water, salt and pepper, and cook the vegetables over fairly high heat for about 10 minutes.
Cook the noodles in abundant salted water. Drain them, arrange them on heated dishes, and pour over the butter in which the vegetables have cooked. Garnish the dish with the vegetables and serve hot.

Wine: Bianco di Pitigliano (Tuscany), 1-2 years

Marinated Rabbit

Coniglio marinato

Serves 4
4 saddles of rabbit, total weight 2 ¼
  pounds (1.2 K)
1 cup (¼ L) *extra-vergine* olive oil
1 garlic clove, crushed
Juice of ½ lemon
2 sprigs of rosemary, chopped
4 ripe tomatoes
1 cup (¼ L) white wine
Salt and white pepper

Salt the saddles of rabbit and put them in the oil. Add the garlic, lemon juice, and chopped rosemary. Marinate for 12 hours.
Put the rabbit along with the marinade in a pot and cook over low heat for about 15 minutes. Add the wine, reduce slightly, and add the peeled and seeded tomatoes, cut into small pieces. Salt and pepper to taste. Continue the cooking for a further 10 minutes.
Cut the saddles of rabbit into thin slices and serve them accompanied by the tomato sauce, which should be quite thick.
Garnish with "flowers" made of carrot cut in paper-thin strips that are curled up to form blossoms and small, round cheese-and-parsley mousses.

Wine: Chianti Classico (Tuscany), 4-6 years

Pigeon in Vinsanto

Piccione al Vinsanto

Serves 4
4 pigeons (or squab chickens), each
  weighing about 8-10 ounces (200-250 g)
1 garlic clove, cut in slivers
Salt
3 tablespoons (60 g) butter
2 cups aged Vinsanto (or Sherry)

Clean the pigeons, reserving the livers. Salt the birds, tie them with kitchen string, and make incisions with a sharp, fine-pointed knife in the pigeons' breasts. Insert the garlic slivers in the incisions.
Melt the butter in a pan and brown the pigeons over high heat for about 10 minutes. Pour off the butter, cut open the pigeons, and remove the breast bones. Put them back in the pan and pour over the Vinsanto or Sherry. Chop up the bones and add them to the pan.
Cook over high heat for 5 minutes. Add the livers and continue the cooking over low heat for 5 minutes more.
Serve the pigeons on heated dishes, pouring over the sauce, after removing the bones and passing the liquid through a food mill to puree the livers.
Garnish the dishes with slices of layered vegetable mousse, made with spinach, Parmesan or ricotta cheese, carrots, and small bunches of white grapes.

Wine: Rosso di Montalcino (Tuscany), 3-4 years

LE TRE VASELLE

*Romano Sartore is the manager of Le Tre Vaselle
restaurant-hotel and his supervision ensures that all
runs smoothly in every way. But the institution's
inspiration is due to Giorgio Lungarotti and his family,
who have put Torgiano on the map.*

Umbrian cuisine is still solidly linked to tradition. The habits of the people, their religion, and their philosophy of life reinforce the conservative spirit of the region, which is expressed in its gastronomy as well. Le Tre Vaselle has not escaped the influence of its environment, although it has still succeeded in freshening some recipes.

Alongside the tradition drawn from old recipe books but above all from the daily cooking of ordinary families, Umbria provides an astounding variety of raw materials, which are the tesseras used by Le Tre Vaselle in assembling its gastronomic mosaic. In Umbria, it is easy to find superb meats, which are provided by the Chianina breed of cattle, a variety that originated in this region and neighboring Tuscany. The meat of the Chianina is now much in demand throughout the world but it is no better anywhere than in Umbria. Trasimeno, the largest lake in south-central Italy, provides a large quantity of freshwater fish, ranging from perch to pike. The land yields the black truffle and the grain used by the pasta industry. The macaroni and spaghetti made in the region are the most highly appreciated in Italy. There are superb vegetables, game, and pork products as well. Throughout Italy, the leading butchers and processors of pork are called *"norcini"* because all these experts once came from the little town of Norcia in central Umbria. Le Tre Vaselle is part of a gastronomic, cultural, and oenological cosmos. At Torgiano, a few miles from the Umbrian capital of Perugia, in fact, Maria Grazia and Giorgio Lungarotti set about establishing a restaurant and hotel but also created the Museo del Vino, a museum dedicated to wine, one that would be unique in Italy for its quality and comprehensiveness. The small town is also the site of the Lungarotti winery, which is one of the most important in Italy, and which operates Le Tre Vaselle. As a consequence,

Le Tre Vaselle represents a complete experience with, at its center, the restaurant and hotel with its impressive collection of old prints on oenological themes. It is difficult to discuss Le Tre Vaselle alone, excluding the winemaking with which it is linked. The Lungarotti Rubesco and Torre di Giano were among the first Italian wines to be denominated by origin – in 1968. The wine museum, which has been installed in the Palazzo Baglioni with its twenty rooms, displays a collection of technical, archaeological, historical, and folkloristic artifacts of great interest. A further guarantee, if one were needed, of the great attention and constant care devoted to wines at the establishment is the fact that one of Italy's most important wine tastings, the Banco d'Assaggio, is held in the fall of each year at Le Tre Vaselle under the sponsorship of the Lungarotti family. To it are invited wine experts from countries throughout the world.

Le Tre Vaselle is not a flashy novelty, capable only of creating a momentary impression, like a passing comet. It is well rooted in the green heart of Umbria, as solid as a stone bastion. It is installed in an old mansion of traditional Umbrian style, situated within the walls of an old town. The cuisine offered here arises as well from the Umbrian soil and follows the seasons. For the products and the way they are prepared marches to the slow rhythm of the passing months. They are products and procedures that have been used for centuries by the people of Umbria. But alongside that conservative adherence to tradition, there is an innovative and imaginative vein that produces new dishes that are envisaged and executed, always, with the firm intention of exalting the flavors, tastes, and aromas associated with the land and climate of Umbria. All the products used in the dishes served at Le Tre Vaselle are supplied by the Lungarotti agricultural estate, the wines as well, obviously.

Via Garibaldi 48 – 06089 Torgiano (near Perugia). The restaurant is never closed. It is directly linked to the hotel and there are two large halls for conferences. Torgiano is 16 kilometers southwest of Perugia and can be reached from SS (Highway) 3 bis, which links Perugia with Terni and Orte on the Rome-Milan Autostrada del Sole (Superhighway A-1). AE, Diners, Eurocard, Visa cards accepted. Tel. (075) 982447

Giorgio Lungarotti, a man of great diligence and considerable intuition, has succeeded in involving his winery, one of the most important in Italy, in numerous enterprises of major significance. Among the activities are the hotel-restaurant Le Tre Vaselle, the Museo del Vino (Wine Museum), which was conceived by his wife, Maria Grazia Lungarotti, and the annual tasting of Italian wines by an international jury of experts, which is known as the Banco d'Assaggio. It is one of the most important of Italian oenological events. The restaurant offers a cuisine that is based on the regional tradition, an extraordinarily rich one, but updated and renewed, while maintaining the authentic goodness of the local ingredients.

Fillet of Beef in Balsamic Vinegar Sauce

Filetto di bue in salsa di aceto balsamico

Serves 4
1 pound (400 g) fillet of beef
2 tablespoons of balsamic vinegar (or a
   highly aromatic vinegar)
4 tablespoons (½ dl) olive oil
3 sprigs of rosemary
Pinch of oregano
Ground white pepper
Pinch of red pepper
Fine salt
Coarse salt

Prepare the sauce in a pan by blending the balsamic vinegar, oil, rosemary, oregano, white pepper, and the red pepper. Blend well over low heat, using a whisk. Allow to cool. Lightly salt and pepper the fillet. Broil or grill over hot coals until the meat is rare. Cut the fillet in thin slices. Baste the slices with the tepid sauce and sprinkle over a bit of coarse salt.

Wine : Rubesco Riserva Vigna Monticchio (Umbria), 6-7 years

Rice al Solleone

Risotto al Solleone

Serves 4
1 ½ cups (350 g) small-grained rice
1 tablespoon finely chopped onion
10 tablespoons (140 g) butter
¾ cup (100 g) grated Parmesan
6 cups (1 ½ L) meat broth
2 cups (½ L) Solleone wine (or dry
   Sherry wine)
Salt

Melt the butter over low heat and lightly brown the chopped onion. Pour in the rice and mix well. Add the broth, a little at a time, as the rice absorbs the liquid. Cook slowly over moderate heat for about 15-20 minutes or until the rice is tender but still with a bite *(al dente)*.
About halfway through the cooking, add a cup of Solleone wine. Two minutes before removing the pan from the heat, add another cup of wine. Finish the cooking and add a small amount of butter and the Parmesan. Blend well and serve.

Wine : Chardonnay (Umbria), 1-2 years

Frascarelli Pasta with Sweet Pepper Sauce

Frascarelli al peperone

Serves 4
For the pasta:
1 ½ cups (200 g) flour
3 eggs
For the sauce:
1 onion
1 celery stalk
2 sweet red peppers
Olive oil
⅓ cup (100 g) fresh tomatoes
1 ½ ounces (40 g) *mascarpone* cheese
Salt
4 tablespoons grated Parmesan

Cut the celery, onion, and peppers into thin slices. Brown in sufficient olive oil over low heat for about 10 minutes. Add the fresh tomatoes cut into pieces. Salt and allow to cook, always over low heat, for about an hour and a half. Pass the sauce through a sieve and add the mascarpone cheese. Blend thoroughly, using a whisk.
Prepare the *frascarelli*. Heat 3 ½ quarts (3 L) of water and a pinch of salt. Sift the flour onto the entire surface of a doughboard in even fashion so that the board seems to be covered by a veil. Beat the eggs and sprinkle the liquid lightly and rapidly on the flour. Carefully gather together the flour and sift it in a fine sieve. The lumps remaining in the sieve are the *frascarelli*, which should be cooked in the boiling water about 1 minute. Drain, add the sauce, sprinkle with Parmesan and serve hot.

Wine: Chardonnay Riserva I Palazzi (Umbria), 3-5 years

Lake Trasimeno "Eel" Pastry

Anguilla dolce del Lago Trasimeno

For a dessert of about 2 inches (5-6 cm) in diameter and about 19 inches (about 50 cm) in length:
10 ounces (300 g) powdered almonds
1 cup (250 g) sugar
6 egg whites, beaten until stiff
2 coffee beans
Pinenuts
1 thin strip of candied orange peel

Combine the powdered almonds with the sugar and the egg whites, and blend well. Stretch out the batter in the form of an eel. Make scales on the back, using the pinenuts. For the eyes, use the two coffee beans. The candied orange peel serves as a tongue. The "eel" should be twisted around so that it forms a circle, placed on a non-stick surface and covered with a buttered cloth. Bake for about 1 hour at 350°F (175°C). Serve cold.

Wine: Solleone Dry (Umbria), 5-10 years, or Vino Santo Lungarotti (Umbria), 5-7 years

ALBERTO CIARLA

Alberto Ciarla's lifelong love for the sea and all things maritime is apparent to all those who dine at his restaurant in the heart of Trastevere, one of the historic quarters of Rome across the Tiber from the center of the ancient capital of the world.

Piazza San Cosimato 40 – 00153 Rome. The one-star Michelin restaurant is closed Sundays and from December 20 to January 10 and August 10 to 30. It is closed at noon, functioning only at night. It is therefore essential to reserve a table. Alberto Ciarla is two blocks west of the Viale Trastevere, the principal street in the district of the same name across the Tiber from the city center.
AE, Visa, Diners cards accepted.
Tel. (06) 5818668

The dishes offered on the menu of Alberto Ciarla play leading roles, like actors in the theater. There is a stimulating succession of preparations based on fish, which vary with the season and the condition of the sea. Ciarla offers his guests only fish, prepared in a wide range of formulas. Fish can even be seen swimming about in the restaurant's tanks. Having as his laboratory a cuisine abounding in marine products, Ciarla knows how to orchestrate preparations that astound and dazzle but also please and satisfy. Contrasts that provoke and stimulate arise from combinations, as does discord when the mixture proves unsuitable. Ciarla knows how to maneuver within that framework, for he is conscious that all excesses must be curbed when experimenting and testing. His cuisine is a combination of experimental and traditional cooking.

During the first act of the meal's performance, the *antipasti* or hors d'œuvres provide an ingratiating whiff of sea air, since most of the dishes are based on raw fish and crayfish. In the next course, there is the substantiality of pasta that lends the Ciarla cuisine its Mediterranean character, creating dishes with sunny natures in which fantasy succeeds in uniting fish or lobster with lentils and pasta or pastry with shellfish. For the principal course, the foods offered depend upon the season and the sea, as well as the creativity, the imagination, and the taste for the spectacular of Ciarla himself.

No one should be surprised to find a restaurant in Rome that serves only fish. Beyond Ciarla's personal passion for seafood, there is the nearness of the sea to the "Eternal City" so that there is a tradition as modern as it is ancient. The Romans of the imperial period grew seabass and other types of fish in saline ponds. In addition, the most famous

Alberto Ciarla's restaurant is situated in the Piazza San Cosimato in the Trastevere section of Rome. It used to be said that no one could call himself a Roman unless his family had resided in the city fourteen generations. And it was also said that most of those who could, on that basis, call themselves Roman lived in Trastevere, where until recently the old dialect, Romanesco, was commonly spoken and understood. At one side of the piazza is the ancient Church of San Francesco a Ripa, in which is displayed a famous statue, by Gian Lorenzo Bernini, of the Blessed

sauce of that day was *garum* (or *liquamen*) made of fermented fish viscera. Its use was specified in numerous recipes in the ancient Roman cookbook attributed to Marcus Gavius Apicius. It was said to enrich the flavors of many preparations. Ciarla is a former national-level rugby player, an expert diver, member of the national and international boards of the International Federation of Sports Fishing, and in his free time a ceramics maker, sculptor, inventor, cart racer, a former Club Méditerranée instructor, builder of boats, professional sommelier and cook. While cuisine is part of Ciarla's family background, cooking was for him initially a marginal element of his life, although it has now become his dominant passion. It is a passion, however, that contains within it another, more ancient and constant, the sea, underwater sports, and, therefore, fish.

Ciarla's establishment is considered the best fish restaurant in Rome. It should not be forgotten that Ciarla, once he had finally decided to dedicate himself to the culinary profession, and being the perfectionist that he is, spent a period working at the French temple of fish cuisine, the La Marée restaurant of Trompier in Paris. From that initial experience and from his own imagination have come the highly personalized preparations offered by the establishment.

Ciarla is indefatigable. He is the sort of man who, while he is doing one thing, is already thinking about what he wants to do next. He recently opened another restaurant, the Grande Italia, in Paris.

And he is known in many countries as "the maestro of Italian seafood."

Ludovica Albertoni. The statue is of great brilliance and undoubted richness. Bernini was known for his theatrical effects and perhaps some of that competence went into the decor and lighting of Ciarla's restaurant, both of which are quite striking. Although Rome is relatively close to the sea, the beaches of Ostia around the mouth of the Tiber being less than twenty miles away, the city is not overly supplied with fish restaurants. Alberto Ciarla has supplied that deficiency with a vengeance, for he offers on his menu an extraordinary range of shellfish and fish prepared in as many fascinating and occasionally surprising – pleasantly so – fashions. He has established such an outstanding reputation for his taste and skill that he recently decided to confront another challenge by opening a restaurant capable of standing in comparison with some of the best French culinary culture has to offer in the very heart of that tradition, Paris.

Raw Fish Salad

Insalatina di Pesce al Crudo

Serves 4
8 slices of filleted and marinated
  salmon, 8 ounces (200 g) total weight
Fennel seeds
Coarse salt
½ cup (1 dl) olive oil
1 tablespoon mustard
1 ½ cups (3 dl) lemon juice
1 tablespoon aromatized vinegar
½ cup (1 dl) cherry brandy
1 small head (200 g) curly lettuce
7 slices of sea-bass fillet, 8 ounces (200 g)
  total weight
2 ounces (60 g) small shelled shrimp
Salt and white pepper
40 raisins, soaked in Cognac
Parsley

Pack the salmon, with the fennel seeds
sprinkled over, in the coarse salt and put the
fish in the lower part of the refrigerator to
infuse for 12 hours.
Prepare a thick vinaigrette, using the oil,
mustard, ½ cup (1 dl) lemon juice and the
aromatized vinegar, by whipping the ingredients in a blender. In another bowl, put 1
cup (¼ L) of lemon juice and the cherry
brandy.
Arrange the lettuce in individual dishes in a
"sunburst" pattern. Salt lightly. Cut the salmon into thin slices and place them atop the
lettuce.
Cut the sea-bass into thin slices and place
them, for a few minutes, in the lemon juice
and brandy mixture. Arrange them on the
plates atop the lettuce, and pepper. Put the
shelled, small shrimp in the lemon juice-
brandy mixture for a few minutes then put a
handful of the shellfish in the center of each
plate. Salt and pepper lightly.
Pour the vinaigrette over the shrimps and
lettuce. Garnish with the raisins and some
sprigs of parsley and serve.

Wine: Spumante (Champagne method)
Brut (Franciacorta in Lombardy, Alto Adige
or Piedmont)

Marinated Fish

Seviche di pesce

Serves 4
Gilt-head bream or sea-bass, about
  2 pounds (1 K)
1 onion
Juice of 1 lemon
8 tablespoons (1 dl) *extra-vergine* olive
  oil
1 tablespoon chopped parsley
Hot red pepper
Salt and white pepper

Clean the fish but do not scale it. Fillet it
after removing the skin, including the scales.
Cut into thin slices, beginning the slice at
the back and cutting toward the head. Put
the fish slices on a serving dish and pour over
the lemon juice, pepper, salt, hot red pepper
in tiny pieces and the onion sliced thin, all
mixed together. Add the oil and garnish with
chopped parsley. Marinate for 10 minutes,
then serve.

Wine: Spumante (Champagne method)
Brut (Franciacorta in Lombardy, Alto Adige
or Piedmont)

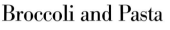

Pasta and Bean Soup with Seafood

Zuppa di pasta e fagioli ai frutti di mare

Serves 4
²⁄₃ cup (150 g) dried white beans
¹⁄₃ pound (150 g) small octopus
¹⁄₃ pound (150 g) small cuttlefish (or squid)
¹⁄₂ pound (200 g) mussels
¹⁄₂ pound (200 g) clams
¹⁄₂ pound (200 g) warty Venus (the French *praire* clam may be substituted; or use 50 percent more of clams and mussels)
2 ounces (60 g) bacon, diced
2 garlic cloves
¹⁄₂ onion, thinly sliced
4 tablespoons (60 g) olive oil
²⁄₃ cup (150 g) chopped tomatoes
Salt and pepper
7 ounces (200 g) dried *maltagliati* or noodles
1 tablespoon chopped parsley

Soak the beans in cold water for 12 hours. Boil them until tender.
Skin, clean, and chop the octopus and cuttlefish. Steam the shellfish for a few minutes, until their shells open. Remove the meat from the shells.
Sauté the bacon, garlic and onion in the oil. Remove the garlic and add the chopped tomatoes, the shellfish, octopus and cuttlefish. Salt and pepper lightly and cook until the octopus and cuttlefish are tender.
Meanwhile, cook the *maltagliati* or noodles in boiling salted water until they are *al dente* (still with a bite). Several minutes before serving, add the *maltagliati* or noodles and beans to the seafood, blend well, and cook together briefly.
Sprinkle with chopped parsley and some drops of good olive oil and serve.

Wine: Merlot di Aprilia (Latium), 1-3 years or Merlot del Collio (Friuli-Venezia Giulia), 1-3 years

Broccoli and Pasta

Bombolotti allo sparaceddo

Serves 4
³⁄₄ pound (400 g) cleaned broccoli
1 garlic clove
1 hot red pepper
²⁄₃ cup (150 g) chopped tomatoes
¹⁄₂ cup (1 dl) olive oil
7 ounces (200 g) *mezze maniche* or *rigatoni*, crushed
¹⁄₂ cup (1 dl) cream
1 cup (¹⁄₄ L) fish stock
6 tablespoons grated Parmesan
Salt

Boil the broccoli until it is virtually mushy. Stew the garlic, red pepper, and tomatoes in the oil. Add the broccoli and blend well.
Cook the pasta in abundant salted water until it is *al dente* (still with a bite). Drain the pasta and add it to the broccoli.
Blend in the cream and fish stock. When the pasta is well coated with the sauce, stir in the grated Parmesan and serve.

Wine: Bianco di Pitigliano (Tuscany), 1-2 years

Sea-Bass Fillet with Almonds

Filetto di spigola alle mandorle

Serves 4
4 fillets of sea-bass, each about ¹⁄₄ pound (130 g)
1 ³⁄₄ cups (400 g) softened butter
2 cups (200 g) breadcrumbs
²⁄₃ pound (300 g) cultivated mushrooms, chopped
1 ³⁄₄ cups (250 g) chopped almonds
2 eggs
1 egg yolk
Rum
Salt and white pepper
1 cup (¹⁄₄ L) white wine
¹⁄₂ cup (1 dl) fish broth
1 sweet onion, chopped
1 ¹⁄₃ cups (300 g) cream, whipped
Vermouth
¹⁄₂ cup (60 g) raisins softened in brandy
8 slices Golden apple
1 teaspoon sugar

Prepare the almond stuffing by creaming the butter and working in the breadcrumbs. Add the chopped mushrooms and almonds. Incorporate the eggs, the egg yolk, a few drops of rum, and the salt and white pepper. Blend well until a smooth paste is obtained. Leave the stuffing in the refrigerator for several hours.
Spread the filling on the fillets and put them in a pan. Pour over the wine and fish stock, add the chopped sweet onion and salt and pepper lightly.
Cover the pan with buttered brown paper (do not use aluminium foil). Cook the fillets in a 350°F (180°C) oven for 10 minutes. Then put the pan under a grill for 10 minutes to glaze the fillets. Arrange the fillets on a serving dish and keep warm. Add the cream and a few drops of vermouth to the liquid in the pan. Stir over a moderate flame and reduce the sauce slightly. Pour the sauce over the fillets, garnish with the raisins, and the slices of Golden apple previously glazed in butter and sugar and serve.

Wine: Montecarlo Bianco (Tuscany), 1-2 years

CHARLESTON

*Palermo may have its problems but it
also has the Charleston, the type of
restaurant that can make any city
forget its worries. Owners Angelo
Ingrao and Antonino Glorioso have
created an establishment that is the
essence of Sicilian hospitality.*

The gastronomic tradition of Sicily reflects the influence of Arabic culture, its geographical reality as an island in the sea, and the character of the Sicilians themselves, who want everything to be extremely rich. Sicilian cooks still prepare *cuscus*, a dish left behind by the Arabs when they were driven from the island nearly a thousand years ago, as well as swordfish, bluefish, tuna, and the shellfish that thrive off the coasts of this fascinating island in the heart of the Mediterranean. Olive oil, tomatoes, and herbs are the island's principal condiments and they lend their aromas, richness, and fullness to a host of Sicilian preparations. The ancient Sicilian tradition has always offered dishes of baroque complexity, never plain but rather brimming with abundance. The desserts are even better examples of this innate urge to display a richness that is virtually overpowering. The island cuisine also owes much to the ancient Greek culture of Magna Grecia, especially in the area of pastries, which have an indefinable personality all their own.

Palermo's link with food begins at the Vucciria market, which is held in a long, narrow street that ends in a small, rectangular square. Anyone walking through that market is immediately impressed by two things: the cries frequently uttered by the sellers, which have given the market its name, for *vucciria* is a dialectal rendering of *vociari* (shouts), and the variety and abundance of the products exposed for sale. It is the Mediterranean market par excellence. The venders' shouts are often confused and they also often seem to be tinged with a suggestion of menace, as if the shopper must be violently persuaded to buy. A visit to the Vucciria is sufficient to provide anyone who does not know the island or its cuisine a complete understanding of the breadth and quality of its diet.

A widespread popular conviction has it that Giuseppe Tomasi, Prince of Lampedusa, wrote a great part of his masterpiece, Il Gattopardo (The Leopard), which represents a milestone of Italian literature of the twentieth century, while seated at a small table at the Mazzara, an historic pastryshop near the market. Angelica and Tancredi were therefore "born" only a short distance away. And he is said to have fueled his imagination with *cannoli* (fried pastry stuffed with sweet cheese and candied fruits), *granite* (ices), and coffees.

The Charleston, one of southern Italy's few outstanding restaurants, is found precisely in this historical area. Even the Charleston pastryshop, Lampedusa's Mazzara, is alive and thriving. It is linked in management and spirit to the restaurant, and both are bound together by one personality above all, Angelo Ingrao, gastronome and sommelier, who, with Antonino Glorioso, a businessman, created the Charleston. Like the dance of the twenties, the Charleston is lively, glamorous, and sunny. Therefore, it should not be surprising if the cuisine in an establishment with such a name is as much a descendant of the sun and of the vivacity of one of Italy's most extraordinary and most contradictory places: Palermo and the whole of Sicily. The Charleston is a bit different from other top Italian restaurants in that it can accommodate two hundred diners. In almost all other leading establishments, the number seldom amounts to a quarter of that figure. It is therefore fair to ask if the Charleston can assure that each of those two hundred diners will receive careful service and attention. It can and it does.

More than that, this restaurant has a tradition of extending hospitality to "*pezzi da novanta*," a slang expression for very important people, including the presi-

Day-to-day management of the Charleston, on the edge of the historic center of Palermo, has been entrusted to Carlo Hassan, an expansive and refined host, by owners Angelo Ingrao and Antonino Glorioso. Hassan has all the warmth of the island itself, the largest in the Mediterranean, and he knows how to put his guests immediately at their ease. The Charleston is a large establishment, capable of accommodating as many as two hundred guests. Yet, despite that considerable number, there is no feeling of being hurried or neglected. In the summer, when the

Piazzale Ungheria 30 – 90141 Palermo. The restaurant, which has been accorded one star in the Guide Michelin, is closed Sundays and from June 15 to September 30. However, during the summer closing, the restaurant shifts to Mondello, Palermo's famous beach resort a short distance to the northwest of the city. AE, Eurocard, Visa, Diners, Comites cards accepted. Tel. (091) 321366

dent of Italy. Obviously, Ingrao has succeeded well in guaranteeing fine service, appealing cuisine, and a warm welcome for all his guests.

There is always another presence at the Charleston: Sicily itself, with its customs and traditions. The establishment has looked carefully into the treasury of island preparations and selected the best dishes of a great cuisine. It offers not only the flavors and aromas of the land but also those of the sun and the sea. The wines offered are Sicilian as well. They are all a part of the inheritance gathered by the Charleston and passed on to its guests.

humidity rather than the heat makes life in the Sicilian capital uncomfortable, the whole staff packs up and moves out to the beach resort of Mondello, along the coast to the west of the city.

The Charleston makes an immediate impression on visitors and it is, invariably, a favorable one. The restaurant is laid out and furnished with great taste and the service is ably attended to. At the side of the Charleston is the Pasticceria (pastryshop) Mazzara, which is operated by the same management and which sums up in its offerings the tastes as well as the richness, whether in form or in content, of Sicilian gastronomy. In approaching the restaurant, the visitor will pass along streets flanked by impressive buildings with large and austere courtyards. And in them, lurking in the shade of their porticoes – shadow, not sun, is the rare element on Sicily – are baroque statues of gods and nobles, heroes and dreamers.

Eggplant Charleston
Melanzana Charleston

Serves 4
4 round eggplants
1 cup (¼ L) olive oil
⅓ cup (200 g) tomato sauce
1 ⅓ cups (300 g) *cannolicchi* (small
  elbow macaroni)
4 tablespoons (30 g) grated Parmesan
1 tablespoon (15 g) chopped basil
Salt and pepper

Preheat oven to 350°F (180°C).
Remove the tops of the eggplants. Cut the
eggplants in half from top to bottom and
remove as much of the meat as possible
without piercing the skin. Using ½ cup (1 dl)
of olive oil, fry the eggplant shells with the
cut side down. With the remaining 8 tablespoons of oil, fry the pulp of the eggplants,
adding the tomato sauce, which should be
blended in well. Salt and pepper. Continue
the cooking for 1-2 minutes.
Meanwhile, cook the *cannolicchi* in abundant salted water, removing and draining the
pasta when it is cooked *al dente* (still with a
bite). Combine the *cannolicchi* with the
sauce. Mix in the Parmesan and basil and,
using the resulting mixture, fill the eggplant
halves.
Bake the eggplants for 5 minutes and serve.

Wine: Regaleali Rosé (Sicily), 1-2 years

Rice with Basil
Risotto al basilico

Serves 4
4 tablespoons (60 g) butter
1 ⅓ cups (320 g) rice
4 cups (1 L) water or vegetable broth
2 teaspoons *mentuccia* (Sicilian mint;
  optional)
4 teaspoons (20 g) basil
2 teaspoons (10 g) chopped parsley
2 tablespoons olive oil
4 grapefruit
½ cup (50 g) grated Parmesan
Salt

Melt 2 tablespoons (30 g) of butter in a pan
and add the rice. Cook the rice slowly, stirring constantly with a wooden spoon, until
the grains become translucent. Add the water or broth and finish the cooking (about
20 minutes). Meanwhile, blend the *mentuccia*, basil, and parsley with the olive oil in a
blender. Two minutes before removing the
rice from the fire, add the blended herbs.
Immediately before serving, stir in the
remaining butter and Parmesan. Stir until
the rice is creamy.
The rice can be served by cutting 4 grapefruit in half, removing the pulp, and stuffing
each half with half a portion of rice. The rice
should be flavored with grapefruit juice
passed around separately at the table.

Wine: Corvo Duca di Salaparuta Prima
Goccia (Sicily), 1-2 years

Stuffed Rolls of Steak

Braciolone della nonna

Serves 4
2 ounces (50 g) salami
2 ounces (50 g) *caciocavallo* (or another
   mild cow's milk cheese)
1 hard-boiled egg
1 pound (400 g) boneless rumpsteak in
   one piece
5 tablespoons (75 g) olive oil
1 cup (300 g) tomato sauce
Salt and pepper

Cut the salami, cheese, and egg into small pieces. Mix well and salt and pepper lightly. Pound the piece of rumpsteak, then lay it out and place salami, cheese, and egg mixture atop the meat. Roll up the steak and tie it so that the ingredients will not come out of the roll.
Brown the roll on all sides in the olive oil. Add the tomato sauce, and cook until the steak is done. Serve the roll cut into slices with the tomato sauce poured over.

Wine : Regaleali Riserva del Conte (Sicily), 5-10 years

Grilled Swordfish Rolls

Involtini di pesce spada alla brace

Serves 4
1 pound (400 g) swordfish
1/3 cup (50 g) sultana raisins
2 large onions
4 tablespoons (60 g) olive oil
1/4 cup (50 g) anchovies
1/3 cup (50 g) pinenuts
2 cups (150 g) breadcrumbs
2/3 cup (100 g) grated Emmenthal (or
   Swiss cheese)
Juice of 2 oranges
Juice of 2 lemons
Bay leaves
Salt and pepper

Cut the swordfish into slices 1 ½ inches by 1 ½ inches (4 by 4 cm). Pound the slices with a wooden mallet, taking care not to break them. Spread them out on a flat surface, if possible a slab of marble.
Soak the raisins in warm water for 20 minutes. Finely chop an onion and put it in a pan with 3 tablespoons (45 g) of olive oil. Add the anchovies, which should be boned and chopped, the trimmings from the swordfish, cut into small pieces, the pinenuts, and the raisins, which have been drained. Brown for about 5 minutes.
Combine half of the breadcrumbs with the grated cheese. Add to the anchovy mixture, with a pinch of pepper, and cook for a few minutes. Then baste with the orange and lemon juice. Stir well. If the mixture is too liquid, add more breadcrumbs. The result should be a thick paste.
Smear the paste on the swordfish slices. Roll up the slices. Moisten the rolls with a bit of oil and dredge in the remaining breadcrumbs. Put the rolls on metal skewers, with, between each roll, a slice of onion and a bay leaf. Grill the skewers for about 15 minutes, turning them once.

Wine : Libecchio Bianco (Sicily), 1-2 years

Tangerines Charleston

Mandarino Charleston

Serves 4
12 tangerines
1/2 cup (1 dl) water
2 cups (450 g) sugar
2 teaspoons (10 g) rennet powder
1/4 teaspoon vanilla extract

Cut off the top quarter of the tangerines. Remove the pulp from the tangerines and place the shells in the freezer. Squeeze the pulp, add the water, sugar, and rennet powder and a few drops of vanilla extract to the juice. Blend well. Allow the mixture to rest for 10 minutes, then pour into an ice cream tray.
Fill the tangerine shells with the frozen mixture.

Wine : Passito di Pantelleria Extra (Sicily), or Marsala (Sicily)

Italian Wines

The family of vines yielding grapes from which wine can be made was introduced into Italy by the Greeks, who settled on Sicily and in the southern reaches of the peninsula nearly three thousand years ago. The vines flourished, and the Greeks gave Italy the name "Enotria," land of vines and wines. The Etruscans, who traded extensively with the Greek colonies and mainland, apparently introduced grape growing and winemaking into central Italy. The Romans, learning from both the Greeks and Etruscans, quickly became excellent winemakers, and they passed on the fruits of their experience to the peoples of the lands they conquered.

By the time of the collapse of the Roman Empire in the West, all the European areas noted today for the production of fine wines were already planted in vineyards. Bordeaux, the Loire, Champagne, Alsace, the Rhône, Burgundy, the Rhine and Moselle, Austria, Switzerland, Portugal, and Spain were producing wines that were distributed throughout the empire.

Italy, however, remained the home par excellence of the vine, which grew virtually everywhere, from the windswept island of Pantelleria, which is closer to Africa than to Sicily, northward along the peninsula to the steep slopes of the Alps. In ancient times as today, there is not a region in Italy where the vine does not grow and wine is not made.

The Italian winemaking tradition is, therefore, ancient, but it has been a rather static one with few changes in concepts or techniques during the many centuries since the collapse of the Roman Empire in the West. It is true that some progress was made, especially in Tuscany, during the seventeenth and eighteenth centuries and especially during the nineteenth. In general, however, winemaking remained essentially at the stage at which the Romans had left it.

In other countries, winemaking evolved much earlier and more decisively than it did in Italy for a host of reasons. France led the way, and even California made great strides forward before the "wine revolution" got under way in Italy around the middle of the 1960s. Since then, however, Italian production has increased despite numerous problems both in volume and quality. Traditional wines have been improved, and a vast array of new products created.

This revolution in winemaking has complicated the selection of wines at table. Twenty years ago, it was all much simpler. In 90 percent of Italian restaurants, the client drank whatever the patron had purchased locally, usually a bulk wine of little distinction. Few restaurants offered more than a few types of wine. Those that did were more apt to offer French wines than products from other regions of Italy. In the average restaurant, the first question the waiter asked his client was, "White or red?" There were no wine lists because there were few wines to be listed. That situation has changed, although not quite as radically as might be expected from the ferment in winemaking. Probably the majority of restaurants in Italy still offer bulk wines made locally and confine their oenological speculations to the sole determination of their clients' preference for white or red wine. And in most cases, there is still no wine list.

However, a great upheaval has occurred at the upper end of the spectrum of Italian restaurant cuisine. A major renewal has been under way now for more than a decade. As in the case of winemaking, much of the impetus to change has come from outside the country. The French nouvelle-cuisine vogue has left its mark on Italian restaurant menus. In some cases, the restaurateurs have been content to ape the French style so completely that the diner is justified in consulting his map to see which side of the Alps he is on. Others, however, while adopting the new mentality, have sought to build upon rather than abandon the ancient tradition. Traditionally, of course, there has never been an "Italian" cuisine. There were many cuisines, each the result of the history and resources of a particular district or region. In general this is still true, despite the "new wave." And visitors to Italy are still well advised to combine the finest local or regional wines with the local or regional dishes, for they usually complement each other in an extraordinarily satisfying way. For the "new" cuisine, the more recently created wines often provide better matches.

In the brief outline of some of Italy's most interesting wines that follows, it should be kept in mind that styles and qualities can vary widely, depending primarily upon the producer. It should also be borne in mind that things are happening so rapidly in Italian winemaking that all books on the subject and nearly all lists and ratings are usually out of date by the time they issue from the press.

Piedmont: For more than a century Piedmont in northwestern Italy has been one of the country's leading winemaking regions. Of its numerous wines, Barolo and Barbaresco are the noblest, longest lived, and most regal. They take some effort, amply rewarded, to get to know. Barolo is more austere and lives longer. Barbaresco is more immediately approachable. Both are made from Nebbiolo grapes, a native variety. The addition of other grapes to Nebbiolo yields Gattinara, Ghemme, Fara, Boca, Bramaterra, Lessona, Spanna, Sizzano and Carema from the Novara-Vercelli hills. They are not as reliable in general, but they are developing more consistency. The variety is also vinified in a youthful version and labeled, simply, as Nebbiolo. It makes pleasant drinking with lighter foods.

Dolcetto is another Piedmontese variety known for its soft grapey flavor. Many versions are produced. Freisa and Grignolino, the first fizzy and rustic, the second dry and slightly bitterish, are traditional Piedmontese vines and wines. They, especially the Grignolino, are being revived and are well worth trying. If Nebbiolo is noble, Barbera is plebeian, a rough-and-ready variety that accounts for a good part of Piedmont's red wine output. Long discounted as a delinquent with no hope of redemption, Barbera is now proving its detractors wrong. An increasing number of producers, applying new technology, are turning out some impressive Barberas. Piedmont also produces a fizzy red, Brachetto, that goes well with most desserts.

The region's best-known and most successful white wines are made from the Moscato and Cortese grapes. The first is the basis of Asti Spumante, the internationally known, sweetish sparkling wine. It is also made as a slightly less fizzy and, some would say, more satisfying dessert wine, Moscato d'Asti. Cortese is used in making dry, crisp whites. The Cortese di Gavi, or simply Gavi, is a good wine but the Gavi dei Gavi is considered as, perhaps, Italy's finest white. A native breed, which is also undergoing a revival but is still scarce, is the Arneis. It produces a soft, almond-flavored white of the same name with a rich texture.

Valle d'Aosta: The Aosta Valley to the north of Piedmont may have the highest vineyards in the world, for many of them cling to Alpine slopes that are often above the clouds. Production is limited, but the white Blanc de La Salle, Blanc de Morgex, and Vin du Conseil are worth tracking down. The red Donnaz, Enfer d'Arvier, and Vin des Chanoines are also interesting, as are the Malvoisies (de Cossa and de Nus), both dessert beverages. The first is white, the second amber.

Liguria: This region on the Mediterranean coast south of Piedmont has a bewildering variety of vines but few wines of distinction. Most are white, probably because of the abundance of seafood eaten along the coast. The Pigato and especially the Vermentino varieties provide the most interesting whites. The Rossese di Dolceacqua, however, is a distinctive dry red.

Lombardy: Two areas of this major wine-producing region to the east of Piedmont, the Oltrepò Pavese hills in the southwest corner and the Franciacorta district to the northeast of Milan, grow large quantities of Pinot – and Chardonnay – for the making of dry sparkling wines, often in Piedmont. The Oltrepò Pavese holds great promise, not yet fulfilled, as a producer of fascinating wines. Three reds of the district – to varying degrees fizzy – offer unusual sensations to match their unusual names: Barbacarlo, Buttafuoco, and Sangue di Giuda. Besides its fine dry sparkling white wines, the Franciacorta makes some interesting and steadily improving reds: Franciacorta Rosso, Botticino, Cellatica, and Groppello, for example.

The Valtellina, far to the north of Milan, is the home of full-bodied, long-lived red wines whose reputations are growing: Valtellina Rosso, Sfursat (made with partly dried grapes) and Valtellina Superiore in four subdivisions: Grumello, Inferno, Sassella, and Valgella. Lugana, which is a graceful, delicately fruity white made south of Lake Garda, is consistently reliable.

Trentino-Alto Adige: This mountainous region between Lake Garda and Austria is without doubt one of the finest winemaking areas in Italy. German is the region's second language, and the wines it makes have something of a Germanic touch. The region is especially noted for its fragrant white wines, but reds account for far more than half of total production. Varietal wines are made in large quantity. Among the more interesting are the Sylvaner, which is relatively rare, Traminer Aromatico (Gewürztraminer), Riesling Renano and Italico, the Pinots, Müller-Thurgau, and Chardonnay, all whites, as well as the red Marzemino and Cabernet Sauvignon and Franc. Caldaro (Kalteresee), made mostly from the native Schiava grape, is a pleasant wine quaffed daily throughout the region, while the Santa Maddalena (St. Magdalener) is a fine dry red that is more popular and better known on German markets than in Italy. No doubt the most impressive red is the Teroldego Rotaliano, which offers a rich color and splendid bouquet. Trentino-Alto Adige also produces excellent dry sparkling wines and turns out a large amount of rosé, the best of which is the Lagrein Rosato, a fragrant and fruity wine.

The Veneto: With its Soave, Valpolicella, and Bardolino, the Veneto has become one of the leading Italian wine-exporting regions. Native varieties are used extensively in all three wines. Those who are not already acquainted with them may want to try the Reciotos, of Soave and of Valpolicella, dessert wines made with semidried grapes. The Reciotto della Valpolicella Amarone, however, is not for desserts. It is a lush, dry red with power and softness, perhaps Italy's closest approach to a Burgundian type of wine. The wines of the Breganze district are worth trying. They are mainly varietals, red Cabernet (Sauvignon or, more often Franc), and white Pinot Bianco, Pinot Grigio, Pinot Nero and Vespaiolo, a local breed. The Breganze Bianco is based on Tocai Friuliano and the Rosso on Merlot. Prosecco, a white that is usually sparkling and may be dry or slightly sweetish, is made in the Treviso area. The Prosecco produced may be even finer, particularly that made in the Cartizze district, which is hard to find. Prosecco is light and lively, qualities that have made it an increasingly popular aperitif.

Friuli-Venezia Giulia : Even more than the Veneto, Friuli-Venezia Giulia, which borders Yugoslavia, is the redoubt of varietals. It has won an outstanding reputation for winemaking with its whites, although reds represent more than half of total output. The areas of Collio Goriziano, Colli Orientali del Friuli, and Grave del Friuli turn out fine whites such as Tocai, Verduzzo, Ribolla, Malvasia, and Picolit, as well as interesting products made from imported varieties such as Sauvignon, Riesling Renano, Traminer, Müller-Thurgau, and Pinot Grigio and Bianco, although a great deal of Chardonnay is often mixed with the latter.

Merlot is by far the leading red, although a great deal of Cabernet (Sauvignon and Franc) is also produced. Schioppettino and Tazzelenghe are both dry reds made from indigenous varieties that are certain to pique the interest of the collector. Picolit is a famous white dessert wine made from the rare native variety of the same name, but it is not easily found. And it does not always contain Picolit grapes alone. The white Verduzzo di Ramandolo is also a native product and a sought-after dessert wine.

Emilia-Romagna : This generous region often produces more wine in favorable years than Portugal or West Germany. However, its reputation in terms of quality is less than brilliant, despite major advances in recent years. Much of the vast annual output of Emilia is represented by Lambrusco ; the best of the numerous subvarieties seems to be that of Sorbara. Other popular wines are the Albana di Romagna and Trebbiano di Romagna, both whites, and Sangiovese di Romagna, a red.

The styles of the region's wines vary enormously, from dry to sweetish, still through fizzy to sparkling. Some of the region's producers manage to make sound, even distinctive wines, but the great bulk of the output is simply pleasant and drinkable without being outstanding.

However, a lot is going on in the hills southwest of Bologna. The Cabernet Sauvignon Colli Bolognesi is a fine red wine that, while usually made to be drunk young, can sometimes be aged with profit. There are also some fine whites, Sauvignons especially, that are beautifully made and as warm and impressive as Sauternes. Gutturnio of the hills around Piacenza, made from Barbera and Bonarda grapes, is a generous, flavorful, well-scented red that has a steadily expanding reputation.

Tuscany : Tuscans are conservative by nature, and they for long resisted the winds of change in winemaking. However, the region is also the home of Italy's finest reds, such as Tignanello and Sassicaia. The furor created by those two wines started the process of renewal in Tuscany, and the oenological revolution is now in full swing, although its course has not been altogether smooth or steady.

Tuscany's most famous wine, nationally and internationally, is Chianti, which is produced in seven zones, the most famous being the Classico district. The entire Chianti area is so large and there are so many soil and climatic variations that generalizations about the wine are almost impossible. The situation is further complicated by the tendency of the makers to put much of their heart and soul into wines and varieties outside the Chianti tradition. Chianti may still have a future as a light, easy-drinking, wine, but there is a danger that winemakers will concentrate their efforts on the new breeds at its expense.

Other fine reds are Brunello di Montalcino, which is a mouth-filling wine that can age spectacularly, although the over-extended stay in wood written into the DOCG discipline does it more harm than good ; Carmignano, complex and elegant ; and Vino Nobile di Montepulciano, which resembles Chianti but has great possibilities, although producers have not yet realized them. Morellino di Scansano is a warm and generous wine that offers much promise, now only in part fulfilled. Montalcino winemakers can elect to forgo the aging required for Brunello and issue Rosso di Montalcino that is intended to be drunk young. Some find its qualities superior to its famous, expensive, and older brother.

Tuscany has never been especially noted for its whites, only Vernaccia di San Gimignano having a long, proud tradition. That venerable beverage is being slowly updated by some enterprising producers. Montecarlo has an interesting mix of grapes that should, in time and with more modern technology, make it one of Italy's most appealing whites. The Montecarlo area also produces a well-structured and fragrant Rosso di Cercatoia that is hard to find but worth the search. Bianco Vergine della Valdichiana, Bianco Pisano San Torpè, and Bianco della Val d'Arbia are not exciting, but quality is improving. Moscadello di Montalcino has recently been revived. Made according to modern techniques, it yields a light, sweetish, bubbly, and appealing dessert wine. Vin Santo is a traditional dessert wine made of light grapes and usually aged for up to five years in small casks.

Umbria : This region, southeast of Tuscany, is one of Italy's smallest, but it is famous for its Orvieto, which is exported in large quantity. The Colli Altotiberini, Colli del Trasimeno, and Colli Perugini all produce red, white and rosé wines under their names. Styles and levels of quality vary enormously, but there is promise of good things to come. The Bianco d'Arquata is an interesting white, as is the Grechetto, a "native" variety imported centuries ago from Greece. However, Umbria's finest wines are made around Torgiano near Perugia by Giorgio Lungarotti. They include the generous, herby, and long-lived Cabernet Sauvignon di Miralduolo, Torgiano Rosso (Rubino), the white Torre di Giano, a Chardonnay, and the Sherry-like Solleone. The Sagrantino di Montefalco is another fascinating local breed, which produces a fat and powerful red wine. *A passito* (raisin wine) version is made from semidried grapes.

The Marches: The region to the east of Tuscany is known internationally for its Verdicchio, although some of the best of it never leaves the region. There are also two fine reds that are not often found outside the region, the Rosso Piceno and the Rosso Conero. The Vernaccia di Serrapetrona, a garnet-purple sparkling wine, is made in dry, sweetish and sweet versions.

Latium: The region, of which Rome is the capital, produces a lot of wine. A great deal of it is shipped abroad, particularly the whites made in the Alban Hills south of Rome: the Frascati, Castelli Romani, Colli Albani, and Colli Lanuvini. They are probably tastier at home than abroad. Torre Ercolana, Fiorano Rosso, and Colle Picchioni are interesting reds that have much to offer, although there is still a disconcerting lack of consistency.

The Abruzzi: The region's main claims to fame currently are the Montepulciano d'Abruzzo, a rosé but even better as a red that is smooth and appealing, and Trebbiano d'Abruzzo, a dry and, in some cases, luxuriant white that is sometimes aged several years.

Apulia: A major producer of powerful blending wines, Apulia has been making a considerable effort to improve quality in the past decade. It is still hard to find its better wines outside the region, although Torre Quarto, a warm and sturdy red, is now known throughout Italy. Castel del Monte, too, is beginning to develop a reputation. It is made in red, white, and rosé types. The latter is quite appealing. Another rosé, with the unusual name of Five Roses, ages well. Other rosés of interest are the Rosa del Golfo and Rosato del Salento, while Locorotondo, a dry white, makes a good companion for fish dishes.

Basilicata: The region, in the instep of the Italian "boot," boasts one of the finest red dry wines in Italy, the Aglianico del Vulture. Aging only brings out its bouquet and broad range of flavors. Unfortunately, the wine is not all that easily found, for it has not yet attained the reputation it merits.

Campania: The region, of which Naples is the capital, once had an outstanding winemaking tradition – about two thousand years ago. Today, its reputation rests almost entirely on the achievements of only one house, Mastroberardino, which produces Fiano di Avellino, an exceptional dry white, Greco di Tufo, a dry, long-lived white, Lacrimarosa d'Irpinia, a delicate rosé, Lacryma Christi del Vesuvio in red, rosé, and white versions, and Taurasi, one of Italy's greatest red wines that is robust in youth and austere and velvety in its maturity. The reds, whites, and rosés made around Ravello above Amalfi provide decent drinking and sometimes even more.

Sicily: The Mediterranean's largest island is also a major wine producer. Unfortunately, the region's reputation still suffers from the emphasis of two decades on the production of bulk blending wines. Yet, there are many fine products to be found throughout the island. The Corvo line of Duca di Salaparuta is consistently reliable and enjoys good sales abroad. The cherry-red Cerasuolo di Vittoria makes interesting drinking, while the reds, whites, and rosés of the Etna denomination, applied to wines produced on the volcano's slopes, are as appealing as they are difficult to find. Two whites, the crisp, dry Rapitalà and Regaleali, are outstanding. For a century and more, Sicily has been noted for its production of Marsala, although the wine's standing had slipped a decade or so ago. A great revival is now under way, however, and Marsala is once again a beverage of fine quality, at least as far as the products of the best, most progressive houses are concerned. Vecchio Samperi, which resembles Marsala but which many believe is considerably finer, is perhaps better as an aperitif.

The Malvasia delle Lipari, made on the islands north of Messina, and Moscato di Pantelleria, produced in extremely modest quantity on the windswept island off the Tunisian coast, are warm and appealing dessert beverages.

Sardinia: Italy's other island region makes a highly distinctive contribution to the country's range of styles and tastes. Typical wines, with strong characters whether in sweet, semisweet or dry versions, include the amber Vernaccia di Oristano and Malvasia di Bosa, and the white Nasco di Cagliari. All three resemble Sherry. Cannonau, Monica di Cagliari, and Giro di Cagliari, all reds, have Port-like characters. The Moscatos of Cagliari and Sorso-Sennori, both whites, are aromatic wines. Vermentino and Torbato di Alghero are distinctive dry whites, which are less extensively produced but perhaps more interesting than the dry white Nuragus. The dry versions of Carignano del Sulcis, Monica, and Cannonau are reds of great strength and fine finish.

Recipe Index